DOGS

WORKING ORIGINS AND
TRADITIONAL TASKS

For Kim

In memory of Crockett, Sparky, Keeper, Jake and Ross.

DOGS

WORKING ORIGINS AND TRADITIONAL TASKS

MIKE LOADES

WHITE OWL

AN IMPRINT OF PEN & SWORD BOOKS LTD.
YORKSHIRE – PHILADELPHIA

First published in Great Britain in 2020 by
Pen and Sword White Owl
An imprint of
Pen & Sword Books Ltd
Yorkshire - Philadelphia

ISBN: 978 1 52674 230 8

A CIP catalogue record for this book is available from the British Library

Typeset in 11/13 pts Ehrhardt by
Aura Technology and Software Services, India.

Printed and bound in India by Replika Press Pvt. Ltd.

Pen & Sword Books Ltd incorporates the Imprints of Pen & Sword Atlas,
Pen & Sword Archaeology, Pen & Sword Aviation, Pen & Sword Discovery,
Pen & Sword History, Pen & Sword Fiction, Pen & Sword Maritime, Pen & Sword
Military, Pen & Sword Military Classics, Pen & Sword Politics, Pen & Sword Select,
Pen & Sword True Crime, Air World, Frontline Publishing; Leo Cooper, Remember
When, Seaforth Publishing, The Praetorian Press, Wharncliffe Local History,
Wharncliffe Transport, Wharncliffe True Crime and White Owl.

For a complete list of Pen & Sword titles please contact

PEN & SWORD BOOKS LIMITED
47 Church Street, Barnsley, South Yorkshire, S70 2AS, England
E-mail: enquiries@pen-and-sword.co.uk
Website: www.pen-and-sword.co.uk

Or
PEN AND SWORD BOOKS
1950 Lawrence Rd, Havertown, PA 19083, USA
E-mail: Uspen-and-sword@casematepublishers.com
Website: www.penandswordbooks.com

Contents

Acknowledgements

A project of this scope would not have been possible without the generous help of many people. Long ago, when I first had the idea for this book, I visited the celebrated dog historian Colonel David Hancock. He welcomed me to his home and was most generous with both his time and his knowledge, also corresponding with me subsequently. I found his views about dogs both refreshing and inspiring, though I should add that all opinions expressed and all mistakes contained herein are entirely my own. I am also indebted to others who gave me their time, advice and expertise, to those who provided locations and especially to those who shared their magnificent dogs with me. These wonderful people include, in chapter order of their assistance, Caroline Woolley, John Whitely, Arwyn Morgans, Mark Giffith and Lynn Kenny, Arctic Dog Adventure, Lizbet Norris, Robert Hurford, Pascal Mathieu, Alison Burgess, Rich and Angie Louter, Susan Liley, The Rt. Hon. Henry Cobbold, Will Duncan, Tim Dow, Karl Jennings, Steve Cross of Shropshire Falcony, Jamie and Helen Cureton, Adeeb Alhasan at Jordan Inspiration Tours, Bill Kane at Digital Grange, Alan Brown, Michael Woodhouse, Kieron Hawkes, Abergavenny Museum, Jeffrey Gladstone and Coleen Burnham-Gladstone. I am grateful to numerous superb photographers. All are credited alongside their images but the following merit special mention for going above and beyond: Whitney McClaren, Gordon Summers, Corin Ashleigh Brown, Andy Collins and Chrissy Stone. I owe an even greater debt to three dear friends, who also happen to be professional photographers. This trio of talent not only accompanied me on memorable dog adventures, capturing unique and wonderful images, but they also gave much needed boosts of encouragement. They are, in order of their photographs appearing, Geoff Dunlop, Ian Potts and Elizabeth Keates. I am most grateful of all however, to my wife, Kim Hawkins. She too is responsible for many of the beautiful photographs in this book and it has been a joy to share some of these canine adventures with her. In addition she has been a stalwart of support and encouragement, patient and understanding during the many long hours of a writer's necessary reclusive withdrawal. I guess I owe her a puppy.

Notes on the Primary Sources

Tracking dog history through old texts is an uncertain business. Historical authors did not have the benefit of photography and all we have for visual reference are some often-unreliable glimpses in art. Nevertheless, historical texts do reveal important detail in terms of practice and function, even if we have to imagine the same type of dog in slightly different physical form than he is today. In the interests of brevity within the main chapters, there follows a brief introduction to the more frequently quoted sources.

The first book, written in English, to have dogs as the exclusive subject matter, was *De Canibus Britannicis* (Of English Dogs) by Johannes Caius. Published in 1570, it gives extensive descriptions of working dogs in sixteenth-century England. Most celebrated for his work in medicine – remarkably he was physician to King Edward IV, Queen Mary and Queen Elizabeth I – Caius was also a pioneer naturalist, writing a treatise on plants and animals as well as his work on dogs. *De Canibus Britannicis* was prepared for his good friend, the Swiss naturalist Konrad Gesner, to feature in his major undertaking, *Historiae Animalium*. Dr Caius' text was never included, although some of his drawings made it into later editions of Gesner's work. His commentary showed a keen eye for observation and Caius clearly experienced dogs at work first hand. Born plain John Keys, he affected a phonetic, Latinized spelling of his name to 'Johannes Caius' after studying as a physician at the University of Padua in 1541. Such pretensions were fashionable at the time. Although the spelling was changed, the pronunciation of his name remained the same and he was known as John, not Johannes. In 1557 John Caius founded *Gonville and Caius College*, incorporating the then defunct Gonville College, which he had attended nearly thirty years earlier, with his own endowment. This has allowed subsequent generations of Cambridge University students to show-off by knowing that correct pronunciation of 'Caius College' is 'Keys College'.

There are earlier mentions of dogs. In the fourth century BC the Greek philosopher, historian and soldier Xenophon (431-354 BC) wrote *Cynegeticus*, which was a detailed treatise on the methods used for hunting with dogs. Five centuries later, Lucius Flavius Arrianus (AD 86-160), known familiarly as Arrian, was a Greek author who wrote a work of the same name. Arrian's opus was largely a copy of Xenophon's original work, although it contained some supplementary commentary. Other early insights into dogs come from natural historians. Aristotle (384-322 BC) wrote prolifically on a wide range of subjects from Astronomy to Philosophy but around twenty-five per cent of his output concerned the classification and organization of the natural world. In his masterwork *The History of Animals*, he includes some details of different dog types. From the Roman period there is really only one author of note. Pliny the Elder (AD 23-79) was a pioneering naturalist during the early Roman Empire. He also served as both a naval and an army commander. His work *Natural History* comprised thirty-seven volumes and dogs were included as part of this encyclopaedic survey.

The most important medieval work concerning dogs was *Le Livre De La Chasse* (The Book of Hunting) written in 1387. Its author was Gaston 'Phoebus', Le Comte de Foix (1308-43), whose luxurious court at Orthez in southwest France was renowned for its elaborate hunting rituals. The treatise not only gave instruction for many and varied forms of hunting but also in the training of dogs. It was illustrated with seventy-eight miniature paintings, each executed exquisitely and packed with instructive detail. Subsequently *Le Livre de la Chasse* was translated and included in the first treatise on hunting to be created in English, *The Master of Game*. This was written by Edward of Norwich, second Duke of York (1373-1415) between 1406 and 1415. He commanded the right wing of Henry V's army at Agincourt in 1415 and was killed during the battle. Although much of his translation is faithful, some sections have been omitted. There are also significant additions by his own hand. It is probable that the two men knew each other. Other medieval works include the *Boke of St. Albans*, which was printed in 1486. It contains a collection of hunting essays that have been attributed to Dame Juliana Berners, a prioress of the Benedictine priory of St Mary of Sopwell, about which little else is known. In all probability the essays are translations taken from various other works that are now lost.

Gervase Markham (1568–1637) was a soldier, poet and writer. He served as a mercenary in the Low Countries and subsequently as a captain in the Earl of Essex's Irish campaign. Markham had numerous works published on subjects ranging from horsemanship and archery to cookery and biography. He wrote original verse and translated poetry from Italian. *Country Contentments*, printed in 1615, was a two-part work. The first dealt with hunting, hawking, coursing and shooting, in addition to other recreations such as bowling and tennis. The second part, under the title *The English Huswife*, was a collection of recipes and remedies together with other household advice.

In 1621 Markham wrote *Hunger's Prevention, or the Whole Art of Fowling*, a work that was largely plagiarized by Nicholas Cox author of *The Gentleman's Recreation* (1674). As with Arrian's rendering of Xenophon and with Edward of Norwich's version of Le Comte de Foix's work, the re-rendering is not exact and also includes both embellishment and original information in places. A dozen years after Nicholas Cox had his *Gentleman's Recreation* published, another countryman, Richard Blome, wrote an entirely different and original treatise on hunting under the same title. In addition to the works cited here, I have accessed a number of public records and read extensively from the works of more modern authors. A brief selection of the more important titles are to be found in the bibliography. Traditional breed histories range from the very good to the far-fetched and fanciful. The story of the dog is as vast and complex as the story of humankind and the truth is not always clear. It sits entwined in a tapestry of false trails. At best I have been able to gather a few threads that connect our modern breeds to their distant ancestors and their original employment.

Introduction

It would be a mistake to assume that our familiar and cherished dog breeds have always been with us or even that they will remain with us. The characteristics of our dogs, in both form and temperament, have changed over time and continue to do so. It is reasonably certain that we have lost many times the number of canine varieties than are currently in existence. Most of the breeds that we have today are relatively recent developments. Nevertheless many modern breeds have a recognizable similarity to historical types; enough to enable us to imagine them in earlier contexts. To some extent, dogs evolved differently to operate in disparate climates and terrain. However the diverse range of dog types that we have is mostly because humans bred them selectively to become specialists; to perform certain tasks for us. Those occupations ranged from herding and guarding to hauling and tracking and all manner of hunting assignments. The fundamental link between form and function is the reason different dogs look and behave the way they do. This book is about exploring those occupational origins, about the social history of this unique and wonderful inter-species partnership and about the enduring power of that connection.

One senses the heightened and alert focus of a dog engaged in work it wants to do; work that it is hard-wired to excel at. There is an adage, which states that the best way to reward a Border Collie for penning sheep is not to give him a treat but to allow him to do it again. It applies equally to sled dogs racing across a wasteland of white and to Labradors hurling themselves into rivers, lakes and lochs to retrieve. Working dogs have an infectious enthusiasm for what they do and the work is its own reward. Not only is there an energized spark between dog and task but also in the way the dog looks to his human companion for instruction. The bond between human being and dog deepens in these moments of working together. In exploring the working origins of different breeds, I wanted to experience first-hand the different circumstances in which the light goes on. This led me to have an assortment of adventures, working at traditional tasks with dogs of an appropriate type. Alongside my accounts of these hands-on experiences, I have sought to weave as much history of both the tasks and the associated breeds as space will allow. In addition to meeting superlative dogs, I encountered their knowledgeable and delightful owners, so these tales of dog doings are also seasoned with a sprinkling of human characters and their worlds.

There is an abundance of literature that deals with the varied and valuable work dogs do for us today; whether it is as guide dogs, hearing dogs, sniffer dogs or rescue dogs. I have chosen to concentrate solely on traditional labours, to glimpse at history through the eyes of the dog. In doing so the trail has often led me to the hunting field. I am aware that this can be a polarizing issue and I wanted, as far as possible, to avoid distraction from factual accounts of historical practice with discussion about present day attitudes to hunting. Consequently, for each of my canine adventures, I maintained a strictly no-kill policy. Where simulations were possible, such as chasing a lure that was the choice. Where substitutions were available, such as taking a pack of hounds on hound-exercise rather than on a hunt, I went for that option. It was irresistible to me to see a Poodle retrieve a duck from water (his traditional job) but when I did so, it was a duck from the freezer, not one that had been shot for the book. I concede that this may seem a slightly artful manipulation of my self-imposed guidelines but the truth is, I have no objection to shooting ducks for food. On the other hand there are certain modes of hunting that I would deplore. You see – we are already in a quagmire of distracting over-explanation! For this reason I wanted to skirt the topic and make this book as accessible as possible to all dog enthusiasts, whether they be anti-hunting or pro-hunting. The intention has been to keep the focus on the dogs and their story. I write about how historical hunts were conducted as a matter of historical record. That is not to say that I approve of their methods. Hunting is an inextricable thread throughout human history. It has been an integral part of our social development and also central to our bond with our hunting partners, dogs. My aim has been to celebrate this extraordinary alliance; the friendship of humans and dogs, banded together in common pursuit. This book is about the history, the process and the custom of that working relationship.

Dogs Chose Us

Even before they met, wolves and humans were predisposed to form an alliance. Both species shared similar social structures, with well-defined hierarchies and an innate instinct to work co-operatively. For instance, they each hunted tactically, with various group members assuming different roles. The raw materials for a synergetic, and mutually beneficial, relationship were present from the start. However something of consequence was required to bridge the antagonistic divide between these two aggressive predators. Whilst the notion of nurturing a wolf pup into some level of socialized animal is not without credibility, it seems more probable that there was first an evolutionary arc that enhanced and encouraged the chances of success. It is undisputed that the domestic dog (*canis familiaris*) evolved ultimately from the wolf (*canis lupus*), specifically the grey wolf, and dog behaviourists frequently explain the behaviour patterns found in today's Chows and Chihuahuas according to their lupine ancestry. However the precise path of that evolution remains a matter of theory and debate. I am most convinced by the idea that there was a phase, over 100,000 years ago, when some wolf packs adapted to living in closer proximity with humankind, in order to exploit the advantages of scavenging around our campsites. These wolves became slightly less fearful of humans and less directly aggressive towards us, enabling them to co-exist nearby without undue threat. The packs that benefited from humans' excess food resources probably didn't mix with wilder packs and so, over time, natural selection produced isolated strains of slightly more docile and sociable wolves. Only some wolves developed in this way and, over many thousands of years, they gradually split from the strains of wilder wolves. Eventually, the theory goes, there were also some slight physical changes, and these wolves developed into a *proto-dog*. At the time of writing no physical evidence for a proto-dog has been unearthed but such a creature remains a strong probability. It was a gambit of evolutionary survival that clearly paid off. Today the global grey wolf population is presumed to be around 300,000; whereas the world's dog population is estimated at 900 million. Of these around 83 per cent are free-ranging dogs, a category that includes street dogs, village dogs, and feral dogs. These all scavenge around human settlement. For them, their dependence on humans remains a one-way contract, just as it was for proto-dog. The remaining 17 per cent, of course, are the dogs we care for, who live with us, mainly in our homes, and with whom we share the symbiotic advantages of inter-species co-operation. Mostly we spoil them and mostly the reward is so much greater than anything we have to do for them. For these dogs and humans it is a two-way contract.

It was the 'pre-evolved' proto-dog that became a candidate for domestication, possibly only a little more than 10,000 years ago, coinciding with the development of agriculture. Only after that, the idea goes, did humans set about the business of selective breeding and the slow process of developing the myriad types that we have now. Despite small evolutionary developments, it remains entirely possible that proto-dog appeared and behaved very similar to a wolf and it was ultimately an act of faith, on the part of both human and dog, to bridge the species divide in order to form such an enduring partnership. My guess is that proto-dog made the first move, even though it took him around 90,000 years to do so. Anyone who doubts a dog's ability to induce a human being to do his bidding has obviously never had a dog.

Pariah Dogs

There is a strain of aboriginal dogs, all of which have a remarkable physical similarity. These include the Australian Dingo (originally from Asia), the Indian Pariah Dog, the Laika, the Basenji, the Avuvi, the Carolina Dog, the Mayan Dog and the Canaan Dog. There are others. It is striking how much these dogs resemble each other in build and shape and size, despite their wide geographical distribution. Some are feral village dogs, others are recognized breeds that have now been fully domesticated and live as pet dogs, though they generally retain a reputation for being somewhat tricky to train. Not only do they all look similar to each other but they also resemble images of dogs in early rock art (petroglyphs) such as those at Shuwaymis in Saudi-Arabia, which are thought to be around 8,000 years old. Here there are hunters with bows and arrows together with a pack of what look like Canaan Dogs.

The Canaan Dog. This breed of the pariah group, bears a singular resemblance to primitive dogs depicted in Neolithic rock art, appearing both as hunting and herding companions. (Photo courtesy of Aleksandra Piorunska, Samorodok Canaan Dog Kennels, Poland)

Collectively, this broad group is referred to as 'pariah dogs' (*canis lupus dingo*), though some organizations have changed the classification to 'primitive dogs'. Pariah means 'outcast' and simply describes a behaviour; that of living in proximity to humankind but not being part of our society. It should not be taken pejoratively. These dogs may be a clue to the earliest form of domesticated dogs, though we are still missing that elusive link between wolf and dog. Common characteristics of pariah dogs are a double coat, pointed, upright ears and tails that curl forward over the back. These features are also exhibited by a group of dogs, from northern climes, that huddle together under the 'spitz dog' umbrella: Akita, Husky, Malamute, Eskimo Dog, Elkhound, Keeshond, Samoyed and Finnish Spitz among others.

There is a phenomenon called the 'long-term pariah morph' (LTPM). Within a few generations, especially amongst feral populations of previously domestic dogs, all mongrels tend to look remarkably similar to the pariah dog type. This suggests that a few thousand years of human tinkering, though apparently dramatic, has nonetheless wrought genetic changes that can be unraveled very quickly. This is something we should be mindful of, if we wish to preserve the priceless heritage of canine diversity that we are privileged to enjoy today.

Classifying Dogs

There are three terms used to classify dogs. The first of these is *landrace*. It describes populations of dogs originating in a particular geographical region that have similar characteristics, recognizable and typical enough to refer to them by the same name but whose physical characteristics vary more than would be acceptable for a registered, standardized breed, according to modern Kennel Club strictures. However breeders of landrace dogs (collie types for instance) had an awareness of the importance of breeding lines, which were either recorded informally in written notebooks or passed on by word-of-mouth recommendations. Maintaining good working landrace strains was far from haphazard.

Secondly we have the word *type*, which describes function – bird dog, sled dog, sheep dog, sighthound, scenthound, flock guardian etc. I have used types as the organizing principal of this book. The third category, of course, is *breed*. A breed is created as soon as the pairing of two similar dogs produces a litter of the same dogs – a Labrador mated to a Labrador yields more Labradors – and that perpetuates through the generations. Breed has the dictionary definition of: '*a stock of animals within a species, having a distinctive appearance and typically having been <u>developed by deliberate selection</u>*'. On top of that we could add the terms *pure-breed* or *pedigree-breed*, which would denote the very specific anatomical requirements for a Kennel Club-approved specimen. In order to be Kennel Club registered, a dog has to have both parents registered as the same breed. Moreover those parents also have to have registered parents and so on. It is about parentage and documented lineage, rather than any innate qualities or abilities of the dog.

The degree of morphologic variation in dogs exceeds that of all other land mammals and the 'dog genome project', which began in the 1990s, has demonstrated that genetic variations between different dog breeds can be as much as 27.5 per cent. There is only 2 per cent difference in DNA between a human and a chimpanzee! This wide divergence of genetic profiles between the varied breeds of dog is highly significant, even though, according to the 'long-term pariah morph' paradigm, after multiple generations of interbreeding with non-breed dogs, the distinctions can fade and they will begin to look broadly similar. Our classic breeds are a precious, yet fragile treasure.

Regional Divergence

Whatever the breed, all dogs can swim, run, hunt, herd, haul, guard, retrieve or any number of inherently canine behaviours. Some, of course, are much better at certain activities than others. My Labrador had a keen sense of smell and delighted in finding hidden objects but he was no match for a Bloodhound who can scent a cold trail. Similarly the Bloodhound would have lost to my dog in a swimming race. Selective breeding by humans singled out the natural talents of particular dogs to create a strain of dogs, originally a landrace and ultimately a breed, with heightened, specialist abilities.

That reservoir of specialist talents might have started to manifest according to regional differences, relating to climate, topography and available food sources. Dogs, or proto-dogs, in colder climes would have had heavier coats and those in the mountains would have been more muscular. Dogs dwelling in vast desert plains, without cover, would have a need to see their prey from afar and be especially swift in pursuit. Those living in dense dark forests would have had to rely more on their sense of smell to find a meal. It seems probable that by the time human beings had a hand in it, the skill-sets required for their dogs had already begun to form according to the landscape. Trade, travel and exchange then created opportunities for almost infinite combinations of managed mating to create the extraordinarily diverse species we see today.

Developing the Breeds

The development of multiple breeds becomes possible because of the large number of pups in the average litter, combined with the number of litters a single dog can sire with different females. Under current practice, these are all allowed to be bred with each other – brothers and sisters, mothers and sons, grandfathers and granddaughters. Although responsible breeders avoid breeding two dogs from the same litter, they will nonetheless put together the offspring from different litters of the same sire and dam. Stud dogs regularly sire well in excess of 100 litters, so a stock of several hundred dogs can be created in a single dog generation – a new breed in less than a decade!

In June 1859, the first dog show was held in Newcastle-on-Tyne, England. It was exclusively for pointers and setters. Following its success, dog shows became increasingly popular and included an ever-widening variety of types. In 1873 'The Kennel Club' was inaugurated in Britain. Other Kennel Clubs and breed societies soon followed around the world. Their emphasis was on the form of dogs, what they looked like, and creating written breed standards for what they should look like.

Giving order and explanation to the world by naming and classifying everything was the spirit of the times. Charles Darwin's *On the Origin of Species* was published in November 1859, just a few months after that very first dog show. However, alongside legitimate scientific enquiry was another influence that fuelled the need to give everything a name: nostalgia. The founding of the Kennel Club coincided with the roar of the Industrial Revolution, whose loud, pulsing beat was the drum to which millions marched as they left the fields and migrated to the cities. A new way of life had been born. People embraced it but they also mourned the loss of an imagined and romanticized rural idyll. In the taxonomical frenzy that followed, every nuanced variety of the same basic dog type, was given its own name. This also meant freezing organic development so that different breeds would comply precisely with their recorded specifications. It was as if the past was being put on ice for all time.

Function, not form, had been the driving force in establishing the diversity of dog types that the Victorians now set about cataloguing as breeds. In the subsequent efforts to preserve these 'old' breeds, ancient wisdom was turned on its head and strict specifications regarding the form of a dog were laid down. Too often these were dictated by fickle fashion. To qualify as a bona fide specimen of his breed, a dog now not only had to meet these physical requirements, he also had to have the right paperwork. In-breeding and line-breeding were adhered to in efforts to 'preserve' dogs of precise form. This was the creation of pedigree breeds; dogs defined by their outward form and their paper lineage.

There have undoubtedly been mistakes both in restricting the gene pools so severely and in the capricious details of how many breed standards have been drawn. However we should be careful not to demonize the Kennel Clubs and breeders too much. Those who make it their business to study, appreciate and adjudicate on matters of breed standards are called dog fanciers. Fanciers existed long before the formal organizations of Kennel Clubs and Breed Societies. From the earliest times dog-people would have had an eye for a good-looking dog, judging its potential ability by its conformation as well as having a mind to its ancestry. They would also have had idiosyncratic preferences for coat and colour. To this extent there has always been an element of breeding according to form and lineage – it is an integral part of the selective breeding process. Some may argue, fairly, that all the Breed Societies and Kennel Clubs have done is to formalize an activity that had been going on for millennia. In the past, however, both form and lineage could be usurped by the requirement for proven performance.

Fortunately the show ring is not the only arbiter of breeding today. Working Trials and Field Trials for some breeds put great store on maintaining function and, when establishing the next generation of working sheepdogs, hill shepherds don't give a second thought to the opinions of the bench judge. As a consequence, those who deal with breeds that still have a working function have had the greater success in perpetuating strains of vigour, ability and character. Sadly, too many breeds are considered on their appearance alone and so become the victims of mercurial trends. Breed standards are modified, little by little, over time resulting in the genetic equivalent of 'Photoshop'– just a little broader here, a touch more curl to the tail here and a smidgeon longer there. Everything becomes exaggerated caricature. Large dogs are bred to be bigger and bigger until they barely function. Small dogs are miniaturized to an equivalent extent and if a dog has a distinctive feature that some find appealing, like a Cocker Spaniel with its judge's-wig ears, then these are often overemphasized until the poor creature has to drag them along the ground. It is a fallacy to presume that different breeds of dog exist in their various forms naturally. Considering their variance to be akin to the differences between a lion and a leopard is a false equivalence. Human beings have determined the form our breeds should take. We cannot say 'ah, poor old Bulldogs, they can't breathe properly, they can't eat properly, they can't walk properly, they are overweight, constantly drooling and wearing an oversized bag of skin that doesn't fit. Poor old Bulldogs, their heads are so big and round that the breed cannot give natural birth. However they are such adorable characters aren't they? So cute to look at, with their grumpy human expressions. What a shame they have all these problems. Ah well, it is just the way the breed is'. No, it is not just the way the breed is. Nor is it how the breed used to be a century-and-a-half ago. It is the way we have made them and we are responsible for that.

Despite the criticisms I offer of some aspects of breed regulation, I have great respect for the responsible and knowledgeable breeders of the world. It would be a sad and greatly impoverished world without the diversity of breeds that we have today. I like to see the specialists, the 'thoroughbreds', who are the best they can be at their job and the healthiest they can be for their type. We have much for which to be grateful to those who have been the custodians of breed integrity. Some have let the side down but others have done a good job. It is a nuanced issue.

New Dogs, Old Tricks

I have always been interested in connecting to history in an experiential way, wanting to see it, taste it, smell it, hear it, touch it. Wanting to feel the weight of things, to know the way of things and sense the thrill of things. I have driven chariots; I have jousted in full plate armour; I have sailed on great square-sail ships as well as on medieval cogs; and for many years I earned a living as a teacher of historical swordfighting. I now live in California where I co-founded a horse-archery club – shooting bows from galloping horses. The past has been both my workplace and my playground. When researching this book, I wanted to apply the same approach by engaging in historical activities with the dogs. However, as already noted, the dogs we have today are often quite different to their historical prototypes.

I have done my best to match selected modern breeds to relevant traditional tasks. It is seldom a perfect analogue but I found them all invaluable guides and they led me on a thrilling historical journey. For each occupation, there was usually a choice between several breeds, yet only time and space to focus on one. Inevitably, many much-loved breeds have been omitted, although I have tried where possible to include some account of other varieties within a group. It has been a selection of my own choosing and one that offered opportunities to dip into a miscellany of cultures and eras. I have followed trails that have led me into surprising places; ones that, without the aid of a dog, I would not otherwise have found.

When referring to breeds and types generically, I have opted to use the pronoun 'he' rather than it. I cannot call a dog 'it'. All general comments address both the male and female of the species, but attention to word count, precludes the more cumbersome 'he or she'. Moreover I make no apology for using language that may be regarded as anthropomorphic and sentimental. To talk about a dog's loyalty, nobility, courage and friendship is the language available to us. We do not have a separate vocabulary that can express adequately what may actually be in the dog's mind. There is always the terrible possibility that if dogs could talk, we may not like them. However we do like them; we adore them and are slightly obsessed with them. Dogs share with us the same four responses to a potential conflict situation: fight, flight, freeze and fawn. Fierce in fight and swift in flight, dogs also use 'freeze' to good effect; just watch a collie working sheep with a stop/start nudging or a pointer hold a bird in situ. However when it comes to fawning, they are the masters of the universe. They can wrap us round their little paws and we fawn back at them in equal measure. There is something in their psychology and form that triggers strong emotional responses in us and we like that.

Behavioural scientists can explain much of why this is so, and it is interesting and revealing as science always is. Having a rational understanding of what makes both dogs and humans tick seems to me to be a good thing and it has never diminished my sense of reverence for the beauty and the mystique of our special relationship.

Dogs have numbered among my most important friends on this journey. I am fascinated by behavioural analytics but my rapport with dogs is intuitive. It functions on a basic animal level, without cerebral interference; for me that is an essential joy of the relationship. Of course, dogs are dogs, not little people (please don't dress them up!); they are driven by different biological and social needs. Nevertheless those needs have meshed with our own and the benefits of co-habitation are reciprocal. When I attribute dogs with human values, it is because these are the only metaphors at my disposal to explain the profound gratitude I have for the wonder and enchantment that they bring to life. Thank you dog for choosing us and for making this world a better place.

Punch cartoon 1889. Its savage lampooning of the trend for 'manufacturing' new dog breeds continues to resonate. (Chronicle/Alamy stock photo)

Chapter 1

Herding and Droving Dogs

There's no good flock without a good shepherd and there's no good shepherd without a good dog

—Traditional Scottish saying.

Border Collie. (Photograph by Geoff Dunlop)

Herding Dogs

Flocking and herding animals such as sheep, cattle, goats and geese are capable of creating unmanageable chaos in response to human requests to move somewhere in an orderly fashion. For the shepherd, a dog is essential. Flocks need to be moved frequently from one pasture to another. Groups of sheep need to be separated from the flock and penned, either for shearing or routine procedures such as pregnancy-testing or inoculation. Stock needs marshalling and selecting for market. For these, and many other reasons, the livestock farmer requires the services of a herding dog.

I lived for ten years on a farm in rural Southwest Scotland, in the beautiful sheep country of Dumfries and Galloway. I was not the farmer, just the tenant of the farmhouse, but I witnessed shepherding activity daily. The roar of the shepherd's ATV, with a pair of Collies riding pillion with the swagger of Hell's Angels, was a thrilling punctuation throughout each day and always drew me to the window to see what activity was about to take place. The farm manager and shepherd, Davey, was a genial and kind-hearted man, a fount of old country knowledge and a colourful character. According to the age-old custom amongst local shepherds, he would castrate newborn lambs with his teeth; an economy both of time and veterinary expense. It was a considerable feat given that he was a number of teeth short of a full set. There was glorious green pasture right outside my study window and also in the fields within my view across the narrow country lane beyond that. Behind the house were the yards and sheep pens, where sheep would be sorted and loaded onto wagons for market, counted, weighed and given veterinary assessments. At various times they were inoculated or dipped; they were wrangled for shearing and generally, constantly, moved from place to place. Above the roar of the ATV, above the bleating of the sheep, sounded Davey's lyrical incantations: 'away, Jess', 'come bye', 'lie down' and, most ubiquitous of all, 'that'll do Jess, that'll do', a command given to instruct the dog to return to the handler's side at the end of a task. The name of the dog would change according to who was on duty, and he usually worked two dogs at a time. The one or two syllables of the dog's name combined with a command gave a mantra-like, sing-song rhythm to it all. Intoned in Davey's thick Borders brogue, the constant chanting of 'that'll do Jess, that'll do' was a poetic refrain that still sounds in my head as powerfully as a favourite old tune.

I lived in beautiful country. It was a painter's palette of green and brown hues; from rich emerald pastures to dun marshland grasses, all accented with sculptural outcrops of grey stone and small copses of mixed woodland. Grazed, green hills undulated as far as the eye could see. These were crisscrossed with an intricate lattice of dry-stone walls, built to separate the pastures. This was the Border country between England and Scotland; the home turf of the Border Collie. To see these dogs running along the tops of the dry-stone walls with the sure-footedness of mountain goats or jumping over them with seemingly effortless bounds was something I never tired of. No wonder these elegant athletes are so superbly adapted for 'agility work'. At just a few weeks old, a shepherd can assess which pups in a litter will have the 'drive' and the right amount of 'eye' to be top-tier sheepdogs. Not every dog is destined to be a star. I took a pup from Davey that didn't make the grade and called him Jake. He was a wonderful housedog and companion. Although he never worked sheep, Jake still got to run freely over rolling Border country and clamber over dry-stone walls, to splash through rushing burns and to watch with rapt attention the goings-on of the farmyard. He never once worried the sheep. He had a good life, full of love and fun, but he was not suitable for breeding and was neutered (by the vet!). Working dogs need to be bred selectively for function and that was not Jake's destiny.

Adventures with a Border Collie

As a result of living there, I had seen Border Collies at work a thousand times but I had never been the handler. So it was with great excitement that I contacted the aptly named Caroline Woolley, when researching for this book. Caroline runs a splendid organization called All About Sheepdogs and organizes training sessions for novice shepherds. She arranged for me to have a session with John Whitley, a shepherd and sheepdog trialist of considerable experience and reputation. John is a Yorkshireman; possessing the bluff, no-nonsense demeanour which that implies. He was also a countryman and naturally suspicious of this chap Caroline was bringing along, a Brit who lived in California! It must have sounded horrifying to him. All my communications had been with Caroline, not John directly, so he had no idea what to expect. Although Yorkshire born and bred, John now lived and worked in Somerset. Set in the wet but milder climes of western England, Somerset has a gentle landscape of verdant pastures that are ideal sheep country. The county was a prosperous beneficiary of the wool trade from the Middle Ages to the nineteenth century, an economic powerhouse in an agrarian age. It is still well-known for its sheep farming.

When I arrived with Caroline around 11am, John was just finishing up a class with four other student shepherds. It was interesting to see them work with their own dogs and a reminder that things would not automatically go well. The working sheepdogs we see on the television or at country shows are exceptionally able and the shepherds at the top of their profession. It is the skill and talent of the expert to make anything appear effortless and easy. Not wishing to interrupt John while he was still taking a class, I stood and watched. I noticed him glancing over, assessing me, for some while before deciding to come up to me. After standard introductions from Caroline he said gruffly, 'What is it that you want to do exactly?' I muttered something about wanting to do as much as possible, to have a hands-on experience of working a dog on sheep, but only to the extent that he was comfortable with allowing me to do. I explained that I was a complete novice but that I was familiar with the basic principles. 'We'll see', he responded and went back to finish matters with his class.

It was ten or fifteen minutes later, as everyone else was leaving, that John came back over to me. This time he was leading a dog, a keen-eyed Collie, on a length of string. He said simply, 'Here's your dog. His name is Joe. Send him out, whichever way you choose'. There had been no other introduction or moment of bonding with Joe and no instruction from John about what to do. Suddenly I was 'at the wheel' and it was a very fast vehicle indeed. An instinct took over. Echoes of Davey in my head brought authority to my voice. Not harsh, not tentative, just strong and expecting to

After a dazzlingly fast outrun, Joe takes it softly with the newly flocked sheep, keeping his distance so that they don't spook. (Photograph by Geoff Dunlop)

be understood and obeyed. 'Joe – come bye' I commanded and in an instant he was streaking out in a broad anti-clockwise arc to gather the sheep from a distant corner. It was beautiful to watch. In an instant he was behind the sheep and the real test was upon me. 'Lie down' I ordered and he did. The sheep, on the verge of stampede slowed and milled in a dense group. I knew in that moment that I had it, the situation was controllable and that if I took it steadily I could have confidence in a good outcome. I was elated but it wasn't the sense of control that had lifted my spirit; it was a feeling of connection.

We had had a successful 'outrun' and 'gather'. Dog and sheep stood stock still, staring at each other. Now for the 'lift', which entailed making the sheep about face and head towards me. 'Walk-on Joe', I said in a relaxed a voice. This was followed immediately by 'ste-ady', intoned softly with lengthened vowels. My heart was in my mouth but Joe nudged them just enough. Now I had to keep them settled as we began the 'fetch' to bring them in. Once more I commanded 'walk-on'. I could tell they were a volatile bunch and I had to bid Joe constantly to 'steady', 'slow', 'stop' and 'lie down', as he pushed them forward in stuttering, staccato bursts of movement. I had not acquired the flow of a true master. However when you have a top dog responding to your commands and a few dozen sheep on the go and everything is happening at lightning speed, it is a thrilling white-knuckle ride. As the sheep drew closer, John quietly instructed me to align myself with the dog, thus balancing the sheep. By doing this, I slowed them from the front, inhibiting a mad charge forward. Although it is the dog that has the greater skill and does most of the work, the shepherd's body positioning and body language becomes integral to the whole operation. At the higher levels this is an art.

From the neutral balance position with Joe at 12 o'clock to my 6 o'clock and with the sheep in between, I found that if I moved a little to my left, the facing sheep veered to their left, away from me. It was rudimentary steering of sorts and I got a sense of the sophisticated precision that might be possible. It was very empowering. Of course, for me, it went wrong in a hurry and suddenly there were twenty or more hooligan sheep making a dash for it, away from the main flock.

The 'lift'. Joe stalks forward slowly putting just enough pressure on the sheep to get them to turn about face but not so much that they will break and scatter. (Photograph by Geoff Dunlop)

'Away Joe', I called and he circled out to his right, to gather them up in a clockwise sweep. He stalled them and I then walked slowly into what I considered to be a good tactical position on their flank, extending my crook to insinuate an invisible barrier between the sheep and a wide stretch of escapable territory. Softly, softly Joe steered them back to the main flock. There were more, smaller breakaway incidents, but we got subsequent renegades under control quite quickly. As the flock, around eighty head of sheep, were marched across the expansive pasture, Joe worked tirelessly and instinctively to keep them together. At one moment he would be sprinting cheetah-quick to reposition himself, then instantly drop with complete stillness to the down position. He would also crouch and stalk, rush with a pouncing leap and side-pass with a dancer's modulated rhythms and grace, all the while fixing the sheep with his eye. Joe had a full repertoire of moves and he delivered a virtuoso performance. It was as joyous to witness as it clearly was for him to perform.

Once we neared the pen, the time came to attempt a 'shed'; that is to split a group of sheep away from the main flock, prior to ushering them into the pen. This was a tricky business. Starting from the balance position, I called Joe to approach the flock very slowly, as I also walked closer to them. Pressure was applied to the centre from two sides until a break began to show. Then I chanted 'that'll do, Joe' a couple of times, calling him to my side. He came straight through the break and the flock

The author assists (probably unnecessarily) with the first breakaway group, who had an especially defiant leader. (Photograph by Geoff Dunlop)

Joe cuts off some rebels, then drops low to stalk them back to the main flock. (Photograph by Geoff Dunlop)

were suddenly divided. Joe and I went to work immediately to stabilize one group and to keep them together. Increasingly I had to play a part, with crook and arms, to create one side of a funnel for Joe to drive the sheep home. It was tense until the end but into the pen they went and I swung the gate shut behind them. It was done. I called Joe in with another 'that'll do' and he came wiggling up to receive the

The 'shed'. Joe has split the flock and is now rounding up the group he wants for penning. (Photograph by Geoff Dunlop)

accolades owed to him. I gave him a brisk ruffling on the scruff, which he accepted gladly but that was it; he then stepped away. This was more of a handshake than a hug. It had been a business transaction and all protocols were now completed and he went back to being an independent being. It was only after we had finished that Caroline confided in me that Joe had not been in good favour – he had misbehaved badly at a sheepdog trial the previous day! I am happy that he was given the chance to redeem himself.

Joe's crouching prowl, giving a strong eye, as he stealthily stalks his unruly mob. (Photograph by Geoff Dunlop)

Joe side-passes with light-footed agility, traversing laterally to close off any lines of escape that insurrectionist factions in the flock might be eyeing. (Photograph by Geoff Dunlop)

The power of the 'Collie eye' is clear to see as Joe thwarts this group of runaways. (Photograph by Geoff Dunlop)

The final drive home, working together to funnel the sheep towards the gate of the pen. (Photograph by Geoff Dunlop)

When the work was done, Joe came in to receive my thanks for his partnership. Collies are immensely affectionate. They may be working dogs but they were often a shepherd's sole companion for many days on the hill. (Photograph by Geoff Dunlop)

Joe showing the double-suspension sprint action that collies are capable of. (Photograph by Geoff Dunlop)

Joe in the 'down' position. The shepherd instructs the dog to drop and stay still if the sheep seem unsettled and under too much pressure. Complete stillness is a vital tool for the controlled movement of livestock. (Photograph by Geoff Dunlop)

Crooks and Whistles

With the sheep securely in the pen, I wanted to learn one more shepherding skill, which was how to use the crook to select and restrain a single sheep for attention. The fleece creates an illusion of a stout animal but its neck is in fact quite narrow and the seemingly tight curl of the crook's hook is exactly the right size. Naturally, the closer one approaches the sheep, the more urgently they run away. One has to be quick but, using the long reach of the crook, I managed to hook one round the neck. Hazel is the wood of choice for crooks. It has tremendous strength and pliability, making it the ideal rod to hold the wriggling might of a hooked sheep. It really was like having a monster fish on the line. I stepped in towards the jiggling and bouncing mass of muscle, simultaneously hauling the ewe towards me as I reached my left hand forward to hold the stick closer to the hook. Then I used my right hand to grab the fleece behind the neck and lift the ewe onto her hind legs, thus reducing the power of four-footed traction. My goodness, sheep are strong.

   Despite my novice errors, I think that I too had redeemed myself with John. We went back to his lovely cottage and enjoyed tea, cake and good conversation. He also showed me a selection of beautiful crooks that he had carved. The hook part is made from a ram's horn, which is boiled to soften it and then flattened in a press. These compressed strips of horn are then sawn to shape before being carved and polished. John also taught me how to use the shepherd's whistle. Throughout my efforts with Joe, I had only given voice commands. Real shepherds make equal use of the whistle, with a simplified Morse code of long and short peeps for each of the voice commands. Traditionally these are made with a broad plate of metal, folded over and with a hole passing through top and bottom of the fold. It sits fully inside the mouth. An expert can produce a surprising range of notes from this simple device and the sound carries far to instruct a distant dog.

The Origins of Pastoral Dogs

The last of the Stone Ages, the Neolithic, began roughly 12,000 years ago. It was during this period that farming first developed. Between then and approximately 10,000 years ago cattle, sheep and goats became domesticated. These animals were able to settle on a relatively limited 'home-range' rather than be truly nomadic and thus could be managed by man, with the assistance of dogs. Dogs performed various functions in this arrangement. Herding dogs could be instructed to sort stock and to corral them into pens, from where they could be sheared, sold or slaughtered. Droving dogs were able to move them over longer distances in an orderly fashion, to take them to market or to different pastures. Guardian dogs were able to defend their charges from large predators. Trade routes and drove roads resulted in an exchange of dogs, as well as the movement of stock, creating a diverse gene pool of shepherding dogs from Asia to Europe. In time distinct regional types emerged - landraces. There was considerable overlap in their duties and most pastoral dogs were multi-purpose. However, over time, many of the pastoral types became more and more specialized. In this chapter I examine the herding and droving aces, the collies and the heelers, reserving the larger flock guardians for a subsequent chapter.

Collies

'*Càilean*' and '*cóilean*' mean 'pup' in Scottish and Irish Gaelic respectively. The word 'collie' or 'colley', as it appears in earlier texts, is almost certainly of Gaelic derivation, though there are other, less convincing, theories. Today, all we can really say is that 'collie' is another word for a sheepdog, which generally, though not exclusively, has a Scottish connection. No discussion of collie types would be complete without first mentioning Lassie, the eponymous canine hero of multiple books and films. Lassie, as portrayed on book covers and in the films was a Rough Collie, a breed that, to many, epitomizes the classic collie type. However, the truth is a little more complex. The inspiration for the first book, *Lassie Come Home* (1940), was a Scottish or Scotch Collie, a much older type that belonged to the author, Eric Knight. Her name was Toots. Scottish Collies were once the most popular working type of stock-herding dog, both in Britain and the United States. Their length of coat, overall size, wider eye and, in particular, length and shape of muzzle resembled more the proportions and morphology of a Border Collie than the Lassie type. So why, then, did they cast a Rough Collie and not a Scottish Collie in the films? For once the fault lay not with Hollywood but with Knight's original work. By the time he was writing, Scottish Collies were an increasingly rare type on farms. Toots was a lucky find. Knights' novel conflated the behaviours and qualities that he observed in Toots with the far more fashionable looks of the Rough Collie. He presumably thought that tuning in to the current doggie vogue would help to sell more copies. However there are important distinctions between the two breeds; differences that underscore the conflict between breeding for form and breeding for function.

Scottish Collie. This is Willow and she is a good representation of the historical type of working landrace collies in Scotland, as evidenced in 19th century art and 19th century breed descriptions. Dogs like this were the foundation stock for many other collie types, including those that developed in America and Australia. The coat is not overlong and the muzzle has 'stop' – the angled indentation just below the eyes that gives the typical canine profile. (Photograph by Becky Davis, Hycottage Farm Collies, Ohio)

Scottish Collie. This profile of Willow shows the archetypal head shape of the true working collie. (Photograph by Becky Davis, Hycottage Farm Collies, Ohio)

Rough Collies were developed for the show bench, not for the farm. They were 'designed' by dog show enthusiasts, utilizing some Scottish Collie genes mixed with other breeds during the last decades of the nineteenth century. Quite soon the flowing, long coats of this new breed became excessively over-exaggerated and, with the probable infusion of Borzoi genes, their muzzles were made overlong and without stop – the steeply angled step down from forehead to muzzle that gives the standard canine profile. Rough Collies were the ornamental cousins of the working Scottish Collie and, given royal patronage by Queen Victoria and Prince Albert, they quickly became fashionable as pets. As well as popularizing them, the royal seal of approval turned this newly developed breed into a Scottish icon. It was their practice to promote a romanticized, and largely false, image of Scottish cultural heritage in general (the patterns of clan tartans are a nineteenth century invention that they also made popular) and the Rough Collie, having what they considered an aristocratic bearing, fitted this narrative. This is not to say that Rough Collies are anything but loveable dogs and good household pets; simply to point out that they are the product of a whim of modish fancy. Half a century later, following the success of *Lassie Come Home* and its many sequels (these were written by others, as Knight died in an air crash in 1943), Rough Collies became all the rage in both the show ring and pet household. This coincided with the rise in popularity of Border Collies and Australian dogs for farm work. As a consequence, the Scottish Collie, a superb archetypal, all-purpose farm-dog and herder, faded into obscurity. Fortunately, although rare, it

Rough Collie. A typical modern specimen in the Lassie mould with the exaggerated coat. Although this breed had some roots in working stock, it was crossbred with other breeds to create an ornamental variety that has achieved great popularity because of its spectacular looks. (Photo: iStock. Credit V Karlov)

Rough Collie. Note the extra-long muzzle with minimum stop together with small eyes, giving the overall appearance of a sheep's head. (Photo: iStock. Credit MOA images)

hasn't yet disappeared completely and the dedicated breeders of the Old-Fashioned Scotch Collie Association and the Scottish Collie Preservation Society in America are working to keep the integrity of this landrace type extant.

The reputation of Scottish herding dogs made it desirable to cross them with local dogs across the border and, long ago, the word 'collie' passed into general usage. There was once the Glenwherry Collie of Ireland (now extinct) and there remains the Bearded Collie (of which more later), the Smooth Collie and the Welsh Collie. Welsh Collies are their own distinctive strain; generally considered to be a cross between the Welsh Hillman (now extinct), the Welsh Back-and-Tan Sheepdog (now extinct) and the Border Collie. Welsh Collies work with a 'loose-eye', which is to say that they vary the amount of eye-contact they give to their flocks, taking care to keep the stock relaxed. They also drop into the crouch less often and to a lesser degree than does the Border Collie. There are considerable style differences in the manner that the different breeds of sheepdog approach their work.

In contrast, the Border Collie is a 'strong-eyed' sheepdog that directs its flocks with an intense gaze and tactical positioning. Border Collies do not bark, bully or bite but, in an imitation of predator behavior, they slink, stalk and stare; thus compelling jittery, swirling flocks to move in precise directions without touching them. They are 'header-stalker' dogs and their peerless proficiency has eclipsed that of other ancient breeds to become the most widely used sheepdog in the British Isles. Working Sheepdog Trials, beginning in the 1870s, became increasingly common as an antidote to the degraded working ability of show dogs fostered by the Kennel Clubs. Today trials are an immensely popular spectator sport and no breed moves the sheep faster or with greater precision and style than does the Border Collie. All Border Collies can trace their ancestry back to Old Hemp, a Lowland Collie born in Northumbria in 1893. Old Hemp had a famously low crawling crouch and was a champion at many a sheepdog trial. These successes put him in great demand as a stud dog. The Lowland Collie, a regional landrace now infused with Old Hemp's crouching gene, was renamed the Border Collie in 1915.

Droving Dogs

Droving is distinct from herding. Herding is rounding up livestock to move them from field to field or to put them in pens. Droving is the act of driving livestock to market or some distance to new grazing. This may be a relatively short journey from the farm to the nearest town or it may be a great distance. Cardiganshire, a county in the far west of Wales, is around 200 miles from the live cattle markets of Smithfield in London and yet the old drovers used to take their famous strain of Welsh black cattle there, walking them steadily along the old drove roads. One of the engines of this enterprise was the Corgi – a short-legged dog, who moved obstinate cattle by agitating at their heels.

The Corgi belongs to a group of dog types known as heelers. Every county in Britain once had its own distinctive brand of heeler. They were known colloquially by old countrymen as 'nip 'n' duck' dogs, because they would nip at the heels and then dodge or flatten to avoid hoofed reprisals. Today the Northumberland Heeler, the Norfolk Heeler and others of their ilk have become extinct and the only British heeler to survive, aside from the Corgi, is the Lancashire Heeler. Overseas, the Swedish

The target for Corgis, and all heeler dogs, is the soft part of the heel just above the hoof. They deliver a controlled and soft nip. (Photograph by Ian Potts)

A Corgi's low-to-the ground profile results in most retaliatory kicks flying harmlessly overhead. (Photograph by Ian Potts)

Vallhund (also a heeler) and the heelers of the Australian stockmen not only survive but are still used extensively to work cattle. By contrast, a working Corgi is a rare find.

The Corgi

It is widely believed that the word corgi derives from the Welsh 'cor' (dwarf) and ci (dog) - the 'c' mutating into a 'g' over time. Some have suggested that it comes from 'cur ci', meaning 'cur dog'. Cur has became a pejorative term, synonymous with a badly-bred mongrel, but it seems likely that this slide in meaning occurred much later than the original use of the word. As late as 1790 Thomas Bewick wrote in his 'General History of Quadrupeds' that,

> The cur dog is a trusty and useful servant to the farmer…they are chiefly employed in driving cattle…They bite very keenly and they always make their attack at the heels.

Swedish Vallhund. Close cousin to the Corgi, these robust heelers still work cattle in Sweden and compete in working trials. (Photo: iStock. Credit GoDogPhoto)

The similarity between 'cur' and 'cor' is inescapable and probably meant the same thing at a time when spelling was not standardized. Moreover 'cur' as it appears in 'curtailed' or 'curt', also means short. Either way, 'corgi' is a Welsh word and the correct plural is '*corgwn*' (pronounced 'corg'n'). However, in common English usage, 'corgis' is the conventional form.

In early Welsh at least, the term 'cur' indicated a working dog of value. References to the worth of herding dogs occur in the laws of the Welsh king, Hywel Dda (r 942 – 950). Book XIII, chapter II states that 'there are three indispensables to the summer resident: a bothy; <u>a herdsman's cur</u> and a knife'. These same laws stipulated the compensation due for various types of injury as well as the value of property, goods and animals. Precise monetary values were given for various types of dog but, for the herdsman's dog, rather than a fixed settlement, the law decreed it should be tied to 'the value of a steer of current worth'. That is a considerable indemnity for anything other than a hunting dog at the time.

An important historical breed that resembles the Corgi is the Swedish Vallhund. Known also as the Viking cattle dog, the Vallhund (literally 'farm–dog') is still worked in Sweden, where regular herding trials are held for the breed. During the century preceding Hywel Dda's reign, Wales largely escaped the relentless Viking invasions that made such deep inroads into English territory and culture. That is, it would seem, except for the Viking dog. It is possible that these little cattle herders from Scandinavia are the antecedents of the Welsh Corgi. Certainly the similarity between the two breeds is compelling. In 2004 a team of archeologists from Cardiff University discovered a foreleg bone of a Corgi-sized dog, dateable to around 900, when excavating a crannog (man-made island) at Llangorse Lake in Wales. By the time of the laws of Hywel Dda, it seems probable that a Vallhund/Corgi type was the sort of dog that was referred to as 'the herdsman's cur'. An alternative view is that the Corgi developed in Wales and was then taken to Scandinavia by the Vikings where its descendants became the Vallhund. However that is not a web that I can untangle.

Today there are two main strains of Corgi, although this distinction wasn't made until the 1930s. The more familiar of the two is the Pembrokeshire Corgi, a breed favoured famously by Queen Elizabeth II. Pembroke Corgis differ in appearance from Cardigan Corgis principally by having a slightly shorter body, shorter ears and a shorter, more slender tail, which in fact is most usually docked. The ears of a Pembrokeshire Corgi are large but those of a Cardigan Corgi are massive dishes that wouldn't look out of place at a satellite tracking station. Cardigans also have an immense brush for a tail, rather like that of a fox, which they use to counterbalance their acrobatic forays of swerves, rolls and lunges into menacing battalions of hostile hooves.

Both 'Cardies' and 'Pembies' are capable of working as drover's dogs, though many believe that it was the Cardigans, the senior breed, who were the long-distance drovers. That is not to say that Cardigan Corgis are not also very useful general purpose dogs around the farm or the market yards, capable of herding cattle, sheep, pigs, goats, ducks, geese and even chickens. Corgis are very good at herding ducks and geese and those that use them for cattle work often train the dog first on these waterfowl. I have seen a corgi herding goats. It was in Jordan, where a Bedouin goatherd was taking his flock along the road before turning onto a track. Annoyingly, by the time we had stopped the car and I had jumped out with my camera, the dog had shyly concealed himself within the herd, leaving outpost duties to others of mixed breeding. From my fleeting observation, the dog seemed to have the longer body and the great tail of the Cardigan Corgi type. Sadly the breed is now endangered in its native Wales; less than 300 Cardigan Corgis were registered in 2010, prompting the formation of the Cymdeithas Cwn Llathen Ceredigion – 'The Ceredigion (Cardiganshire) Yard Dog Society'.

A name, which crops up when rummaging around Corgi history, is *'ci llathen'* (also rendered as *'ci llathaid'*). It translate as 'yard dog'. In English a 'yard dog' is a farmyard watchdog but in Welsh the term *'llathen'* is a unit of measurement; a yard. The Cardigan Corgi is said to measure a yard from the tip of its nose to the tip of its tail. Thus *ci llathen* defines a dog by its size not its function. According to the very helpful folks at Geiriadur Prifysgol Cymru (the Welsh Dictionary) the term *'llathen'* is first recorded in the fourteenth century, where it was the equivalent to an English yard of 36 inches. It is impossible to know when the portmanteau expression *'ci llathen'* first entered everyday language but the first written evidence for it is not until 1933, where, in different texts, it is ascribed both to the Corgi and, erroneously, to the Dachshund. To complicate matters further, another term - 'llathen Gymreig' - occurs from 1816

George, a Cardigan Corgi who measures exactly 40 inches (a Welsh yard) from the tip of his nose to the tip of his tale. (Photograph by Ian Potts)

onwards. It means 'Welsh yard' and a Welsh yard is 40 inches. In Wales, Corgis are still known colloquially as 'yard dogs', though whether they are supposed to be an English or a Welsh yard long is something people differ about.

My Adventure with a Corgi
The chairman of the Ceredigion Yard Dog Society is Arwyn Morgans. He is a butcher in Builth Wells and he works his herd of Welsh black cattle with a Cardigan Corgi. I went to visit him at his farm on the outskirts of Builth in the lush, rolling hills of

central Wales, where he breeds both racehorses and Welsh black cattle. Arwyn, himself Cardiganshire born and bred, is passionate about his Cardigan Corgis and his eyes twinkle when he talks about them. 'I had my first Corgi when I was seven years old', he tells me proudly in his rich, lilting Welsh tones that make even prosaic statements resound with the most beautiful poetry. 'My mother had said "no" to me having a dog', he continued, 'but I saw this Corgi pup and I just fell in love with it. I had half a crown pocket money and it was enough to buy him. I called him Carlo and I hid him in the barn. At meal times I would put a little in my mouth but most of the food went into my pockets. It was several weeks before my mother found out. She was furious but it was too late.'

Arwyn owns three Corgis today: Seren a lovely tri-colour bitch, who was curled up on a chair in the kitchen demonstrating what delightful, gentle house companions these dogs can be; George, the strutting stud dog, a dazzling dandy in his fox-red coat; and Sian, the main worker of the trio. She has a black and white coat, which she wears daubed with large patches of thick farm mud, a badge of honour for a proper working dog. Although Arwyn undoubtedly holds his current dogs in high esteem, there has never been a dog to match his first love, Carlo. 'What a dog', he eulogizes, 'there was never a dog quite like Carlo. He was fearless and would really get into a bull – hanging from its tail or its nose and refusing to let go until it did what was required of it.'

This is Sian, a black and white Cardigan Corgi belonging to Arwyn Morgans. She is fast, she is fearless and, in a David and Goliath contest, she triumphs in constant duels with belligerent bovines. (Photograph by Ian Potts)

He recalled the time when an extremely aggressive and bad-tempered Charolais bull, which had been hired out to inseminate some cows, was proving impossible to load onto the trailer. 'Three men and four dogs spent two hours trying to get this bull in the trailer', he told me. 'Eventually someone suggested fetching Carlo. Within two-minutes the bull had been loaded!' He beams with pride at this oft-told anecdote before delivering the punchline: 'The farmer then exclaimed "Why on earth didn't you send for the Corgi sooner?"' Arwyn chuckles infectiously at this ringing endorsement of Carlo's aptitude for controlling belligerent bovines. Latching on to show who is boss, however, is an extreme measure not usually required.

A major difference between moving cattle and sheep is that sheep will instinctively flock and run from a dog, whereas cattle have to be made to move with rather more physical coercion. A sheepdog therefore works relatively far away from the flock, manoeuvring them on a wide axis. Cattle dogs have to get in amongst the action. In the Welsh language, the Corgi is also referred to as a '*ci sodli*'. '*Sodli*' translates as 'to heel' and the means by which the Corgi moves cattle is to nip at their heels (heeling) to move them forward or at their noses (nosing) to stop or turn them. I choose the word 'nip' carefully – it is a nip rather than a bite, albeit executed with piercing eyes, curled back lips and a snarling ferocity that belies the damage inflicted. When wanting Sian to pose with me for a photograph, she was at first reluctant, being wary of and uneasy with strangers. I took hold of her, making a fuss of her, tickling her stomach and then trying to set her into position. She wriggled and wrestled and nipped in protest. Her teeth must have closed around my hands many dozens of times but not once was I in fear of her puncturing the skin. She was cross but not angry. When Corgis are working cattle they aim their nip very low on the soft part of the heel just above the hoof. It is an act of high-speed precision and great daring. In practice the dogs seldom need to make contact; once the cattle in a herd have had a few nips they know what to expect and most of a Corgi's lunges are merely feints.

'Bring 'em on', Arwyn called to Sian, as he swung open the gates to the cowsheds. Sian had the confident swagger of a matador as she took to the arena; she knew she belonged there. The cattle looked fierce and lowered their heads. One or two attempted to charge but Sian was far too nimble for them, dodging multiple assaults and immediately dashing back at them with renewed authority. Welsh Black Cattle are an ancient breed and like most old breeds, they can be pretty aggressive. We started off with them in the sheds and the mission was to take them up to the top field. I was surprised at what a contest it was. These beasts had no intention of moving without at least putting up the pretence of a fight. Undeterred, Sian faced them down – a dozen ticked-off, large and hefty heifers who resented the disturbance. The little Corgi hurried about her business with great leaping bounds, looking not dissimilar to a bucking bronco; first with her fore-quarters up in the air and then plunging down to lift her hindquarters. It was a to-and-fro rocking motion that created a great deal of energetic movement, stirring the cattle, but which enabled her to stay at finely judged distances; almost like running on the spot. I wondered if these great leaps, and she reached quite a height at times, were also a means of making herself appear bigger to her opponents.

Sian getting ahead of a runaway heifer in order to turn him. If necessary a heeler will nip at the nose, an action referred to as 'nosing'. However a bark and a snarl is usually all it takes (Photograph by Ian Potts)

A feature of Corgi anatomy that also now made sense to me was the distinctively turned-out forelegs. At times she would crouch. With her large broad head lowered and these feet splayed wide she was able to shift from side to side with tremendous alacrity and balance. The ability to dart sideways at the same speed you can go forwards is a useful talent when attacked by either end of an irate critter. 'Get behind', Arwyn ordered, once all the cattle had been provoked from the sanctuary of the sheds and Sian set about their heels. This was not a timid dog. The feisty young heifers did their best to kick her. Mostly the hooves swept harmlessly over her head but there were occasional brushes that bowled her over. She just rolled with it – there are advantages to having the anatomy of a barrel – and was straight back at them.

Once in the field, she occasionally had to return to the front end to turn an animal. In one instance she was sucker-punched. As she came from behind to have a word in the heifer's ear about the direction he was going, he hooked his hind leg forward, up and over the dog. Raking it back, he deftly knocked Sian to the ground. At one point during the assault, she appeared to be underfoot, though this was an illusion created by the hooking kick – the energy was travelling rearwards not downwards. 'She'll be all right,'

Sian faces up to some
very menacing beeves.
She was utterly fearless
(Photograph by Ian Potts)

Note that the heifer's hoof is
raised to strike. The author
looks concerned but Sian
saw it coming and swerved
deftly to avoid it entirely.
(Photograph by Ian Potts)

This kick connected, raking over from the top, but Sian simply rolled and got up unharmed and unperturbed. She resumed her duties immediately with undiminished confidence and determination. (Photograph by Ian Potts)

Arwyn assured me and sure enough, though she looked momentarily affronted by the audacity of this impertinent beef, she was entirely unharmed by the experience and immediately resumed her duties, snarling and nipping with gusto.

By now, Arwyn had stepped back and I was notionally working the drive. Sian, however, knew where her charges were supposed to go and she knew how to get them there and she had little inclination to listen to either me or Arwyn. 'Stand' was shouted by both of us periodically in order to settle things down into a facsimile of a drove and there were moments when she did stand and laid back a bit and the herd steadied. Mostly though we went at quite a pace as we pushed on up the hill towards the top field. It was not a pace that bothered Sian. Her attack was undiminished by the ever-increasing gradient; her energy seemingly inexhaustible. After periods of standing back, Sian would need to put on a burst of speed to get back in contact with the cattle. At the gallop a Corgi has a spectacular leaping action, whereby all four paws leave the ground and she flies over the ground. The short muscle fibres of those little legs deliver an explosive energy. Arwyn rued that he had not been able to work her recently as much as he'd like. Moreover this was a routine movement from shed to field that both dog and cattle knew well. Sian was perhaps a little unruly that morning but she certainly didn't disgrace him. In fact quite the opposite; she showed a talent for the work, a talent and an instinct she was clearly born with.

To keep the meat on the cattle and to conserve the stamina of all – stock, dog and man – for a long-distance journey, a drove would have to be conducted at a steadier pace. Nonetheless I had been given a glimpse of how intuitive the task was to these courageous little dogs. Once the herd is moving on as required, a Corgi just pushes from behind, generally standing back several yards. However as soon as there is a straggler or a wanderer, the dog is quick to round it up and re-unite it with the herd. The rich green pasture of Arwyn's fields provided ample temptation for errant beasts to deviate from the line of our drove, giving Sian plenty of 'incidents' to sort out. It was a very exciting rodeo to witness.

The Drover's Road

A distinctive feature of Welsh Black Cattle, like many old breeds, is that they are browsers as well as grazers. This means that they eat leaves, plants and hedgerow (browse) just as much as they eat the grass (graze). Consequently Welsh Blacks can be raised on relatively poor pasture, such as is found on the rocky hill farms of the Cardiganshire coast. On a drove road, where many herds of cattle had passed previously, the feeding would be sparse and so breeds that could do well on a little were best suited to the longer routes. Despite the relatively barren grazing of a drove road, there were often opportunities for browsing to one side or other. Cattle would meander, snatching what they could as they trudged along. Consequently drove roads follow the natural winding trail of browsing cattle. Moreover well-trodden roads set boundaries to land. Thus when old drove roads were transformed into tarmacadam roads, they continued to follow their original course. It is because of this that country roads in Britain are so notoriously winding.

I asked Arwyn about looking after the dog's feet on a drove of 200 miles. 'Ah', he said, 'they used to make them little leather boots'. I wished that we had had a pair for Sian to model but sadly we didn't. 'When they didn't do that', he added, 'they would walk them through hot tar, which then hardened and protected the paws for the journey'. For the longer droves the cattle were shod, like horses, with metal shoes. The return journey could be altogether more agreeable for the dog. Wealthier drovers might ride a horse for a drove from Wales to London and even those who went on foot often had a packhorse for supplies. Without cattle to drove the little Corgis would get a free ride home in panniers slung across the horse. Whilst fierce and fearless when facing down rambunctious steers, Corgis are nevertheless quite happy to be cosseted as the gentle companion dogs that they also are. A drover's life could be a lonely one and a Corgi made a good friend on the long road. However on a short trip to a local market, the drover was more likely to find his companionship in a nearby public house and the Corgi left to find his own way home.

Whether outward or homeward bound on the long droves, the Corgi had an additional function – that of watchdog. A drover would have to make many overnight stops with his herd, resting in unlit and unfamiliar countryside, vulnerable to local rustlers. Perhaps this is why the Corgi has such very large ears – to be on the alert for any sounds of disturbance throughout the night. Corgis have a reputation for vigilance. Drovers' dogs also have an uncanny ability to know each of their charges. In his book *Dogs and Their Ways* (1863), the Reverend Charles Williams recounts the tale of a drover's dog in which:

> a man had brought seventeen out of twenty oxen from a field, leaving the remaining three there mixed with another herd. He then said to the dog 'Go, fetch them,' and he went and singled out those very three.

Such remarkable stewardship was a frequent necessity on the road, when herds from different droves pastured together overnight. 'Losing' cattle to another herd was almost as great a risk as having them stolen by gangs of rustlers.

As well as the risks of having stock rustled, highway robbery was a significant problem for the drover. Travelling as he did from isolated rural areas through large towns and onto big cities, the drover doubled as messenger and courier. He took letters, rents and taxes from these small communities to the big landlords and authorities in distant towns and he journeyed back with letters and news. The road home could be equally perilous. On the return trip a drover might also be carrying gold coin from the sale of his stock. During the eighteenth century, at the height of droving activity, highway robbery was endemic. As a consequence, drover's banks began to spring up along the drove roads. These small banks were licensed to print their own banknotes. In 1799 one such bank, David Jones and Co of Llandovery, Wales, featured on its banknotes an image of a black ox, an emblem that signified the economic importance of Welsh Black Cattle to the region. It became know as the Black Ox Bank (*Banc yr Eidion Du*) and was a highly successful institution. Llandovery was an important drover's town and it is home today to a magnificent bronze statue of an eighteenth century drover. The plaque informs us that 'Over 30,000 cattle and other livestock were taken by drovers to London from Wales each year'. The Black Ox Bank was taken over by Lloyds Bank in 1909, by which time the railways had put an end to the drover and his dog. Before tentacles of rail had coiled their iron grasp across the entire land, the only way to get stock from farm to market was to walk them there. In Britain, geese, sheep and cattle were driven in their tens of thousands from all corners to the markets and fairs held at great centres of agrarian commerce such as Norwich, Canterbury, Guildford, Barnet and, of course, Smithfields in London. Equivalent journeys were made in other countries. Wherever there were livestock farmers, they had to get their herds and flocks to market and they needed canine assistance to accomplish the mission. The Old English Sheepdog was a drover. He had the regular energy-efficient gait of the endurance walker. Herding and droving wasn't always about dash and hurry. Every region has its own 'specialty' herding breed with coat, conformation and capabilities suited to the local terrain and climate.

Bearded Collie

Frequently mistaken for the Old English Sheepdog is the Bearded Collie, a lighter, more agile dog who wears a similar style of coat. The Bearded Collie is a Scottish sheep-herding and droving breed that has such a developed sense of smell that it can herd a flock of sheep in zero-visibility fog! This is a very useful skill in Scotland. A 'Beardie' possess a stentorian bark, which it uses to gather a flock. Even when dispersed over rough country, the sheep clump together and fall in line like raw recruits responding to a stern drill sergeant. Once sheep are gathered and moving, the Beardie maintains a steady rhythm, keeping the flock on the move. It is an entirely different style to the stop/start precisions of the Border Collie. Their herding instincts are innate but these dogs are independently minded, preferring to be left alone to get on with it, rather than entering into a partnership with the shepherd as does the Border Collie.

Bearded Collie. The coat of the modern show Beardie has been exaggerated in modern times, especially over the face. However working strains still exist and in some instances still work sheep. (Photo: iStock. com / Zuzule)

Although the modern Kennel Club style of Bearded Collie dates to a very limited bloodline originated in 1944, dogs of a similar type have a much longer history. In 1514, a Polish merchant from Gdansk, Kazimierz Grabski, put into the Scottish port of Aberdeen with a shipload of grain. He had come to trade it for sheep and had brought with him six Polish Lowland Sheepdogs (*Polski Owczarek Nizinny*) to assist in loading his ovine cargo. One Scottish shepherd was so impressed with how well these Polish dogs worked the sheep that he traded further sheep in exchange for one male and two female dogs. According to tradition these Polish dogs were bred with local Scottish dogs to produce the strain known as the Bearded Collie. The similarity between the breeds is certainly striking. It is difficult to be certain of the story, which is contested, but there is a general truth that sheep are traded throughout the world and dogs travel with their sheep. As a consequence the dispersal of the gene pool for herding dogs is probably far greater than for other types.

Although they were useful herding dogs on the home range, Bearded Collies also drove large flocks of sheep from Scotland to Smithfields (London's leading livestock market). These hardy Scottish sheep were then sold for export, where they established the great flocks of Australia and New Zealand. The same dogs that had

Hungarian Puli. Its distinctively corded coat of matted hair serves to protect against weather and also has a fleece-like appearance enabling these dogs to blend in with their flocks. The Puli's larger, flock guardian accomplice, the Kommondor, has the same 'dreadlocked' coat. It is said that this defends against wolf bites. (Photo: iStock.com /ssss1gmel)

brought them from the moors drove their charges onto the ships at London docks. In fact the dogs were usually sold with the flock to facilitate their disembarkation at the other end. There is an Australian 'breed' of sheepdog that greatly resembles the Beardie; they call it the 'Smithfield'. It derives from those Scottish dogs who, by dint of their profession, took passage for a new life. Both Bearded Collies and Smithfields are still worked today.

A major consideration for all droving breeds is that they are out in all weathers – night after night and day after day after day. Bearded collies, like Old English Sheepdogs and many other herding/droving breeds have long, dense coats, though those of the true working dog were nothing like as long as they have become for today's show dogs. These help to shield them from wet and windy weather as well as allowing the mud of the trail to cake and drop off relatively easily; though not as easily as modern day owners may wish! Corgis and Vallhunds are spitz dogs, having the double-coat insulation possessed by all 'dogs of the North'. A distinctively alternative type of 'weatherproof' coat appears on herding dogs from Hungary. The Puli and Kommondor wear the densely matted coils of a corded coat to resist the biting winds of the *puszta*, Hungary's vast and featureless grassland plains that offer no natural shelter. It is said that these dense cables of matted hair also resist the bite of a wolf. However not all droves are conducted in the cold, wet climate of Northern Europe. Droves also take place on hot, arid and dusty trails.

Hall's Heelers

Thomas Simpson Hall (1808 – 1870), the son of a first generation migrant to Australia, was a cattle rancher in New South Wales. By the end of his career he controlled over 1,000,000 acres of prime grazing. In order to bring his beef to market in Sydney, the vastness of these holdings led to cattle droves of epic proportions. Furthermore the ruggedness of the terrain together with the harshness of the climate made such undertakings especially arduous. A letter from Hall recalled that he once lost 200 head of cattle in scrub. This was virgin country without fencing or natural barriers. The cattle were left, untended, to fatten for months on end, which created somewhat ornery beasts. Moving thousands of head of quarrelsome cattle for many hundred miles could only be done with the aid of exceptional dogs.

According to traditional breed history, Hall imported a number of Northumberland Blue Merle Drovers Dogs, a hardy type from the north of England, and crossed them with hand-reared Dingoes (it is speculated that Dingoes – Australia's feral dogs were brought over by early seafarers from Indonesia around 6,500 BC). The notion that Hall crossed his heelers with Dingo blood has been scoffed at by some modern dog historians (notably Hancock, *Dogs of the Shepherd*, 2014), considering it an unfounded mythology. He sees no benefit from the admixture, since all the alleged attributes of colouring, silent working and heeling instinct were present in a variety of British working types that were imported to the Antipodes, along with their sheep and cattle.

Whatever the truth of the Dingo infusion, there is no doubt that, by 1840, Thomas Hall had developed a type of dog that possessed extraordinary

Australian Cattle Dog. Also known as a Blue Heeler or Queensland Dog. These are exceptionally hardy cattle dogs. (Photo: iStock. Credit GoDogPhoto)

intelligence, toughness and endurance. He was protective of his unique strain and didn't sell his dogs to anyone. They were exclusive to the Hall ranching empire and a key component in giving it a competitive edge. However. after his death in 1870, his estates were split up and auctioned off, complete with stock and dogs. From these dogs emerged Australia's famed Blue Heeler, Red Heeler, Queensland Heeler and the Australian Cattle Dog. Aside from minor variations in colouring, these are all really the same dog. Jack Timmins, a contract drover, who formerly worked for Hall, developed a variant of these fierce little warriors. In the late 1840s, Timmins acquired a pair of Hall's Heelers and bred a line that he heralded as 'great biters'. They became known as 'Timmin's Biters.' Despite romantically bucolic images of cows grazing gently in verdant pastures, cattle can be fierce and aggressive creatures, especially beef cattle. It takes a dog of great courage and tenacity to move a large number of them. A long cattle drive is work for tough humans and even tougher dogs and for droving large herds over open space, the dog par excellence is the Australian Cattle Dog. They remain in widespread use today, not only in Australia but also in the United States. Cowboys mount up and move herds a great distance over harsh terrain, assisted by these peerless little dogs from Down Under. Whilst heelers may not have the precision of a Collie, they have the appropriate level of confrontational aggression that is needed to get large, angry and stubborn bovines to move.

Australian Shepherd Dog

Australian Shepherd Dogs differ from Australian Cattle Dogs in two principal ways. Firstly they are collie-type dogs, rather than heelers. Secondly, 'Aussies', as they are popularly known, were not developed as a breed in Australia but rather in the United States. Following the Mexican-American War (1846-1848) the United States purchased vast tracts of land, including California, from their defeated foe at knockdown prices. There was the instant reward of gold, of course, but of greater value was the extensive expanse of land now available for settlement. Abraham Lincoln's Homestead Act (1862), in which land titles could be purchased for $1.25 per acre, accelerated this westward migration. Sheep ranching offered great opportunity to those prepared to work hard and take the gamble. It was mostly scrub grazing, so many settlers purchased imported strains of sheep from Australia, sheep that did well in a dry climate. Australian sheep were imported in prodigious quantities. Shepherding dogs were necessary to marshal the flocks on and off the ships and into holding pens at

Australian Shepherd Dog. Known affectionately as the 'Aussie', these dogs were developed in the Western United States in the 19th century and remain extremely popular on farms and ranches in the area. They are hardy Collie-type dogs able to endure all weathers. (Photo: iStock.com / Zuzule)

the dockside markets. A notice in the 21 April 1858 issue of the *Alta California* (a San Francisco daily newspaper) recorded that,

> The ship *Eli Whitney*, recently arrived from Sydney, brought two dozen well-trained Australian shepherd dogs, whose valuable services will be henceforth applied to tending sheep in some of the ranches in this section of the country. They have sustained the voyage without accident, and landed in fine condition. The Australian shepherd dog is celebrated for his courage, sagacity and powers of endurance…Wonderful stories are related of the faithfulness of these dogs, and their almost human intelligence.

The use of the term 'Australian shepherd dogs' in this instance does not imply that there was an established breed of that name at the time; it is merely a collective term to indicate a group of sheepdogs arriving from Australia. It was a common story and ships carrying sheep and dogs from the Australian outback unloaded not only in San Francisco but also in Seattle where they could be fattened quickly on the greener pastures of Washington, Oregon and Idaho. The dogs voyaging with these ovine cargos were the direct descendants of the dogs that had taken the sheep from Europe to Australia in the first place, just a few decades earlier. They were mixes of various British strains. Over the next several decades in America, they were interbred, not only with other antipodean immigrants but also with stock dogs that had been brought from the Midwest by other Europeans in search of the new ranching bonanza. Consequently it is likely that genes from sheepdogs originating in Spain, Germany, and France, as well as Britain were added to the mix. Function, not appearance, was the driving force for all selective breeding. However by around the 1920s the Australian Shepherd Dog, as we know it, was recognizable as a distinct breed and was breeding true, although the AKC did not recognize the Aussie officially until 1993! His ancestors were mostly, if not exclusively, British. Nevertheless he is the product of systematic selection by American breeders; he is an American dog. He carries his name as a throwback to his migrant ancestors, though he is not a breed in regular use in Australia. Aussies have become ubiquitous general-purpose dogs on American farms in the West, where they serve double duty as watchful guard dogs. Although they can exhibit a variety of coat colours, the most characteristic is the black, white and tan tri-colour. When working sheep, Aussies use a trinity of bark, nip and eye to coerce their charges into compliance.

Kelpie

According to a popular saying, 'Australia was built on the back of the Kelpie'. It acknowledges the central role of this muscular, medium-sized herding dog, in the establishment of Australia's principal source of wealth – sheep-ranching. As with other Australian breeds there is folklore that suggests an infusion of Dingo blood but that is far from certain fact. Some breed histories claim Russian ancestry for these tireless workers but various types of Scottish collie are the more likely antecedents. Nineteenth-century accounts report that crofters in Scotland's Western Isles used

Australian Kelpie demonstrating 'sheep backing', a manouevre in which these dogs run across the backs of sheep in a jammed pen to get to the cause of the bottleneck. (Photograph by Martin Pot ©)

cattle dogs that they referred to as kelpies. These remarkable stock-dogs must have had fierce powers of persuasion, since they were able to compel curmudgeonly cattle to swim from one island to another at low tide. It seems probable that 'kelpie' was a variant pronunciation of collie and that the word migrated to Australia with Scottish settlers, as a generic for sheepdog. Whatever the truth of that, the Kelpie is an exceptional herding dog, famed for its ability to traverse a crowded pen of sheep, by hopping onto their backs and padding lightly across the undulating sea of wool with the balanced finesse of a funambulist.

German Shepherd Dog

Sitting somewhere between herding dogs, droving dogs and livestock guardians are German Shepherd Dogs. They work without 'eye' or 'balance' but are nevertheless able to control sheep, intimidating with their size and by constant activity. In areas where grazing juxtaposes crops, or another farmer's land, without a robust physical boundary, German Shepherd Dogs are taught to 'work the furrow'. Having been shown the limitations of where the sheep may roam (traditionally this was literally a furrow), they will patrol constantly to keep the sheep within bounds. Transhumance – the practice of taking flocks to the high pasture for the summer and bringing them back down to the low pastures before the snows come – required a particular style of shepherding. German Shepherd Dogs were used extensively in the mountainous areas of Germany for such work. Sheep were kept away from neighbours' crops as they were taken from one pasture to another and during the summer on the hill, the GSD remained with the sheep, and the shepherd, as guardian.

German Shepherd Dog (Alsatian) guarding its flock of sheep and Haflinger horse. (Photo: iStock. Credit fotokate)

For centuries the Eurasian wolf had been the GSDs principal adversary but their numbers had been decimated by hunters and trappers throughout the nineteenth century. The last wolf in Germany was shot in 1904. As the need to guard against wolves began to diminish, the German Shepherd Dog – then at best a loose descriptor of a general type – morphed into more of a general herding dog. It was from these dogs – a varied assortment, each distinct to its own locale – that the German Shepherd Dog, as we know him today, was developed. A group of enthusiasts, calling themselves the Phylax Society, got together in 1891 with the aim of creating a standardized version of the German Shepherd Dog, one that was emblematic of the newly formed German state. They disagreed on detail and the plan floundered. In 1899, a former member of the Phylax Society, Captain Max von Stephanitz, attended a dog show where he saw a specimen that he considered was the right type to represent an ideal form of the German Shepherd Dog. He bought it and bred from it. That dog, whose name the captain changed to Horand von Grafrath, is the ultimate source of all German Shepherd Dogs today. There is no doubt that these are spectacular dogs, justly respected for their intelligence, courage and high level of trainability. There are places where they are still worked with sheep but the type has changed quite a bit since their early shepherding days.

In German he is called the *Deutscher Schäferhund* – German Shepherd Dog – but for most of the twentieth century these dogs were known in Britain as Alsatians. During World War I, a time when, to appease anti-German sentiment, the British Royal family changed its name from Saxe-Coburg and Gotha to Windsor, there was a similar bowdlerization applied to these German dogs. The British Kennel Club listed them as Alsatian Wolf Dogs. Alsace is geo-politically in France. However the region has German cultural links and the old Alsatian dialect has a characteristically Germanic brogue. Pastoral dogs from the Alsace region were just one of many varieties from a wider area of German lands that were all broadly similar. They were also much like the Belgian Malinois, a pastoral breed of common heritage. During the last quarter of the nineteenth century, at the time of the German Shepherd Dog's establishment as a singular breed, Alsace was administered from Germany/Prussia following its victory in the Franco-Prussian War in 1871. Alsace was returned to French administration at the end of World War I. The dogs, of course, knew nothing of these nuances. Although the sensational 'wolf dog' suffix soon fell out of use, it wasn't until 1977 that breed enthusiasts lobbied the Kennel Club successfully to have the name revert to German Shepherd Dog. Even so, 'Alsatian' persists in common parlance and was only removed from Kennel Club listings as an alternative name in 2010.

As with so many breeds that have enjoyed extreme popularity and have therefore been bred in quantity without sufficient thought to the animal's well-being, there are controversies concerning alterations to the breed's anatomy. Far too many modern GSDs have an acutely sloping topline, with the hindquarters sunk low. This design modification was thought by some to give the dog a menacing appearance, the angle implying that it was constantly on the verge of springing forward to attack. Sadly it has resulted in dogs that cannot run properly and are prone to discomfort in the hips. Fortunately, away from these aberrations, many working specimens are still bred to have a functional straight back. Today German Shepherd Dogs are used extensively as guard dogs, arrest dogs and search-and-rescue dogs, especially by the armed services and police forces. The GSD's natural flair for these tasks draws on the heritage of his former life as both a herder and a livestock guardian. Though now engaged only rarely for this original employment, the ancestors of the German Shepherd Dog reigned supreme in the high pasture.

There are many other herding and droving breeds of distinction, such as New Zealand's Huntaway, the French Briard and the Basque Gorbeikoa. Indeed every region of every country has its own distinctive herding and droving type. Terrain, climate and the character of the stock they have to command have influenced their form. Different tactics – be it barking or barging, nipping or nudging or giving the eye – are matched to the different temperaments of particular breeds of cattle and sheep and their environments. For these reasons herding and droving dogs are a very diverse family and a full gazetteer is not possible in a work of this size. There is one other group of pastoral breeds however, that demands attention. These are the livestock guardians, who protect the flocks from predators. They are the subject of the following chapter.

Chapter 2

Livestock Guardian Dogs

'The shepherd's hounde is very necesserye and profitable for the avoyding of harmes and inconveniences which may come to men by the means of beastes.'
—Dr Caius, *Of English Dogges*, 1576

Anatolian Shepherd Dogs lined up on sentry duty, patrolling the perimeter. (Photograph by Kim Hawkins)

Livestock guardian dogs are large, powerful and courageous dogs that live out on the high pasture with livestock in order to guard them against predators. Depending on the region, these may include wolves, bears, mountain lions or coyotes. Most commonly, livestock guardians are used with flocks of sheep but they are also employed to guard herds of goats and even flocks of poultry. In extremis they will do battle, to the death, with a predator but generally their presence is enough to deter an attack.

Predators are put off by dog behaviours that are designed to confuse their normal hunting pattern. Although at first sight the dogs appear to blend in with the flock, a potential predator is unnerved by actions that are not characteristic of the prey animal. Once a dog senses a predator in the vicinity, he will put on all manner of display threats. At a distance these include ferocious barking, charging around aggressively and aggressive tail postures; at closer proximity the dog will bare his teeth, snarl and feint with sudden lunges. Most predators err on the side of caution. According to the size of the flock and the level of danger, there may be any number of guardian dogs and when this is the case, they work together as a pack to face down any threat. A friend who has a pair of livestock guardians, reports that the local coyotes can deploy quite sophisticated tactics. Some undertake to lure the dogs away from the flock, while others attempt an ambush. Her dogs outwit them though. Only one will go and remonstrate with the decoy bandits, while the other remains stolidly with the flock.

Pyrenean Mountain Dog (aka Great Pyrenees) guarding a young flock. (Photo: iStock/DMU)

The patient and vigilant eye of a Pyrenean Mountain Dog. Whilst more docile strains have been bred as house-dogs, the working strains of these powerful animals have the potential to confront ferocious predators. (Photograph by the author)

Livestock guardian breeds include the Pyrenean Mountain Dog (known in the USA as the Great Pyrenees) from Spain and France; the Ovtcharka from the Ukraine and Russia; the Kuvasc and the Komondor from Hungary; the Maremma from Italy and the Anatolian Shepherd Dog from Turkey. There are others. Anatolians vary regionally from a black-faced variety known as the Karabash and a white-faced variety called the Akbash. The AKC designates the Akbash as a separate breed but given that such small distinctions of breed variation are man-made constructs, this is really splitting hairs. I prefer to call all Turkish livestock guardians by the name they are revered by in Turkey: Kangals. These are the livestock guardians most in use in the United States today and can be found on active duty on ranches throughout the country.

A number of livestock guardian breeds continue to serve as working dogs in various parts of the world. They perform their traditional roles in remote areas where flock predation by large predators is still a problem. Livestock guardians are a much sounder, more humane and more ecologically responsible solution to predation than are the traps and poisons that are used otherwise. In Italy, for instance, the use of the Maremma to protect flocks in some wilderness areas has allowed the re-introduction of wild populations of wolves, without posing an undue threat to the sheep.

The key to creating an effective livestock guardian is to ensure that it is socialized and bonded with the species it is going to guard. This is achieved by introducing a dog to his future companions at the puppy stage. At a few weeks old even the toughest pup

Known as Anatolian Shepherd Dogs in the West and as Kangals in their native Turkey, these dogs have an imposing muscular power and an intent watchful gaze. They are a popular choice as livestock guardian in the United States. (Photograph by Kim Hawkins)

Kangals with sheep. Note how the dark face of the dogs blends with the black-faced sheep. (Photograph by Kim Hawkins)

will learn his manners if he receives a sharp peck from a goose or a hefty butt from a goat or a sheep. His adopted species also become his playmates and his friends. Without this process, which is close to imprinting, a livestock guardian could itself become the predator. However if it is done correctly, the bond between dog and sheep is so strong that the dog will, if necessary, lay down his life in their defence.

Adventures with a Livestock Guardian Dog

When I received the e-mail alerting me to the impending introduction of a Kangal pup to some sheep, I made immediate plans to be there. Mark Griffith and Lynn Kenny run the Rare Breeds Ranch in Cottonwood, California, just a few hours' drive North from where I live. Their beautiful ranch is situated in the magnificent wooded foothills that nestle beneath the snow-capped majesty of Mount Shasta. In addition to Peruvian Paso horses,

Shire horses and Suffolk sheep, Mark and Lynn breed Anatolian Shepherd Dogs – Kangals. They have eight of them! A recent litter had produced only one pup, Autumn, and it was time for this very spirited and self-assured young lady to come face-to-face with some sheep. Since she was four weeks old, she had been spending a few hours a day in a pen adjacent to a couple of ten-month-old lambs but had not yet been let loose with them. When I arrived, Autumn was just eight weeks old and I was able to witness that very first physical meeting. The lambs were in a pen that measured around 12 feet by 12 feet. Without any hesitation, Autumn bounded up to them, wagging her tail. At ten months, the lambs were considerably larger than Autumn and were also accustomed to having dogs around. They were not at all startled and the little pup was able to get nose-to-nose with them for a very friendly greeting. Although polite, the lambs showed little interest in Autumn and she quickly became bored, as pups do, and started ferreting around in the straw to see if there were any food scraps. There were slim pickings, so she became bored again and decided to see if her new friends were interested in a game of chase. Lynn grabbed her immediately and rolled her on her back, rebuking her with a very stern 'No!' Any notions of chasing sheep have to be nipped in the bud at the earliest possible stage. Once these dogs grow larger, games take on a far less innocent character quite quickly.

Autumn, the bold Kangal pup, introducing herself to a much larger sheep for the first time. (Photograph by Kim Hawkins)

Autumn practises her adult sentry stance, while the sheep look on suspiciously. (Photograph by Kim Hawkins)

Good behaviour can only be sustained for so long by a spirited pup. Autumn succumbs to chasing her new friends. After a coupole of gentle human rebukes came a not-so-gentle head-butt from the pursued. This admonishment had the desired effect and Autumn was well-behaved for the rest of the session. (Photograph by Kim Hawkins)

Autumn tries the nonchalant approach, but she is about to get short shrift as an ovine head lowers in readiness to butt. (Photograph by Kim Hawkins)

Autumn was clearly going to be a handful. She possessed confidence and curiosity in equally abundant measure, mixed in with strong-willed and stubborn streaks. 'No' was not a word that she regarded as important. Soon she was at it again and, although it remained playful, this time it was with snapping jaws. Again came a swift reprimand from Lynn. There was pause. However after a few moment of desultory nosing around, Autumn provoked her companions once again. This time one of the lambs responded to her advances with a lightning strike. She head-butted the little pup and sent her tumbling over. Peer pressure triumphed and little Autumn was very well behaved after that. Although not in the least dismayed or intimidated by this robust reproach – she still felt comfortable rummaging around the straw beneath their noses – Autumn resisted any urges she may still have had to chase. In the coming weeks she would be spending more and more time with the lambs and a bond would form between them. Autumn would become more and more protective of her sheep.

After spending time with Autumn, we set off to see the big dogs on the hill, who were getting ready for their night patrols. On arrival, the moment we exited the car, a great, galloping, barking pack of eight Kangals descended on us with energetic exuberance. I had been aware of the reputation of these dogs as being fierce, dangerous even. I knew that we might need to be wary around them. However, it was immediately obvious that no danger existed. These Kangals had been thoroughly socialized with people and were as gentle and demandingly affectionate as spaniels. This was a credit to the training given to them by Mark and Lynn. The male, Khan, weighs in at around 120lbs of lean muscle but he was perhaps the soppiest of them all; an adorable fellow. These are dogs that are as big as people. When you give them a hug, you need the full length of your arms to wrap around them and you can give them a huge squeeze. They roll on their backs and want their stomachs scratched just like any other dog. Nonetheless these are not an average pet dog and should not be owned by anyone without the appropriate knowledge and facilities. They require an advanced level of canine keeper.

Among the livestock guardian breeds that are common as domestic pets are some strains of Pyrenean Mountain Dog. There remains working Pyrenean stock, who retain their ancestral dominance over predators. However there are others who have been bred to be more placid. These make wonderful pet companions but the more docile strains are unlikely to be able to make it on the high pasture when the wolves or the coyotes come around. Facing up to large, carnivorous predators is not a problem one has in Surrey and so, to the dog-loving English, the aggression required in a working livestock guardian can seem a little shocking.

Kangals not only have large reserves of residual aggression, they are also very independently minded. They do not sit, come or stay on command with the same punctilious adherence of a Labrador but wander off at will and do their own thing. They will respond to human requests if it suits them but generally they believe that they know best, that they are always on duty and that if they need to patrol the fence-line now or check on some sheep over there, or dig a hollow to shelter in then that is what they will do. It is yet another reason why these dogs do not make suitable domestic pets. That independent spirit, that ability to be the decision maker rather than the recipient of human decisions, is what makes them good at their job. When they are out on the hill with their flock, they are in charge. After all they are the ones who will be aware of any danger from predators long before the shepherd will.

We had arrived mid-afternoon in December and after observing the pup's induction with the lambs, we headed to the hill around 4pm. Sunset approached around 5.30pm. It was a period of intense activity as the dogs stationed themselves at various points looking even more alert than usual. A few of them were busy digging; Kangals are compulsive diggers and their territory often looks like a moonscape. Like wolves, they are capable of excavating deep-tunnel dens. However, to shelter from the worst of the wind and the cold when on duty on the hill, they dig a shallow trench, which they can tuck into, keeping their underside and internal organs warm and dry. It was going to be a cold night. Others were watching, listening and scenting the air. Every so often there would be a burst of activity. Sometimes it was frenzied barking. At other times the whole pack would race to a corner of the compound and then, with their tails

A Kangal excavating a deep tunnel. The digging gene is not exclusive to terriers. Dogs that live outside in harsh weather need to dig for shelter. (Photograph by Kim Hawkins)

A Kangal taking a rest, while others are on watch. She has curled up into a hollow that she dug for the purpose, shielding her underbelly from the biting winds. (Photograph by Kim Hawkins)

Spot the dog. Note how, when amongst the flock, a Kangal lets its tail hang straight, simulating the hang of the sheep's tails. When patrolling the boundaries, however, the tail is curled over the back. (Photograph by Kim Hawkins)

curled and flagging, stand sentry with steadfast stillness. Their tails are important signalling systems. When standing with the flock during the day, their tail unfurls and hangs straight, a mirror image of the sheep's tails. However, when on the alert and reporting to each other, it coils tightly over their backs.

For the most part livestock guardian dogs are very unexcitable, moving around slowly so as not to disturb the flock. They spend much of their time just standing or sitting and watching, always watching. However dusk is a prime time for opportunistic predators to creep out from the gloom and so it is a moment in the day when the dogs become especially energized, sending out strong messages, for any predator thinking about it, not to try anything in the night. The ranch sits on 110 acres and it is surrounded by a high fence. This means that these dogs do not actually come into direct physical contact with predators as they would on the open range but that they are able to exercise all their natural guardian instincts. They have sheep to protect and they have a large area that gives them the twin stimuli of strategic positioning and rapid-response deployment to a suspected trouble spot. Although, if it comes to it, a livestock guardian will engage in combat with a predator, most of its work is in deterring such an event by employing display aggression. Here the dogs had ample opportunity to exercise this ancestral dance of defiance and it was exhilarating to be standing in a spot when the pack would come hurtling close by, with all the fury and intensity that would be expected for an imminent confrontation with a pack of coyotes.

While I was there a spirited play-fight broke out. It is a common occurrence among livestock guardians and serves to teach them tactics and to keep them in readiness for the real thing, should it ever occur. Working livestock guardians may have to confront a coyote, a mountain lion or a wolf in the service of their flock and they need to keep their fighting reflexes sharp; they need to train. One typical move is to rear, getting higher than the target animal and use bodyweight to wrestle it to the ground. They did a lot of this. Most impressive though was how harmoniously they worked together as a pack. When the girls ganged up on Khan, the dauntingly large male, there was clearly co-operative tactical deployment. When fighting a real predator in earnest, teeth may be used but it is more typical for Kangals to kill by choking, using a leg and their bodyweight against the throat. Although I am happy to report that not so much as a scratch was received in the drill that I witnessed, these are very tough dogs with

A play-fight, witnessed by the author at close quarters. It was apparent that this was just high-spirits and an instinctive training session. They were using play to simulate how they might work together co-operatively to neutralize a dangerous predator. Khan was the surrogate victim surrounded by the girls. One faced off to him, drawing his gaze and growl, while a second dog seized his tail, halting him and upsetting his balance. A third then barrelled into him, body-slamming him to the ground, while the fourth attacker stood close-by in reserve. Subsequently they all piled onto him on the ground, but only briefly. It was a well-orchestrated team effort and they soon got up and resumed their patrol as friends. (Photograph by Kim Hawkins)

the potential for serious aggression. Their combat training sessions can and do get out of hand. Once in a while, the dogs have to be separated and stitched up. It all sounds very brutal but in order to be an effective deterrent against coyotes preying on a flock, these sentinels have to be battle-ready.

There was no lack of coyotes in the area, which was very apparent once we had gone to bed. The dogs, of course, remained outside – on duty. Throughout the night there were numerous eruptions of belligerent barking – a raucous cacophonous, canine concerto as predator and guardian dog challenged each other with vocal animosity. Amidst the barks swelled waves of synchronized howls, adding an eerie, ancestral tone to this choral duel. It was a sound, the call of the wild, that shepherds in remote regions must have heard for millennia and it was a reminder of the harsh realities of nature in isolated areas. In this case the remoteness was a blessing – you would not want to be too close a neighbour to these nocturnally noisy dogs. One of Mark and Lynn's neighbours also has Kangals. These protect a flock of sheep on the open range and Lynn told me that they had come out one morning to discover that their dogs had killed a bear in defence of their flock! Such stories are common. There is one about a goat rancher in Texas, retold in the book *Livestock Protection Dogs* (Dawdiak and Sims, 1990). The rancher had come out to find his large herd of Angora goats missing from their usual feeding station. As he searched for them, he came across pools of blood and scraps of hair. Then one by one, he found seven dead coyotes. Sadly two of his guardian dogs had also been killed in the fight. However one dog had survived and he found him walking in tight circles around the huddled herd of goats. Not a single goat had been harmed. A local wildlife officer estimated, based on footprints and the number of coyotes found dead from bite wounds during the next few days, that the three livestock guardian dogs had thwarted an attack from a pack of over twenty coyotes. The instinct to chase prey animals (which includes the neighbour's cat) is inherent in all dogs, it is part of their wolf heritage. Livestock guardian dogs have been kept especially close to their wolf ancestry in order to maintain levels of aggression, strength and animal-cunning that make them a match for these predators. However wolves also have the potential for trans-species empathy. Livestock guardians have been selectively bred over the millennia to take advantage of that empathetic trait but it has to be reinforced with training because it will always sit alongside a suppressed predator tendency. It is a fine balance to produce a dog that is as tough as a wolf and as gentle as a lamb.

As with all species, the teenage phase can be a challenge and once a young dog is put out on the hill with a flock, unsupervised, chasing can become a problem again. There are two pieces of traditional training apparatus designed to curtail these adolescent rampages – the 'drag' and the 'dangle-stick'. This first was a small log attached to a long chain, which slowed and inhibited a dog's ability to chase. However, unless the dog was under constant human supervision whilst wearing it, there was a risk that the drag snagged on something. A safer solution was the dangle-stick or 'dangler', a small log that hangs from the dog's neck. It allowed him to move around slowly but if he tried to run or chase, the log would knock uncomfortably against his legs. Although it may look rather awkward, these big powerful dogs supposedly got used to it quickly and pottered around with it quite unperturbed. They generally didn't need to wear one for very long, although there could be circumstances that caused them to be put back 'on the log'. For instance if one of the flock is injured, the flock guardian's instinct will be to cull it; injured animals attract predators, which threaten the whole flock. A watchful shepherd may wish to override this, knowing that he can bring the animal back to full health but needs to restrain his guardian dog for a few days. Dangle-sticks were the precursors of the electric shock collar and arguably a gentler option for dissuading dogs from chasing stock. Even so they are seldom employed these days.

Another piece of specialist equipment for the livestock guardian is a spiked collar. This ferocious looking device is not for attack but for defence. Whether it be wolf, coyote or mountain lion, predators attack the neck and throat as primary targets. A spiked collar removes that lethal threat entirely. Medieval and some later period hunting dogs often wore spiked collars when going up against dangerous game for the same reasons. Here the spikes were often mounted on a leather collar but the

A Kangal posing with a traditional 'dangle-stick' or 'dangler', which was used to dissuade young dogs from chasing their flocks, when they were first let lose with them on open land. They had complete freedom to roam but were deterred from chasing because the stick would have knocked against their shins. (Photograph by Kim Hawkins)

traditional Turkish Kangal collars are always made entirely of metal, which, despite problems of rust, is less perishable and more durable than leather versions. Some are a plain metal band, while others consist of articulated metal plates. Mark and Lynn had quite a collection of different styles and although their dogs do not wear these on an everyday basis, they (the dogs) were nonetheless happy to model them for us. They appeared to be entirely comfortable in them.

A Kangal modelling a traditional spiked collar. The neck and throat are primary zones for attack by predators and these collars offered useful protection against such assaults. (Photograph by Kim Hawkins)

Despite appearances, I was also entirely comfortable in the traditional Turkish shepherd's coat that Lynn urged me to try on. As sunset approached it became very, very cold on the hill. In fact the following day, shortly after we left, they had the first snows of the season. Yes, in parts of California, at higher elevations, there is snow. Shepherds spend the night on the hill, alongside their dogs, snatching periods of sleep, with no other warmth or protection than one of these coats. It was like wearing a house on one's back and I felt about as mobile as a tortoise. Fortunately I didn't have to move very far and, even more fortunately, I didn't have to spend the night outside. As soon as the sun went down we went inside, where Mark prepared us a fine gourmet meal.

At dinner Mark produced a giant tooth and told us the story of Zor. Zor was the foundation stud dog for their kennel and, although he is now dead, it was clear that he had been loved above all others and that his memory remained fresh. One day

The author trying on a traditional Anatolian shepherd's coat, made from a very thick felt, which is a lightweight and extremely good insulating material. It is half tent, half cloak. The shoulders are extremely wide, making the whole thing hang away from the body. As a consequence, neither wind nor rain act directly against the body through the textile, as they do with other weather-proof garments. Moreover an insulating pocket of air, warmed by body heat, is trapped in the large space between body and robe. It was effective and Turkish shepherds would sleep on the hill in sub-zero temperatures with nothing but this coat for shelter. (Photograph by Kim Hawkins)

Mark accidentally reversed his truck over Zor – we all know how easily such a terrible thing can happen. An indignant Zor had retaliated by biting into one of the tyres and puncturing it. That tyre is where the tooth, having been dislodged from Zor's gums, had lodged. Though he had some bleeding, miraculously nothing was broken and Zor recovered from the incident. These dogs are tough beyond measure. When he subsequently passed away, his grave on the ranch was marked with the tyre. It still stands there, in memory of a wonderful dog. However Zor's most enduring legacy is the contribution he has made to save cheetahs from extinction.

Saving the Cheetah

Cheetahs are an endangered species and the vast majority of the remaining population, around 2,500 animals, are located in Namibia. The greatest threat to the cheetahs in Namibia is that they are shot, poisoned and trapped by small farmers, who blame them for preying upon their flocks of sheep and herds of goats. The Cheetah Conservation Fund, co-founded and run by Dr Laurie Marker, pioneered an ingenious solution. In addition to ongoing education programmes, the fund donates livestock guardian dogs to the farmers. The dogs of choice are Anatolian Shepherd Dogs (Kangals). Zor was selected to donate semen to the cause and he is an intrinsic part of the gene-pool for the dogs now being bred in Namibia. Farmers who have accepted livestock guardian dogs have seen predation rates drop by eighty per cent and more. The scheme has been an unqualified success and attacks on the cheetah population have been reduced dramatically. Cheetahs are naturally timid predators and do not confront the dogs; they simply move on in search of undefended prey. It is a beautifully elegant solution in which everyone is better off as a result. This outcome has only been possible because good working strains of livestock guardians have been preserved.

By far the greater majority of dogs in the world today are household pets. Although immensely affectionate to their owners, most working livestock guardian types are not suitable pets for the city-dweller or indeed anyone without the proper facilities. To do their jobs and to survive, a high level of aggression is required in a livestock guardian. The appropriateness of keeping livestock guardian dogs has to be considered very carefully but it is important that the right people continue to breed types with the vigour, courage, build, and aggression necessary to do their traditional job. They have an enormous contribution to make in maintaining a balance between man and nature in our few remaining wild places.

It is not without irony that one may note that cheetahs are the only species of feline to be used by man in the manner of a hunting dog. They were used in Ancient Egypt, where wall paintings show them running alongside hunting chariots. They were similarly valued as trained hunting partners by the Assyrians and the Persians. Charlemagne hunted with cheetahs, as did Genghis Khan. In Renaissance Europe, the gentry used cheetahs for coursing deer; the cats sat on padded cloths, riding pillion on the backs of their horses. Cheetahs were especially popular for hunting in India. The Mughal Emperor, Akbar the Great (r.1556-1605), had over 1,000 hunting cheetahs in his stable. When hunting antelope the cheetahs were taken out on bullock carts and leashed with a simple rope. Cheetahs are triggered to hunt by sight and were kept calm by wearing a leather mask. It worked in the same way that a hood quietens a falcon. When quarry was sighted the mask was removed and the cheetah slipped to give chase. Akbar's cats were a sub-species known as the Asiatic cheetah (also as the Indian cheetah or the Iranian cheetah). Tragically Asiatic cheetahs are now extinct in India and on the critically endangered list in Iran. We may hope that, thanks to the work of the Kangals in Namibia, the same fate doesn't befall the African cheetah.

St Bernard

Now famed for his majestic and imposing size, the St. Bernard is another well-known breed that derives from livestock guardian types. Sadly many of today's specimens demonstrate exaggerated breeding and a preference for caricature. Old photographs of St Bernard dogs show large, but still powerfully athletic dogs, whereas modern specimens have been overly enlarged. The breed received successive infusions of mastiff and Newfoundland blood for the sole purpose of making a bigger dog, just for the sake of it.

In the Alps between Switzerland and Italy there is a monastery, situated in the Great Saint Bernard Pass. Called the Great Saint Bernard Hospice, it also serves as a hostel for travellers. The monks here sponsored the development of the breed as a guard dog, using a mixture of local flock guardian stock. Breeding was not done at the monastery but outsourced to local shepherds, who introduced some mastiff blood into the strain. They were large dogs with immense power, as the terrain demanded, but initially they were very far from lumbering. Livestock guardians have the ability to detect, both by scent and thermal sensitivity, a warm body beneath the snow. They find and dig out lambs from snowdrifts as part of their job.

A typical, heavy-set modern version of the St Bernard dog with a young lamb. The lamb's attachment to the dog is apparent but one wonders if this lumbering giant would be a match for a lean, muscular predator. (Photo: iStock/mb-fotos)

It is unsurprising that they were equally useful at finding lost travellers. However, although there are some accounts of rescues, the principal role of these dogs was to act as guides rather than saviours. Moreover the practice of these dogs carrying a small barrel of brandy around their necks is a myth. It possibly derives from an error by Sir Edwin Landseer, the famous animal portraitist, whose 1820 painting of a Saint Bernard depicts such a reviving cask. It seems probable that he conflated an image of a livestock guardian with a dangle-stick and the renowned hospitality of the monks who operated these canine rescue missions.

Maremma

The Italian livestock guardian is the Maremmano–Abruzzese Sheepdog, known colloquially as the Maremma. Native to the high hills of the Abruzzo and Tuscany

A Maremma (the Italian Livestock Guardian) guarding its young flock beneath the shade of an olive tree. (Photo: iStock/RalphRenz)

regions of central Italy, these dogs are still employed by shepherds, guarding sheep from wolves which are a protected species in the area. In 2006 a pair of Maremmas were recruited to stand guard over an endangered species of penguin (little penguins), native to Middle Island, which lies off the South Coast of Australia. Non-native red foxes from the mainland had colonized the island and were predating the penguins. When the dogs were first stationed there, only ten penguins remained. A report in 2013 announced that the penguin population had expanded to 200 birds and that there had been no penguin losses attributable to foxes during the seven years of the Maremmas' stewardship. It is a reminder that we never know what helpful tasks our galaxy of specialist breeds may offer in the future. This is just one more reason why these classic breeds are worth preserving.

Chapter 3

Sled Dogs

'The toil of the traces seemed the supreme expression of their being, and all that they lived for and the only thing in which they took delight.'
—Jack London, *The Call of the Wild* (1903)

The author mushes a team of Siberian Huskies in Alaska. (Photograph by Whitney McLaren)

Dogs have been used to haul sleds, carts and wagons for the transport of both people and goods for hundreds of years. Sled dogs remain in active service and are the central focus of this chapter. Famous long distance sled dog races such as the Iditarod have recently attracted criticisms of cruelty from animal rights organizations. Instances of individual abuse, such as the beating of dogs, have been cited. Such actions, though always deplorable and indefensible, can occur in any walk of life and are not endemic to the vast majority of those who race sled dogs. Of greater consequence are concerns that the Iditarod race is simply too long, both in terms of distance (over 1,000 miles) and duration (around twelve days) in unrelenting hostile weather and over severe terrain. This chapter, in attempting an account of the history of sled dogs, also references the genesis of races like the Iditarod. My sole purpose has been to chronicle the historical record, not to attempt to weigh the arguments nor stand in judgment of modern practice. That is for another forum. I condemn wholeheartedly any suffering caused by poor human management or behaviour but the sled dog folk that I have spoken to, and there have been several, have all been beyond reproach when it comes to the care and welfare of their animals. The sheer joy of a sled dog team about to set off is both electrifying and contagious. This is what they were bred to do and by all appearances, when well cared for, they love to do it.

We cannot be certain when man first harnessed dogs to a sled but the archeological evidence is that it was at least 8,000 years ago. Excavations on Zhokov Island, a small

The author and a team of six dogs, making swift progress on a pristine trail. (Photograph by Whitney McLaren)

and remote island in the East Siberian Sea, have revealed traces of a dog harness, a sled runner and dog bones; all of which were radiocarbon dated to around 6,000 BC. The Mesolithic inhabitants of this tiny and inhospitable outcrop bred two sizes of dog: large mastiff types for hunting reindeer and polar bear, and a more compact type for pulling sleds. Certainly dog sleds were used as a means of winter travel across the flat tundra and the boreal forests of the Northern Hemisphere long before recorded history and long before the invention of the wheel (that didn't happen until around 3,500 BC). The use of sleds and dogs is ancient and only superficial elements, such as the materials for building the sled, have changed over time. Sled dogs have answered a great practical necessity for millennia but their functional advantages are transcended by something else. That is the timeless thrill of riding the graceful, glissade glide of a sled pulled by a team of beautiful dogs – dogs whose names you know – and travelling silently through a pristine and majestic landscape. A person driving a sled dog team is called, in English, a 'musher'. The word derives from the French word '*marcher*', which has many shades of meaning, including to walk, to advance and to move on. French trappers were prevalent in Canada from as early as the seventeenth century. 'Mush' (*marche*) is the command for dogs to set off and is also called out to urge greater effort. It is used throughout the North American continent and the activity of running sled dogs is today called 'mushing'. It is uncertain when that term became commonplace and the older term was to 'drive' a team of dogs, in the same way that one 'drives' a team of horses. 'Driver' and 'musher' can be used interchangeably. Of all the experiences I embarked on for this book, the one I had most looked forward to was that of being a musher.

My Dog Sled Adventure

I flew into Fairbanks, Alaska. There is probably a greater concentration of commercial dog-sledding operations there than any other single place today. I chose to go with Lizbet Norris and the Artic Dog Adventure Co. Lizbet came highly recommended and rightly so! Also important for me was the fact that her dogs are all Siberian Huskies. In these I had a good example of a traditional, not to mention spectacularly striking, working breed. I had hired Whitney McLaren, a talented local photographer, to capture some of the action and she picked me up from my hotel and drove me out of Fairbanks for nearly an hour, winding up into higher ground. She had arranged with Lizbet where to meet and, after turning down several unmarked tracks we eventually came to a halt high on a hill by a stand of snow-covered birch. The vistas were sweeping and breathtakingly beautiful – a true, expansive wilderness covered in pristine snow, which continued to fall lightly. There was nothing that I could discern that announced 'this is the spot'. However, we didn't have to wait long before Lizbet's truck came into view. It had two basket sleds strapped to the roof. The bed of the truck had been converted to create two tiers of wooden dog housing. Each dog had its own box with a grill-fronted door. As soon as Lizbet parked the truck, a great deal of din arose from the boxes. Sharing the excitement of the howling canine cargo, I ran to greet them. Eyes – piercing, ancient, alert, primal eyes – stared at me though the grills.

It was a powerful moment. After the meet-and-greet, a few basic instructions and some preparations, we lifted down the sleds and then disembarked the dogs. I walked each of the dogs on a leash from the truck to where we had set up a picket line by the trail. This consisted of a wire secured to the slender trunks of young birch trees. Extending from the taut wire at 6-foot intervals were wire leashes that clipped to the dogs' collars. A sled dog cannot be let loose in open country. It will run and run and run. There is no human recall that can override the sled dog's instinct to run. A loose dog will almost certainly become a lost dog.

Of course, there are always exceptions to every rule. During the 1925 antitoxin dash to Gnome, Leonhard Seppala rested after passing on the serum to the next relay. After a few hours, he set out on a more leisurely trip home. En route his dogs picked up the scent of reindeer. His lead dog, Togo, and another dog broke free of their lines and went off in pursuit. Huskies are by nature hunting dogs every bit as much as they are hauling dogs. Seppala fretted that the dogs would be shot as wolves by hunters or, worse still, get a foot caught in a snare or a spring trap. Even today such risks are very real in backcountry Alaska. Happily, several days later the two dogs wandered back to Seppala's kennels. A similar tale was told by Sidney Huntingdon, a man raised in Alaska's remote outback during the early twentieth century and whose spoken memoirs are chronicled in *Shadows on the Koyukuk*. Huntingdon reminisced that on a sledding trip in 1937 his sled rolled, sending him tumbling down a bank into the frozen waters of the mighty Koyukuk river. It was that time of the year when the ice was beginning to break up. His dog team continued steadfastly along the trail with the sled bouncing on its side behind. Sidney was swept downstream. After around an hour of struggle – fighting a strong current, numbing cold, and lacerating, jagged ice floes – he eventually managed to drag himself onto the slippery ice and thence ashore. He was close to death and passed out. Sidney awoke to find his lead dog, Dakli, licking his face. His team had returned. He noted that this was not usual behaviour for a dog team. Later he saw the paw prints, about 5 miles further along the trail, where Dakli had led his team, off trail, in a sweeping semi-circle to turn them around and trek back in search of their master. After managing to right the sled, Sidney crawled into the basket and his loyal dogs took him home.

Such occurrences are so rare that it is worth retelling another of Sidney Huntingdon's experiences. On this occasion he had encountered some wolves. He had shot at them and chased them away. Shortly afterwards, he had tied the sled to a tree, while he checked on one of his traps. The dogs got wind of the wolves again, broke their line and went off in pursuit. He predicted that 'they would tangle the sled, harness, or towline in trees or brush, or if they happened to catch and fight the wolves, some of the dogs might get chewed up or killed'. He set off on snowshoes to make his way to the next camp. Some time passed when, suddenly, his team came into view, heading towards him and with the sled still upright. He was rightly pleased with his dogs but the perils he paints of a runaway team are all too real.

The character and skill of the lead dog is everything. I had immediately taken a shine to my lead dog, Dirka, the most wolf-like and, with her brindled russet coat, the most striking and beautiful of them all. However it was a one-way adulation. She was gentle and responded to affection but she was also a little retiring. I certainly wouldn't be able to count on her to turn the team around for me on so slight an acquaintance. Before even setting foot on a sled, I had already had the first three rules of dog sledding drilled into me by both Lizbet and Whitney:

Rule 1: Don't let go.
Rule 2: Don't let go.
Rule 3: Don't let go.

All the dogs jumped and jinked like jack-in-the-boxes as I walked them down. Their excitement for the impending trail was palpable. Although some were a tad more aloof than others, the inherent friendliness of these wonderful dogs was also immediately apparent, responding affectionately to a scratch and a squeeze as I hitched them to the picket line. That friendliness became even more apparent, when we took a break for a flask of hot soup at lunchtime. The dogs had curled in the snow, nose to tail, for a quick nap. I decided to follow suit and lie among them. Several of the dogs moved over to lie with me and lick the snow from my face. One can imagine being very appreciative of the warmth generated from a pack huddle in the event of being out alone in the wilderness and perhaps spending the night without fire.

The five-dog team taking a break after a morning's work. So that they may lay comfortably, the dogs have been released from their tug lines but remain attached to the central towline by their neck lines. (Photograph by Whitney McLaren)

Without doubt these were well-socialized dogs, part of a family pack that received nothing but kindness from their human pack leader. Lizbet hitches them to sleds and exercises them all every day throughout the long winter and in the summer months they lounge contentedly in a large compound, which is all a sled dog wants to do on a warm day. There were a couple of moments where, in the impatient excitement before setting off, one dog snapped at another. This was normal hierarchical pack behaviour and although, for a moment, a tiny bit of blood flowed on broken skin (rinsed off with a handful of snow) it was not serious. Despite their striking resemblance to untamed wolves, these dogs were far distant from the stereotypical savage beasts portrayed in *Call of the Wild*. Aside from the obvious influence of Lizbet's tender care, Siberian Huskies are known to be an especially social breed of sled-dog. Chukchi dogs were valued highly and treated with kindness because the Chukchi people believed that they embodied the spirits of dead ancestors. Consequently they shared their food and shelter with them, even during times of hardship. While some Chukchi dogs pulled sleds to carry home the bounty of a hunting party, others remained behind to care for the children, while the family was away. They were bred to be part of the family.

My day began with a five-dog hitch – a number in keeping with the historical model. Alongside my lead dog, Dirka, was Ravni who had the most piercing of blue eyes. Twin leads are a relatively modern idea but these two highly-intelligent alphas worked together harmoniously and effectively. The positions on a dog team are termed as they are for a horse team, so that the two closest to the vehicle are called the wheelers. My 'wheel dogs' were Jasmine and Bidey. In between the leaders and the wheelers are the 'team' dogs. For this first shift, I had just the one, Strawberry. One-by-one I hitched the team to a modern basket sled; a type used for both racing and touring. During this operation, the team were held in place by an anchor known as a 'snow hook'. This is a great iron claw, attached to a lanyard, tied to the sled. Its long curled prongs are thrown to spike the snow and then kicked in to bite at an angle. As each dog joined the hitch, the excitement rose to fever pitch. The barking and howling was deafening. Human conversation was no longer possible, other than by improvised sign language. Accompanying this cacophonous riot was a balletic display of rearing and vertical leaps, as each dog leaned into its harness eager for the off. Hot breaths steamed in the frozen air and the canine choir-song ricocheted with joy against the White Mountains across the valley. We were in a big place, with unspoiled vistas; epic views that stretched ethereally through a low hanging mist into a distant horizon. A yellow sun sent dazzling light to dance and sparkle on the crisp, freshly fallen snow. On one side of the trail, forests of birch and pine stood with their branches glistening and bent low with a heavy frosting. It was a majestic auditorium for the raucous husky hullabaloo that was taking place.

In order to show me the way Lizbet had stationed her sled ahead of mine on the trail. I stepped onto the runners and immediately pushed down on the foot brake. Getting in position was a further cue to the team. It energized them to a crescendo, so much so that the snow hook alone could barely hold them. The foot brake was a twin-pronged affair, fixed to the back of the sled, with a pedal bar along the top that allowed one to drive its broad, curved spikes into the trail. Once on the move, additional braking was offered by the drag mat. This ingenious contraption consisted of a plastic panel (it could equally have been made from rawhide) that was attached, in the manner of a flap, to the back of the sled. On the underside was an array of small spikes, similar to those worn by track athletes. In operation it allowed slight adjustments to speed – for steadying on sharp turns for instance – either by applying slight pressure with a heel or by standing on it with all one's weight. Further nuances, that affected the way the sled could be slewed round corners, were achieved by applying pressure to just one side. It is not clear when these drag mats were first introduced but the old sled-dog men were probably able to achieve a similar affect by digging their heels in the snow, with their toes on the runners. A further function of the drag mat is to ensure that the towline remains consistently taut, for instance in undulating ground or when travelling downhill. It is better for the dogs to sustain an even pull, rather than to have the harness jerk in fits and starts. So much for theory – it was time to set out!

I pulled the snow hook and released the foot brake. Without the need to even whisper 'mush' under my breath, we were off at a sizzling pace. At once, all fell silent. The dogs

Top left is a snow hook, which attaches to the sled by a line and anchors the team when standing-by. Rubber treads on the runners offer a good grip and the musher's weight can favour one side or the other to affect direction in the same way as it does with skis. Between the runners is the drag mat with its spiked underbelly. When approaching corners or to keep the lines tight downhill, one or both heels press on this to slow the sled. The metal arch with prongs attached to the back of the sled is the foot-brake; its claws bite deep into the snow. (Photograph by Whitney McLaren)

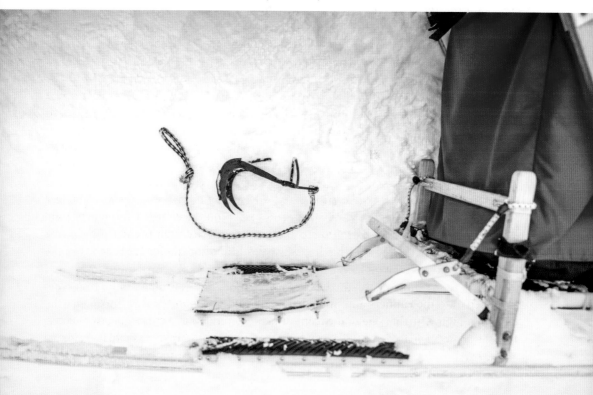

stilled their tongues and put all their energy into pulling. There was a serene quiet that I hadn't anticipated; it was as if the roar of the engines had been turned off and we were now gliding through this enchanted landscape. Hauling happily with an easy, loping jog, the dog's footfalls made no sound and the runners were equally mute. Such utter silence, whilst in motion, was slightly eerie but in a wonderful and magical way. Different snow or ice conditions can produce a range of sounds from the runners, but today we had the muffling hush of fresh snowfall and they withheld their song. Lest this all sound too idyllic, learned I quickly, with a mixture of surprise and admiration, that a sled-dog can crouch, defecate and yet still keep up with the team and lean into its harness to pull a little. Once they are going they stop for nothing.

As we approached the first bend in the trail – a pretty sharp right-hander – I assumed that my team would follow on behind Lizbet. Consequently I didn't command them with the customary 'gee' for right. I was wrong. They didn't follow; they ploughed ahead into deep powder until they were plunging like dolphins. The command for stop is a softly cadenced 'whoa', slowing them with a lulling voice, together with stamping a foot on the brake to send its twin fangs tearing into the snow. My team halted. Lizbet kicked in her snow hook and came to assist. On this occasion her team held with the snow hook. A more secure alternative is to attach the sled to a tree with what is known as a 'snub-line' but this takes time. Fortunately Whitney was close by and able to step on the foot brake. You certainly would not want to trust to just a snow hook if the need arose to go out of sight – to check on a trap line for instance. Other needs for absence may spring to mind and indeed, later in the day, Lizbet did ask me to look away for a few moments; an insight into a sledder's life that I hadn't anticipated!

Meanwhile the immediate task was to get them back on the trail. It was not an easy matter to get the dogs turned round in the narrow tree-lined space. Lizbet took Dirka by her harness and led the team to line out in the opposite direction, while I manhandled the sled with lifting and bumping. This was exhausting work in thigh-deep snow. However we managed and off we went. It was exhilarating, the view was sublime and the pure air filled my lungs. The trail at this point was slightly downhill, well-packed and fast. It meandered very slightly and there were small undulations, all of which made for an exciting ride. I had applied a light pressure onto the drag-mat in order to keep the towline taut but, apparently, I had not slowed sufficiently for the next big right-handed bend that was ahead. Dirka and Ravni heeded my 'gee' and turned at just the right moment. They raced round the bend. The sled swung out wide, just catching a small mound off to the side of the trail and we rolled. I hung on to the driving bar and both arms felt as if they would be torn from their sockets. 'Whoa' I called as calmly as I could muster, and the team heeded my command. I then made the mistake of trying to right the sled whilst I was still on the ground. Not a good idea. Once on its runners, the team just wants to pull away again. I hung on resolutely whilst being dragged along and pulled the sled onto its side again. In this mode the sled is harder to pull and signals the dogs to pause. First, I learned, I must get myself upright. Only then did I right the sled and as quickly as possible apply the foot brake. Now I had control. Once again, I was able to set off on the winding trail. I had learned a useful lesson; subsequently I rolled the sled about half a dozen times.

Having just rolled the sled, the author hangs onto the straining team as he clambers to his feet before righting the sled. It is essential not to set the sled upright until you have got to your feet. A rolled sled acts as a partial brake. Once it is back on its runners, the dogs are off and if the musher is still on the ground he just gets dragged along. (Photograph by Whitney McLaren)

The dogs would gulp mouthfuls of snow to hydrate themselves, even whilst running and every so often we stopped to give them a quick breather. A key procedure during a stop was to check their pads for snowballs. This is a particular problem when there is fresh, soft snow on the trail. In such conditions, build-ups of compacted snow form between their toes. These icy spheres stick to the hair on their pads and can cause discomfort in the same way as a stone in a horse's hoof. Certain individuals seemed far

After a steep hill and coming into a bend, there is plenty of power in this six-dog team. (Photograph by Whitney McLaren)

more susceptible to them than others. At regular intervals I checked the pads and with warm bare hands eased the little ice marbles from their lodgings. The dogs seemed to enjoy the attention.

After lunch, I was given an extra dog, Honeybee. It is extraordinary how much more powerful it feels to have six dogs, rather than five. This was especially apparent when the sled capsized and I felt the full strain of the team tugging on my arms. One of the pitfalls that occasioned so many crashes, apart from my predilection to go as fast as possible, was that the team sometimes cut the corners. Once they came to realize that we were using a looping trail and that their mission was to follow Lizbet's team, Dirka and Ravni decided to start cutting corners. This resulted in going off-trail and into deep snow. Undeterred, they would lean into their harnesses with extra determination and, with bellies against the snow, continue to pull. Unfortunately there was hidden terrain beneath the snow and hillocks and hummocks, invisible to me, would suddenly tip the sled one way or the other. Should I put a foot down to steady it, it sometimes disappeared thigh-deep into a void. I would then stumble and, because I stuck to the 'don't let go' maxim, the sled had to roll with me. Clambering in deep snow in order to right the sled became increasingly draining as the afternoon wore on. However I also got better at reading some of the corners and knowing where the dogs would go. One can, to a limited extent, affect where the sled goes by putting weight on one runner, in the same way that one puts weight on a ski to turn. Furthermore one can sometimes

Cornering with the sled swinging wide off the compacted trail. It is necessary to lean appropriately to keep it from toppling. (Photograph by Whitney McLaren)

When sledding over rough terrain, as here, or uphill, the musher assists the dogs by 'pedalling' – that is using one foot to help scoot the sled along. It is hard labour. (Photograph by Whitney McLaren)

counter toppling by leaning out at extreme angles, like a motorcycle sidecar passenger. When it works, it is immensely satisfying. The trick is being able to read (or at least remember) the land beneath the snow.

The nature of taking a trail that loops, albeit a magnificently long loop, is that as well as thrilling downhill sections, there are laborious uphill sections. Even with a six-dog team, some of the uphill stretches required the driver to assist his team. If the going was very heavy, the driver simply had to get off and, if necessary push. Mostly though it was enough to 'pedal'. This involves transferring one foot to the opposite runner (say right foot onto left runner) and then using the free leg (in this example, the left leg) to scoot the sled along. In this way the musher partially relieves the weight and also aids locomotion. It was exhausting work, especially in patches where fresh snow had drifted onto the trail. On my excursion it had been cold enough for snow but only just; the sun shone and it was a beautiful crisp day. Not for me the savage lash of an icy wind, nor cruelly low temperatures, nor long days of winter darkness, nor blizzards, nor white-outs. My modern-day recreation of gliding, almost effortlessly, on a well-packed trail and on a fine day was a luxury seldom experienced by the men of 'Old Alaska' - the pioneer trappers, the stampeders and those who mushed the mail sleds. I had gone in April. There had been a risk that I would be too late for the snow but I was fortunate. I doubt conditions could have been more perfect.

Polar Explorers
Since the beginning of the twentieth century, dog sleds have been employed for exploration in both the Arctic and Antarctic. In 1994, however, an international environmental protocol agreement banned all dogs from Antarctica, for fear that they might introduce distemper to the seal population there. On 14 December 1911 the Norwegian Roald Amundsen famously beat the Englishman Robert Falcon Scott in the race to be the first to reach the South Pole. Much of Amundsen's success has been attributed to his expert use of sled dogs. It was an arduous trek that took a ferocious toll on the dogs. Of the fifty-two dogs that set out, only eleven returned from a round trip of 1,860 miles. Dogs that became weak were killed and fed either to the other dogs or to the men. Amundsen's rival, Scott, was opposed to using dogs for the entire journey, though he did take thirty-three to assist with haulage during the initial stages of the journey. He had hoped to rely mostly on mechanical sleds and ponies. In the event, the engines failed, the ponies died, the dogs died and, after man-hauling the sleds to

the pole, so too did the men on this tragically ill-fated expedition. To his credit, Scott's resistance to the use of dogs was in part his understanding of the brutality that such a long journey in extreme conditions would impose on them. He wrote:

> One cannot calmly contemplate the murder of animals which possess such intelligence and individuality, which have frequently such endearing qualities, and which very possibly one has learnt to regard as friends and companions.

Although the rigours of such a prolonged and relentless Antarctic journey proved too much, the type of dogs that were used possessed both physiological and temperamental qualities that suited them for harsh winter conditions. Like all 'dogs of the North', traditional sled dogs are all 'spitz' dogs (though not all spitz dogs are sled dogs). Spitz dogs have a characteristic double coat. A dense covering of fairly long, thin, wiry hairs forms an outer layer. This is wind resistant and water repellent. Beneath this waterproof coat is a thick, soft-textured undercoat that traps pockets of insulating air. This 'woolly' undercoat was traditionally spun into a yarn in some cultures. Being of hollow-fibre construction, the undercoat of the Samoyed, for instance, has been calculated to be eighty per cent warmer than wool from sheep. Dogs do not have sweat glands; rather they cool themselves by panting. Consequently they are less vulnerable to the cold than many other mammals. Blood vessels in a Husky's legs are configured in such a way as to be resistant to frostbite. Their distinctively bushy tails serve as effective insulators for their noses. When they curl themselves into a tight ball to sleep, the tail covers the face and traps the warm air from their breath. Ears are short and cocooned, both inside and out, with a blanket of thick hair that mitigates the risk of frostbite on extremities. Similarly, the feet have insulating hair on the underside of their extra-thick, leathery pads. Their eyes are almond-shaped, which enables them to squint to an extreme degree and still see when running forward into the harshest blizzard. Husky-type dogs have been bred for thousands of years to be able to deal with gnawing cold and biting winds, with snow and ice and sleet and slush. Their biology has equipped them for it and they were more than strong enough and willing enough to pull the sleds. On these early expeditions, however, they faced the additional hardships of excessive distances, endless working hours without respite and inadequate food supplies. On top of that, as they neared the South Pole, the Antarctic served up daily extremes of cold and blizzard that exceeded even the worst of regular Arctic weather.

Sled Dog Breeds

Scott had recruited Samoyeds, a characteristically 'fluffy', medium-sized dog bred by the people of the same name (also known as Nenets) who live in Northern Siberia. Samoyed dogs were used to hunt and herd reindeer as well as pull sleds and the Samoyed people huddled with them in their shelters at night as an additional source of warmth. Although Samoyeds occur in several coat colours, pure white has become the fashionable choice. Their affectionate nature has endeared 'Sammys' as pets. They were popularized in Britain in 1886, when, as Prince of Wales, the future Edward VII

A team of Samoyed dogs hauling a sled. These are the breed that Scott had chosen to take on his ill-fated Polar expedition. (Photo: iStock/Irina Orlova)

(r. 1901–1910) received one as a gift from the German Chancellor Otto von Bismark (r. 1871–1890).

Amundsen chose Greenland Dogs. These were large, powerfully built dogs, native to Greenland. Although not common in other parts of the world, there are an estimated 30,000 living in Greenland today, where they work primarily as sled dogs throughout the long, dark winters. Tests have indicated that the Greenland Dog and the Canadian Eskimo Dog are, in genetic terms, the same breed. Current thinking is that both dogs originated with the Thule people, progenitors of the Inuit, who spread to Alaska from their homeland in Siberia's Chukchi Peninsula, from around the tenth century AD, and thence westwards as far as Greenland. Coincidentally, the Vikings not only colonized Greenland in the tenth century but they also settled in Newfoundland. Neither colony was to last but it might be that they influenced the canine gene pool in both locations. The Norwegian Elkhound, a spitz dog, has strong associations with the Vikings and is also reminiscent of a classic sled dog type. Elkhounds had a primary function as hunters' dogs, a utility which is retained by many sled dog breeds. Archaeology, art and literature indicate that the Vikings enjoyed strong bonds with their dogs.

The Norwegian Elkhound. This is the hunting dog of the Vikings, still used as a general hunting companion today. These dogs have clear similarities to sled dogs and both belong to a general category known as spitz dogs. Spitz dogs are 'dogs of the North' – they have insulating undercoats, short prick ears, hairy feet and bushy tails. All sled dogs are Spitz breeds but also under this umbrella are the Japanese Akita, the Chinese Chow Chow and the Karelian Bear Dog – a Finnish breed that is used in Arctic exploration because of its unique ability to herd polar bears and keep them away from human explorers without confrontation or harm. (Photo: iStock/Rolf Johnsen)

Early adventurers to Canada, and subsequently to Alaska, wrote about 'Indian dogs' when referring to native types, suitable for sled haulage. Although most have now disappeared, there is one ancient breed in Alaska that has survived. It is the Alaskan Malamute, an iconically powerful sled dog. Malamutes are large, robust dogs, ox-strong and bred for endurance. Although they move at a relatively slow pace, they were suited perfectly for hauling heavy freight over long distances. Known affectionately as 'Mals' or 'Mallys' these dogs were named after the Mahlemut people who live between the Kobuk and Noatak rivers. Generally thought to be among the oldest of all domestic dogs, the Malamute probably migrated to Alaska, along with the first settlers from Siberia, at a time when there was a land bridge between the two continents. Like other ancient breeds of sled dog, the Malamute was also used for hunting. This included holding bears at bay, as well as being able to scent the whereabouts of seals' breathing holes in the coastal ice. As draught dogs, a team of Malamutes was capable of hauling around 700 pounds of mail on a single sled. In order to service the tens of thousands of 'stampeders' who had flocked to the Yukon gold fields after 1896, the United States Postal Service sub-contracted dog sled drivers to deliver mail to the tent cities that had sprung up

A Malamute. These are a very powerful sled dog. Larger and stronger than Siberian Huskies, they are especially suitable for freight-hauling (Photo: iStock/ TRAVELARIUM)

in the area. Prospecting was a lonely life and the stampeders were desperate for letters from home. Mail sleds, hauled by trains of Malamutes, ran the entire length of the Yukon River until 1963, when they were finally decommissioned.

Also hailing from Siberia are Siberian Huskies, dogs which are indigenous to the Chukchi Inuit. Indeed the word 'husky' appears to be a mangled rendering of the word Chukchi and, in turn, 'husky' has become a widely use generic for all the sled dog types. Siberian Huskies are spectacular wolf-like dogs with especially mesmerizing eyes. Although smaller than other sled dogs, they combine considerable pulling ability and resolute drive with greater speed. Siberians have less stamina than a Malamute but, pound for pound, they are capable of hauling heavier loads. This made them ideal for personal transport between villages, for short hunting excursions and, of course, as racing dogs.

Siberian Huskies. The lighter of the husky breeds. However these dogs are fast and have immense stamina and drive. (Photograph by Whitney McLaren)

Although sharing the name Husky, Alaskan Huskies are entirely different from Siberians. They are not a breed but rather a type of dog, of mixed appearance, that is used in the competitive world of modern dog sled racing. During the past century many have been mixed with non-Northern dogs, including Salukis, German Short-haired Pointers and Anatolian Shepherd Dogs, in order to produce stronger, faster dogs that do not overheat when run for hours on end in modern marathon races such as the Iditarod. It may be that the core stock originated with a dog type bred by the Athabascan Indians of the Alaskan interior; however Alaskan Huskies today are not a traditional type.

Teams and Trains

Accounts from the golden age of dog sledding – late eighteenth to early twentieth centuries – frequently use the term 'train', in reference to the linear nature of a harness system that placed one dog behind the other in tandem. A dog team may be in a train or it may be in some other configuration, such as a fan. Travelling along frozen rivers and across frozen lakes offered particular challenges. Not least of all was the risk of falling through thin ice! One precaution was to harness the dogs in a 'fan hitch', where they were spread out, like a fan, in front of the

These Greenland Dogs are set up in a fan-hitch as they cross a frozen lake. Such an arrangement would be a disaster in timber country but when crossing terrain such as this it is a safety precaution, not only to lighten the weight distribution but also, in the event that one dog falls through thin ice, he can be rescued quickly without the whole team tumbling through. (Photo: iStock/ RubyRascal)

sled. This distributed the weight over a wider area and, if one dog were to crash through the ice, it was not fatal for all. This method was especially common in the Greenland tradition. For obvious reasons the fan formation was only feasible in open country and would court disaster on timber trails. The key thing in wooded country was to use as narrow a trail as possible, one that could be made by a single human treading it down.

Today, we are used to seeing dogs hitched in pairs, with one pair behind the other in tandem. However, this is a relatively modern arrangement. In 1862, John McDougall, a Methodist missionary who journeyed through the Canadian plains, described the typical set up for a winter trek along the frozen Saskatchewan River:

> Four dogs to each team form a complete train, though three and even two are used, and are harnessed to the cariole by means of two long traces. Between these traces the dogs stand one after the other, with a space intervening between them of perhaps a foot.

The dogs in this instance were hitched in single file between traces. Trace is a term borrowed from horse harness. It means 'pulling line' and has the same etymological root as tractor. A pair of traces extends from a harness, one either side of the animal, back to the sled or vehicle being drawn. McDougall went on to explain that the reason they hitched their teams in single file was 'so they might negotiate the narrow trails most efficiently'. He also described the harness system that was in use at the time:

> A round collar, passing over the head and ears and fitting closely to the shoulder, buckles on each side to the traces, which are supported by a back band of leather.

The word collar is misleading here. It was not as we imagine a dog collar today, but rather it functioned in the same way as a horse collar, with the traction engaged from the chest of the animal, not its neck. These pulling collars were often padded. McDougall noted that the natives expected everyone to make their own harness for the journey ahead and that the harness for the dogs was sewn out of tanned moose skins, whereas that for horses was made from buffalo hides. It is difficult to determine the specific advantage of one over the other, though both required fingertips inured to pain, when pushing a needle through thick hide on a cold night.

It wasn't until the very late nineteenth century that the scheme of hitching dogs side-by-side, harnessed to a single gang line (also known as the 'towline'), was developed. This advance enabled twice the pulling power whilst maintaining a manageable length to the team. Long teams are only practicable on exceptionally well-defined trails that are railroad-straight. The United States Army were brought in to make the trail for the first Iditarod race; such logistics support was not available to the early trappers!

Mail Team leaving Circle City for Fort Gibbon, Alaska. *Wm. H.*

This postcard, dated 1900, shows contract mail carriers preparing their dog sled team to carry mail through the snow from Circle City to Fort Gibson, in the Alaskan Territory. The teams are harnessed by traces and arranged in tandem – in a train. This is the most suitable hitch for narrow trails. There are only six dogs per sled. (National Postal Museum, Curatorial Photographic Collection)

The dramatic and majestic image of a dog sled with fourteen dogs leaning into their tug lines in a powerful dash across the snow was not a commonplace historical sight. In fact such a long train of dogs is a relatively modern phenomenon. Early dog teams comprised of only a few dogs. Writing in the thirteenth century, Marco Polo (1254 -1324) painted a picture of winter travel in Siberia. He claimed that the dogs were the size of donkeys, though this is doubtless an exaggeration, a retelling of other travellers' tall tales. Intriguingly he also remarked that the sleds were useful for sliding over muddy terrain as well as snow:

> carriages without wheels and made so that they can run over the ice, and also over mire and mud without sinking too deep in it…and the sledge is drawn by six of those big dogs that I spoke of.

Four to six dogs were a typical number for most early sled travel. Marco Polo reported that the region was crisscrossed with a series of post houses, each having a kennel of around forty dogs. Both freight and passenger sleds were entirely unmanned. The keeper of a post house would journey aboard a separate sled in caravan to lead the way and the convoy followed on. Once he reached the next relay, the sled caravan would be furnished with fresh teams and the keeper of that post would guide them to the next destination. Meanwhile the other teams returned with their keeper to their original station. Distances between post houses are not specified but there is a critical relationship between the size of team required to share the load and the length of the journey.

The gang-line system has a central line attached to the front of the sled. Dogs are hitched either side of this at two points: a neck line connecting the dog's collar, and a tug line fastening to a chest harness. The neck line keeps the dogs 'in line' and, by leaning into their chest harness, the dogs provide their motive power to the gang line via the tug line. (Photograph by Whitney McLaren)

In 1749 the Swedish explorer, Peter Kalm, wrote:

> In winter it is customary in Canada, for travellers to put dogs before little sledges, made on purpose to hold their clothes, provisions, &c. Poor people commonly employ them on their winter journeys, and go on foot themselves. Almost all the wood, which the poorer people in this country fetch out of the woods in winter, is carried by dogs, which have therefore got the name of horses of the poor people. They commonly place a pair of dogs before each load of wood. I have, likewise, seen some neat little sledges, for ladies to ride in, in winter; they are drawn by a pair of dogs, and go faster on a good road, than one would think. A middle-sized dog is sufficient to draw a single person, when the roads are good.

This notion of very small dog teams for regular work is borne out in several accounts of the Canadian fur trade. From 1779 to 1821, the North West Company, based in Montreal, was a fierce competitor to the Hudson Bay Company. There were riches to be made from furs at the time. Pelts were at their thickest in winter and trappers ventured deep into the frozen outback in search of the finest beaver, mink, muskrat, fox and marten. After a winter on their trap lines, the long journey back to the trading posts with a heavy cargo of skins could only be accomplished by means of sleds. One of the North West Company's traders, Daniel Williams Harmon, recorded his experiences in *Sixteen Years in Indian Country*. An entry from December 1801 indicates that it was common for as few as two dogs to be used:

> Our goods are drawn on sledges by dogs. Each pair of dogs drew a load of from two hundred, to two hundred and fifty pounds, besides provisions for themselves and their driver, which would make the whole load about three hundred pounds. I have seen many dogs, two of which would draw on a sledge, five hundred pounds, twenty miles, in five hours. For a short distance, two of our stoutest dogs will draw more than a thousand pounds weight.

Such relatively short journeys place lighter demands on the dogs than either polar exploration or today's 1,000 miles-plus races. They are more representative of a working sled dog's daily routine. H.M. Robinson in his travel memoir *The Great Fur Land: Sketches of Life in the Hudson's Bay Territory* (1879) reported that slightly larger teams had become more usual for hauling similar loads. He noted that:

> An average train of four dogs will trot briskly along with three hundred pounds' weight without difficulty. Trains loaded to travel short distances with a barrel of liquor and two sacks of flour, or about six hundred and eighty pounds avoirdupois, are not an uncommon sight.

James Carnegie, a Scottish explorer and poet, who was also the 9th Earl of Southesk, wrote of his 1859 expedition through Canada and recalled, presumably with affection, the names of a small three-dog hitch:

> My team consists of three middle-sized Indian dogs, sharp-nosed, bushy-haired and wolfish. Chocolat, the leader, is dark red; Casse-toute, grey, shaded with black; and Fox, reddish fawn-colour.

Sidney Huntingdon recalled that during the 1920s and 1930s, a five-dog team was considered large among the Koyukan people. Five- or six-dog teams were the norm for trappers and those making local journeys. A team this size provided ample pulling power, was more economical to feed and did not stretch too far ahead. This last was a crucial factor for those who had to break trail. An exception, other than for marathon racing, arose in the last days of the mail sleds. By the 1920s, the mail sleds had to compete against the new bush aircraft. This, together with a massively expanded population, created a demand for extra-large cargos of mail to be hauled. Sometimes this was achieved by employing two large freighting sleds, coupled together, and hauled by a train of up to twenty-five dogs. Such sledding leviathans only operated on straight, major highways, trails that were well-maintained by the postal service. More local tributary services continued to be pulled by five- or six-dog trains.

Breaking Trail

Dog sleds do not travel over unprepared ground; they require compacted trails. It is a binary choice; there is trail and there is no trail. Once dogs go off trail and are in deep snow, at one moment up to their chests and then, within a stride, above their heads, they can no longer pull effectively. Moreover the sled itself will sink and become unstable on one side or the other depending on the terrain beneath; it will plough great heaps of snow into its basket and the hapless musher will be grunting waist-deep in an opaque and frozen sea, exerting himself beyond endurance to make every step. Breaking trail was an exceptionally arduous business, requiring the musher to go ahead of his dogs on snowshoes. Once a trail had been created, between villages and trading posts or along regular trap lines, it was maintained with regular traffic. Some fresh snowfall on top was of minimal consequence, provided that there was a firm trail beneath. A passage in *Call of the Wild* (1903), Jack London's visceral novel set during the Klondike Gold Rush, points to the contrast between travel on a good trail and having to break trail:

> That day they made forty miles, the trail being packed; but the next day, and for many days to follow, they broke their own trail, worked harder, and made poorer time. As a rule, Perrault travelled ahead of the team, packing the snow with webbed shoes to make it easier for them. Francois, guiding the sled at the gee-pole, sometimes exchanged places with him.

London had travelled to the Klondike and experienced these conditions at first hand. He understood well the grunting slog of tramping ahead in snowshoes and of manhandling the sled with a 'gee-pole'. Mushers use the commands 'gee' and 'haw' to command a lead dog to turn right and left respectively. A gee-pole was a stout, freshly cut length of timber, usually springy spruce, that was lashed to the right-hand 'gee' side of a sled. When breaking trail or on an infrequently travelled trail, the gee-pole helps to guide the sled from the front. A person manning a gee-pole usually wears short skis or has to run in snowshoes. They are positioned directly behind the dogs, in front of the sled and straddling the gang-line – a potentially perilous position with a strong team. At best the dogs make reasonable progress, pulling sled and person along, and all that is needed is some judicious leaning on the tiller to keep the sled upright over choppy terrain. However, where the going is especially rough, the gee-pole has to be used to lever and bounce the sled around turns on the trail. It could be backbreaking, heart-straining labour that frequently involved righting a toppled, fully laden sled.

Navigating the trails became particularly challenging in the spring, when the snow melt was intermittent. Moreover the dogs could overheat if worked too hard in milder temperatures. In his memoir, John McDougall recalled the expedient of night travel for such circumstances; he also bemoaned the drudgery and discomforts of sledding late in the season:

> As the days grew warmer, we who were handling dogs had to travel most of the time in the night, as then the snow and track were frozen. While the snow lasted we slept and rested during the warm hours of the day, and in the cool of the morning and evening, and all night long, we kept at work transporting our materials to the site of the new mission. The night-work, the glare or reflection of the snow, both by sun and moonlight; the subsidence of the snow on either side of the road, causing constant upsetting of sleds; the melting of the snow, making your feet wet and sloppy almost all the time; then the pulling, and pushing, and lifting, and walking, and running – these were the inevitable experiences.

Sadly, it wasn't just the humans who suffered. The traditional image of gnarly men with snarly dogs was not without foundation. Sidney Huntington recollected that while he valued his own dogs, giving them both care and kindness, such an attitude was not universal. He remembered that some owners didn't believe in treating these work animals gently and that he had seen teams of dogs so wild and vicious that he feared to be near them. It was standard practice in earlier centuries for the driver to carry a whip. In itself this did not signify cruelty; a whip can be used to crack, giving a sonic signal to pay attention to the trail, without touching so much as a hair on the animal's back. In extreme sub-zero temperatures, with a muffled face, using the voice was not always a convenient option. A whip can also be used as a simple extension of the arm, allowing the driver to lightly touch an individual dog, to let it know to listen up. However in the wrong hands whips were instruments of abuse and cruelty. This led to brutalized and dangerous dogs. During the days of the fur trade and the Gold Rush, the Arctic frontier was a harsh environment that attracted equally harsh and ornery individuals. It is mean men that make mean dogs, not genetics. John Franklin, a Captain in the Royal Navy, and author of *Narrative of a Journey to the Polar Sea* (1823) recalled with considerable distaste

> the wanton and unnecessary cruelty of the men to their dogs, especially those of the Canadians, who beat them unmercifully, and habitually vent on them the most dreadful and disgusting imprecations.

Writing in 1879, H.M. Robinson presented a similarly heart-wrenching account of extreme brutality:

> Dogs are often stubborn and provoking, and require flogging until brought into subjection; but lashings upon the body while laboring in the trains, systematic floggings upon the head till their ears drop blood, beatings with whip-stocks until nose and jaws are one deep wound, and poundings with clubs and stamping with boots till their howls merge into low wails of agony, are the frequent penalties of a slight deviation from duty. Of the four dogs attached to the provision sledge, three underwent repeated beatings at the hands of the Cree.

Beatings were just part of the story; many trains of dogs were forced to travel long distances with inadequate provisions and for excessive hours. At the end of their useful working life, which given how poorly they were treated may have been just a few years, retired dogs were simply turned loose to fend for themselves. Weak and broken, they soon starved or succumbed to predators. Although there will always have been men, like Sidney Huntington, who nurtured true devotion in his dogs, the historical reality of dog sledding amidst the grasping greed of both the fur trade and the Gold Rush was all too often a dark chapter and a terrible stain on our own wretched species.

Sleds

Sir Martin Frobisher was an Elizabethan explorer and privateer. He set sail in 1576 to try to find the Northwest Passage and subsequently spent time in the Hudson Bay area searching, without success, for gold. The *Historia Navigationes* is an account of his travels and in the 1675 edition (a century after his actual voyage) is a woodcut, showing a small kayak, pulled over snow by a single dog in traces. Certainly there would be times of the year, spring for instance, when the river ice had begun to melt but when the sled trails were still firm with compacted snow, that a kayak or a canoe might double for both land and water transport. The smooth base would glide smoothly on a compacted trail and although there is a mechanical advantage to runners (they offer less friction) they are not essential. Runners, however, were a feature of a classic style of Inuit sled, called the '*komatiq*'. This was fashioned from driftwood and animal sinew. In an area where timber was scarce to non-existant, there was considerable jeopardy if any of the wooden parts, especially the runners, were to break. Scavenging supplies for repairs might be challenging. Consequently the komatiq sled was designed with tremendous resilience. Holes were drilled in the two thick, wooden runners and horizontal slats of bone were secured onto these by means of one continuous length of sinew rope, secured by locking knots. These sinew lashings were immensely strong and provided the right amount of flexibility to the structure. When heavily laden, a sled had to withstand significant strains from twisting as it was hauled over uneven terrain, especially over sea ice. In the most remote areas, when no driftwood was available, runners were sometimes fashioned from whole frozen salmon, wrapped in hide and lashed to the sled.

Where timber was abundant, however, an entirely different design was prevalent. In the Canadian outback, the preferred sled was the toboggan. The modern English word derives from the Algonquin Indian word, '*thapakan*', via the Canadian-French '*tabaganne*'. A toboggan resembled the modern basket sled. It had a slatted wooden bed mounted on wooden runners. At the rear these runners extend behind upright posts with a crossbar. This is called the 'driving bar'. Rails, supported by vertical stanchions, extend either side of the driving bar in a diagonal line towards the front

A splendid example of a 19th century, komatiq-style sled in the British Museum. It has driftwood runners shod with a veneer of walrus ivory to make it glide more smoothly. Other parts of the sled, such as the transverse slats, have been fabricated with a whale's ribs. (© Trustees of the British Museum)

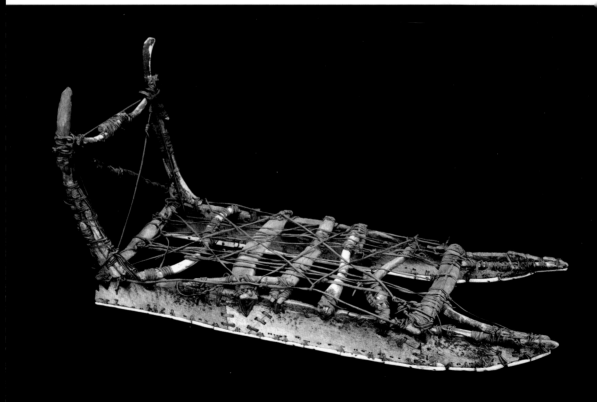

The German explorer Prince Alexander Philipp Maximilian zu Wied-Neuwied captured the essence of a cariole-style sled in an unfinished watercolour dated to 1833. It shows a trapper, with his bundle of supplies, setting out from Fort Clark in North Dakota. The cariole is being pulled by a train of just three dogs. (Wikicommons)

of the sled, giving structural support and providing a frame for hides to enclose the basket. Instead of cargo, a passenger could sit at the back, muffled with buffalo hides.

Another common type, encountered in the eighteenth and nineteenth centuries, though seldom seen today, was the 'cariole'. It had no runners but rather a smooth, flat bottom. Made from steamed laminations of wood that were turned up and curled over at the front, carioles were long and narrow in order to slot into narrow trails. They were an exceptionally tough historical type of freighting vehicle, which being flush with the trail, offered both easy loading and a low centre of gravity for a heavy cargo. With their distinctively curved prow, these flat-bottomed sleds not only bulldozed any recently piled snow, they also acted like steam-rollers to compact the trail evenly.

Sled Dog Racing

I have little doubt that the second person in the world to put a team of dogs to a sled had a race with the first person to do so. Almost every means of transport ever devised cries out to be raced. Certainly there is a long history of mushing races among the peoples who live in frigid climes, though mostly these were short distance events. However, a longer race took place in Alaska. Between 1908 and 1917, the All-Alaska Sweepstakes ran a course from Nome to Candle and back, a total distance of 408 miles. It tracked alongside the coast of the Seward Peninsula that jutted into the icy waters of the Bering Sea. Running parallel to the route were telegraph lines. These linked the camps, villages and gold-mining settlements that had sprung up after gold was discovered there in 1899, a year after the Klondike Gold Rush further south. Mushers were able to telegraph their checkpoint times to the media and this ready means of communication was a boon to those betting on the outcome. They could follow the race from the comfort of a warm saloon. At a time when the solemn thunder of artillery reverberated on the battlefields of Northern France, a young Norwegian musher by the name of Leonhard Seppala was making a name for himself in these races. He won the sweepstakes in 1915, 1916 and 1917. He was to became a significant influence on the development of sled dogs in Alaska.

During the 1920s, single-propeller biplanes began to replace the dog sled for delivering mail to outlying areas in the Arctic bush. Some routes were still served by the sleds and local travel, haulage and hunting trips remained the unchallenged domain of the Husky and the Malamute. That was to change with the coming of the snowmobile. Although experiments with a mechanical means of snow travel had begun as early as 1908, a viable snowmobile wasn't produced commercially until the early 1960s. Once these 'iron-dogs' became available affordably and in quantity, they soon ousted the dog sled as the primary mode of transport in snow-covered landscapes.

It was soon apparent that snowmobiles threatened the loss of sled dog lore, know-how and culture, not to mention a diminished breeding stock of true sled dogs. A potential salvation came in the form of newly created sled dog marathon races. In 1967, the centennial of the US purchase of Alaska from Russia, Dorothy Page and Joe Reddington Senior organized the first Iditarod race. It was a mere 56 miles but run on part of the old Iditarod trail linking Anchorage to Nome – Iditerod being the name of one of the villages along the way. This was a primary freighting route for the early settlers, particularly during the Yukon Gold Rush. In 1973 the race route was extended to link Anchorage to Nome. It also meandered to take in some villages that were not on the original route. Slightly different routes exist, depending on snow conditions, which may change annually, but all are within 25 miles of a daunting 1,000-mile journey. When the Iditarod trail was an arterial highway, it wasn't the norm for a single sled to make the entire journey. Shorter trips to nearby destinations and relays, transferring goods, passengers and mail, for longer journeys were more usual. These did not require the massive dog teams employed by the marathon racers. It was these twentieth-century marathon races that ushered in the age of the large dog team. Today they typically start the race with a fourteen-dog team. This doesn't mean that they go any faster (they can only go as fast as the slowest dog) but it means that each dog is pulling less, so stamina is conserved. According to the rules they must finish with a team of at least five dogs.

In 1925 there was a legendary feat of mushing along part of the Iditerod trail. Known as the Great Race of Mercy, this was not a race between different teams but rather a race against the clock. In the harshest of conditions, relays of dog teams rushed a cylinder of antidote serum to combat a diphtheria epidemic that was devastating the population of Nome. It was deepest winter and Nome could not be

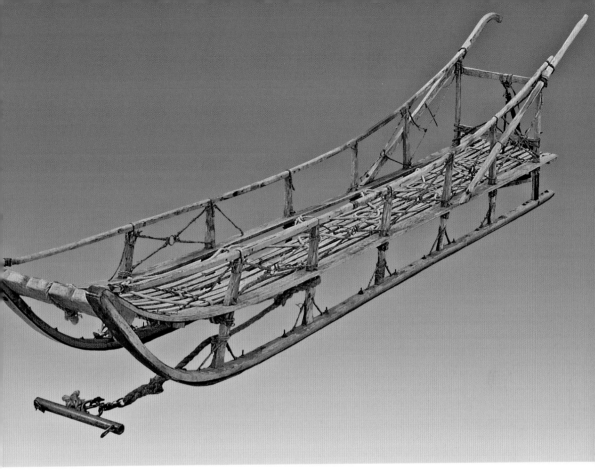

Contract mail carrier Ed Biederman (1861-1945) used this sled for his 160-mile route between Circle and Eagle, Alaska. Sam Olson built the sled of hickory in 1922. It has moose hide lashings and iron runners, brake, and springs, with cotton cords for securing mail loads. In 1935 frostbite crippled Biederman, after which he retired. His son, Charlie Biederman (1918-1995), took over the route briefly. Charlie's days as a dog-sledding mail carrier ended in 1938. Mail carriers and their dogs were made warmly welcome at 'road houses'. These Arctic inns offered their best beds to carriers and it was usual for the lead dog to be able to sleep inside. (National Postal Museum, Curatorial Photographic Collection)

reached either by sea or by air. The nearest serum was in Anchorage, a thousand miles away. A train from Anchorage carried it to Nenana, where it arrived just before midnight on 27 January. It was from here that it was transported the final 674 miles by relays of sled dogs. Twenty different mushers and over one hundred different dogs took turns to hurry the emergency remedy to its destination. Leonhard 'Sepp' Seppala, and his lead dog Togo have been hailed as the greatest heroes of the mission, covering a staggering 91 miles across the most perilous section of the route, by far the farthest distance of any single team. At 5:50 am on 2 February, another Norwegian, Gunnar Kaasen, with his lead dog Balto, delivered the serum to Dr Curtis Walsh, the town's doctor. Many thousands of lives were saved. A statue of Balto was erected in New York's Central Park.

Perhaps a majority of the dogs that ran in this relay were Malamutes, relatively heavy-set native dogs that were ideal for freighting heavier loads. However, Balto and the rest of Gunnar Kaasen's team of nine dogs were Siberian Huskies. So too were Togo and Leonhard Seppala's six-dog team. Seppala was an ardent fan of the slightly sleeker and faster Siberian Husky. He worked as a dog musher for a Swedish gold-mining company based in Nome and operated a breeding kennels, importing dogs from Siberia to improve his stock. He referred to Togo, who was just that bit smaller than the average Siberian, as 'fifty pounds of muscle and fighting heart'. In later life, Seppala recalled, 'I never had a better dog than Togo. His stamina, loyalty and intelligence could not be improved upon. Togo was the best dog that ever travelled the Alaska trail.'

Another 1,000-mile sled dog race held each year is the Yukon Quest. It follows routes parallel to the Yukon River from Whitehorse in Canada to Fairbanks, Alaska, linking together several historic trails from the days of the Yukon Gold Rush. The world's longest race however, The Beringia, is in Siberia with a 1,300-mile route from Kamchatka to Chukotka. It too is a creation of recent times. The current dominance of these marathon races can sometimes obscure the working traditions of sled dog culture. For the vast majority of their history dog sleds were not primarily sporting vehicles. They were used to carry mail; they were a means of personal transport, ferrying people between their remote villages; they freighted crucial supplies and trade goods and they carried peripatetic priests, doctors and judges across remote snow-covered regions. Hunters, trappers and explorers, venturing deep into the

Statue of Balto in Central Park, New York. He was the Siberian Husky lead-dog of Gunnar Kaasen's team in the 1925 serum run that was the inspiration for the founding of the Iditerod race. (Photo: iStock / Raghu_Ramaswamy)

wilderness, travelled by dog sled. Dog sleds were the life-blood, powering the arteries of communication and supply, throughout the snow-lands of the Northern Hemisphere.

Summer Months

Generally 'dogs of the North' are not suited to hard labour in the summer months; they overheat. For the most part they spend the summers out of work, lazing and lounging. However, in his memoir, *Alaska's First Free Mail Delivery in 1900*, Fred Lockley recalled that on making a spring landing in Nome, he saw freight on the beach 20 feet high and stretching 50 yards deep. It had been ferried there from the landing craft by dog carts:

> Dog teams, consisting of eight or ten Huskie or Malemute dogs hitched tandem, were straining at their collars to drag their carts through the soft and yielding sand.

Wheeled vehicles were an obvious answer to the absence of snow; dogs that could pull sleds could also pull carts. In Alaska, at the turn of the twentieth century, this meant using sled dogs for the summer work. In both Europe and Asia, it had long been the practice to harness dogs for hauling goods by means of a wheeled dog cart, a task for which various dog breeds were used. This function is the subject of the next chapter. In North America, however, the wheel was not introduced for transport until after European settlement in the sixteenth century. Instead, Native American tribes, from the snow-lands to the prairies and from the forests to the deserts, used a device called a 'travois'.

Travois Dogs

The travois, or 'drag sled', carried loads on a platform of horizontal staves, which were lashed to two long poles. These dragged on the ground behind the draught animal. It was an effective, and simply constructed, means of carriage for nomadic tribes who followed seasonal hunting and gathering routes. It remained the primary means of transporting goods and personal effects even after the introduction of the wheel. Wheels were relatively expensive and required a particular skillset to make. Horses were also introduced to the Americas in the sixteenth century and rapidly adopted by many Native American tribes. Horses were used to pull large travois, carrying the tepee and other communal items, whereas the dog travois was employed for smaller domestic items, food or small children. Sometimes two dogs would be paired to pull a travois carrying an elderly or sick person. When not travelling to seasonal hunting grounds, the travois still found daily use, going out with the women to bring back water, stores of firewood or buffalo chips (the name given to dried buffalo dung; it was used as combustible fuel where wood was not plentiful). After a buffalo hunt, the women would be sent out with their travois dogs to haul back the cuts of meat and the heavy hides.

George Caitlin, the pre-eminent chronicler of the customs of America's native peoples during the 1830s, wrote, after seeing several thousand Plains Indians on the move:

> At least five times that number of dogs fall into the rank, following in the company of the women. Every cur is encumbered with a sled on which he patiently drags his load – a part of the household goods and furniture of the lodge to which he belongs. Two poles, about fifteen feet long, were placed on the dogs' shoulders, leaving the larger ends to drag upon the ground behind him...faithfully and cheerfully dragging his load till night.

Dogs pulling travois to carry water for Native American women on Western Plains. 19th century hand-coloured woodcut. (North Wind Picture Archives / Alamy Stock Photo)

An average-sized 'Indian dog' was probably comfortable with loads of around 30 pounds, depending on the terrain. These were generally of a spitz/pariah-dog type and were common to native peoples throughout North America. So-called Indian dogs, similar to those seen in art, can still be found today but they are not from an ancient line. The historical type, which according to analysis of archaeological evidence carried a unique genetic signature, is now extinct. A travois had two significant advantages over either snow sleds or wheeled vehicles: it could be quickly assembled from nearby scavenged materials; and it could travel over any terrain, whether jouncing over a rocky landscape or scything through dense sage brush. Useful and expedient though the travois was, it could not compete for mechanical efficiency with the wheel.

Chapter 4

Draught Dogs: Cart Dogs

'*All the milk and similar commodities were distributed silently, quickly and early in the morning by dog-carts…[and] most of the fish taken from Grimsby to Nottingham was by dog-drawn carts.*'

—*Country Life magazine* (September 10th, 1904)

Milkmaids in Belgium using a dog cart. (Wikicommons)

Using dogs to haul loads was not unique to the snow-lands. Throughout Europe it was once common for dogs to pull wheeled carts, both for personal transport and for goods. When putting a cart, any sort of cart, to a dog, balance is everything. A properly balanced cart and load will not bear down onto the dog. The dog's sole effort should be in pulling the load not in carrying it. Anything else breaches good standards of animal welfare. In the nineteenth century abuses with poorly balanced and overladen carts motivated the Royal Society for the Protection of Cruelty against Animals (RSPCA) to lobby Parliament, calling the use of draft dogs 'cruel servitude'. Their efforts were successful and the use of dog-carts was made illegal throughout Britain. By the nineteenth century cities had become dense warrens of narrow streets and dog-carts were an expedient way of purveying goods door-to-door. Driven by this commercial advantage, there is no doubt that many impoverished, brutalized and uncaring people inflicted cruelties on their working dogs. In part, some dogs suffered from poorly balanced and excessive loads. However much of the worst abuse arose from their general mistreatment, not the 'principle' of a dog pulling a cart. Common sources of suffering were beatings, severe undernourishment, neglect and overlong hours. Moreover for the dog's comfort, harness had to fit properly and be maintained in good, supple condition. Without question there were appalling abuses in need of regulation. However, putting a dog to a cart is not inherently cruel. Those that are bred for it – Bernese Mountain Dogs, Rottweilers, Newfoundlands, Belgian Mastiffs *inter alia* – are invariably wag-happy to drop their shoulders into a comfortable harness and haul. What matters is the ratio of dogpower to the load and the general treatment that the dog receives from its human provider. The scandal of nineteenth century animal cruelty was not exclusive to those with dog-carts; it was endemic to society. An article in *Country Life* magazine in 1904 by an English traveller to Holland, commented on the continued use of cart dogs in that country. He noted that in some of the poorer areas, the dogs did not fare too well but that in the wealthier cities:

> The cart dog is a high-spirited, eager creature, which, as a rule, takes a great deal of interest in its work and needs neither beating nor scolding.

Our correspondent went on to detail that at The Hague:

> the dogs that bring the vegetables into market lie under their carts, while the cargo is being sold. In the afternoon, when the time for going home approaches, they bark loud and excitedly, and with their owners sitting in the carts, often race other dogs home.

Whichever way we thread the needle to nuance the rights and wrongs of using dogs for haulage, it is an activity that is an indelible part of canine history and the *raison d'être* for certain types of dogs.

Carting as a recreation for draught breeds has become increasingly popular in the USA today and, provided that the harness is of good quality, that it fits, that

OUZOUER-sur-LOIRE (Loiret)
Le Boulanger et son attelage

French baker with dog cart in 1918 (Mary Evans Picture Library)

the loads are perfectly balanced and sufficiently light, the dogs appear to love the work, every bit as much as a Husky relishes pulling a sled. If they are cared for properly, dogs that are bred for it pull a cart with cheerfulness and enthusiasm. Modern carts are built from lightweight tubular steel and have a platform upon which verifiable weights are stacked. Competitions begin with a judged assessment of how well a dog backs into its shafts and gets hitched. Next is an obstacle course, which involves navigating tight turns around traffic cones, passing through narrow chicanes and behaving correctly at gates – stopping, waiting, moving on when the gate is opened and stopping again when it is closed. After that they go on a cross-country freight-haul. For obvious reasons, larger dogs are favoured and these are generally either mastiffs, livestock guardians or Newfoundland Dogs. Among the most popular choices is the Pyrenean Mountain Dog. When a shepherd went up into the high hill with his flock for the summer, he required a substantial quantity of supplies. Willing Pyreneans hauled a cartload of provisions in a steep climb before being set loose to patrol the flock.

Present-day carting dogs taking a break. It is essential that a properly fitting harness allows a dog to lie down comfortably between the shafts. (Photograph by the author)

Carting enthusiasts in California with a convoy of Pyrenean and Newfoundland cart dogs on a 'freight-haul'. This is a cross-country hike with uniformly weighted carts. (Photograph by the author)

Dogs of Yard and Market

Several dog types originated as general helpers to the farmer. They could guard and, to some extent, they could also herd and drove livestock– though not as expertly as the specialist collies and corgis. One of their main occupations, however, was to pull carts and wagons. Carts are two-wheeled vehicles, for which it is essential to have a finely balanced load that sits over the axle. A wagon on the other hand is a four-wheeled vehicle. It is less able to turn tight corners, as found in city alleyways, and is harder

A Bernese Mountain Dog about to deliver a wagonload of hay to a cattle pasture. Lightweight loads such as hay could be transported in considerable bulk by a single dog with little effort. The joy that this dog derives from his work is plain to see. (Juniors Bildarchiv GmbH / Alamy Stock Photo)

work to pull over rough terrain. The benefit of a wagon though is that all the weight is on the wheels, therefore it can carry a much heavier load without putting any weight at all on the dog's shoulders. Bernese Mountain Dogs were wagon dogs *par excellence*. When harnessed to a wagon in pairs they were capable of carrying considerable loads but a single dog could haul considerable bulk of lightweight materials such as hay. Bern is a vast canton of Switzerland famous for its lush pastures and herds of dairy cows. Wagonloads of heavy milk churns were trundled to town and village, to manor and market, by these sturdy dogs; their powerful hindquarters drove the climb up many a hill. Wagons were also used to ferry feed and equipment around the farmyard.

Another general-purpose yard-and-market breed is the Rottweiler. They too worked as guard dogs and drovers but pulling carts to market was a chief occupation. These tremendously strong, muscular dogs were usually driven as pairs or three abreast and had the ability to haul heavy cargo. Rottweilers are well known for their smooth trotting action and they can maintain a steady pace for miles. Popular legend claims that the breed originated with the Romans and that they were used to drove cattle behind the baggage train of a marching army. Before canned meat or refrigeration, it was usual for armies to transport their meat supplies on the hoof. The Romans made several incursions into German lands and, so the story goes, their dogs remained behind. It is certain that the Romans used herds of cattle, marshalled by droving dogs, to feed their troops. It is unproven whether or not the Rottweiler is a direct descendant, though there are dogs in Roman art with a distinct facial resemblance.

The official name of the breed is the Rottweiler Metzgerhund, which means the 'Rottweil butcher's dog'. Rottweil is a town in southwest Germany, founded by the Romans in 73 AD. Rottweilers have an ability to herd sheep as well as cattle but

Rottweiler with butcher's cart, depicted in this reproduction poster (Photograph by the author)

A pair of strong Rottweilers. The form of these muscular, deep-chested dogs fitted them well to lean into a harness. Frequently used in pairs, they were cart dogs, guard dogs and general purpose herding dogs. (Photo: iStock/ Callipso)

the soubriquet 'butcher's dog' stems largely from their work pulling carts laden with slaughtered meat to market. Although in reality Rottweilers can be extremely affectionate with their owners, their seemingly fierce appearance and protective instincts served double duty when it came to guarding the day's takings. Whether journeying to or from the marketplace, it was not uncommon for either farmer or butcher to hop on board the cart or wagon and take a ride.

Personal Transport

In the 1920 silent film *Polyanna*, Mary Pickford drove a dog-wagon. The diminutive actress played the role of a child in the film, although she was in fact twenty-eight at the time. Her vehicle was a four-wheeled wagon, placing no weight onto the dog's back. She carried a passenger, a toddler in a tin bathtub. Her dog is wagging its tail and appears both happy and lively. Scaled down versions of horse-drawn vehicles that were pulled by large dogs were a popular novelty for well-to-do children from the mid-nineteenth to the mid-twentieth centuries. With small children, properly fitted harnesses and correctly balanced carts, the exertions would have been minimal for large, strong dogs. Two-wheeled carts, with the driver's weight over or behind the axle were equally kind to the dog, provided all the other parameters were in place. I have some experience of this from the dog's perspective. For television programmes about Ancient Egypt, I have on a number of occasions placed myself in the shafts of an Egyptian chariot with a strap over my shoulders and pulled a chariot with two, sometimes three, full-grown men on board. The point of this was to demonstrate that, provided the weight is on or behind the axle, there is virtually no load bearing on the shoulders; one simply has to pull.

John Lawrence, writing in *The Sporting Repository* in 1820, refers to a gentleman having a carriage drawn by six dogs, stating that these were the largest and most powerful he had ever witnessed. One may imagine that this fellow fair zipped along with no detriment to his team of dogs. Another entry in the same publication recalls a Mr Chabert, who journeyed from Bath to London by means of a gig (a light two-wheeled carriage) drawn by a single 'Siberian wolf dog', presumably a large Husky. In the process of offering the dog for sale, at the princely sum of £200, Chabert claimed that the dog could pull him for 30 miles a day. There are a number of early photographs that show adults sitting on dog-drawn carts that are well-balanced and appear to be comfortable for the dog. However there are other, more questionable images – photographs and cartoons – that show undersized dogs, carting plump matrons, surly soldiers or obese burghers, where the overall weight and load distribution is clearly inhumane. By the 1840s, there were debates in the British Parliament to ban the use of cart dogs. Speaking on one occasion, Lord Brougham opined that:

> Nothing could be more shocking or disgusting than to see the practice of great, heavy men being drawn by dogs…Indeed, I have seen near the place where their lordships assemble, all sorts of articles drawn by small dogs who could hardly get on.

French soldier driving a dog-cart, c1914-18. His weight seems to be over the axle and the dog, a strong mastiff, appears to be moving easily and carrying his tail high. (The Print Collector / Alamy Stock Photo)

Another issue that affected the welfare of cart-dogs was the state of the roads. Outside the smooth cobbled streets of the towns, road surfaces were of variable quality. After animal welfare legislation came into effect in 1836, there were numerous prosecutions against those who forced their dogs to continue pulling a cart after jagged flints in the road had cut their feet. During the eighteenth and nineteenth centuries in England the principal road network was built and maintained by local trusts. These raised money for the work by means of tolls, although a great deal of the labour – breaking rocks – was done by prisoners. A majority of surviving toll boards use phrasing such as 'drawn by horses, asses or other beasts of burden' when referring to the charges for bringing wheeled vehicles of various descriptions through the toll. However on a toll-board from outside the Sussex town of Northchapel, now exhibited at the Weald

Unidentified American Civil War Union veteran in a wagon pulled by two dogs in front of C.F. Cook's photography studio, Wilkes-Barre, Pennsylvania. With a wagon (four wheels) even an unbalanced load has no weight-bearing effect on a dog. (Library of Congress)

and Downland Museum, there is specific reference to canine-powered transport. It declares the following toll:

> For every Dog drawing any Truck, Barrow or other Carriage for the space of One Hundred Yards or upwards upon any part of the said Roads, the Sum of One Penny.

This compared favourably with the toll of 4½ pennies for 'every Horse, Mule, Ass or other beast (except Dogs) drawing any Coach…Cart, Wagon, Wain… or other vehicle'.

Not only did such charges encourage the thrifty trader or traveller to use dog-carts, where such transportation was feasible, but it also dissuaded such persons from harnessing any more dogs than they could get away with. This undoubtedly led to single dogs having to haul unduly heavy loads – and people!

City Carts

By far the greater use of dog-carts was by tradesmen and vendors in the towns and cities. A dog-cart could deliver goods, such as bread or milk, through winding back alleyways that were inaccessible to a horse and cart. Daily door-to-door milk deliveries were made with dog-powered wagons laden with churns. Dog-carts were also the preferred transport of tinkers, knife-grinders, greengrocers, butchers, bakers and candlestick makers. Organ-grinders used dog-carts to transport their barrel organs

Pre-war photograph of the greengrocer Levie Pais with his dog cart in Harlingen, Netherlands. Behind the cart is his delivery boy, Piet Mensonides. Tragically, Levie Pais was killed in the Auschwitz death-camp in November 1942. The cart appears unbalanced, sloping forward at the front. However the unstressed demeanour and upright stance of the dog, a strong Belgian Mastiff, implies that he is bearing very little weight. This indicates that the load has been distributed so that there is more weight behind the axle, thereby lifting the shafts in the tugs. (Griet de Jong Fotos, courtesy of Tresoar, the Frisian Historical and Literary Centre)

and entertain the crowds. Dog labour was ubiquitous. These enterprising merchants were predominantly poor, barely making a living from long hours of work. Apart from the convenience of access to narrow passageways, dog-power was less expensive than using horses; dogs were both cheaper to buy and to maintain. In theory a dog could be fed scraps from the table, though to those in penury, scraps too were a precious resource. A sole-trader's dog could provide some companionship to a lonely life and be a source of heat on a cold winter's night. Many traders' dogs would have been treated with great affection by their human partners but, sadly, this was not the case for all. Abject poverty in squalid living conditions can brutalize and pervert a man's soul. Enslaved to such oppressed wretches, the poor dogs often became the victims of cruel abuse and neglect. As a result there were many calls, particularly in Britain, for the prohibition of dog-carts. After years of lobbying the RSPCA had its first success when parliament passed a Dog Cart Nuisance Law in 1839, banning the use of draught dogs within 15 miles of Charing Cross. It did not pass without protest and London costermongers (fruit and vegetable sellers) petitioned Parliament, declaring that their kindness to their dogs was well known and that the new law would ruin their trade.

Nowhere was the dog-cart more popular than in Belgium. Many of the dogs used by the poorer tradesmen were what people today would call mongrels but there was a basic landrace type – the Belgian Mastiff – that was purpose bred for the task. Belgian Mastiffs became extinct but a group of enthusiasts in Belgium have now bred a dog that appears to be exactly like this old breed. The Belgium Kennel Club recognizes it as a 'reconstructed' breed. According to W.E. Mason whose book *Dogs of All Nations* was published in 1915, around 50,000 carting dogs were estimated to be working in Belgium, of which 10,000 were in Brussels alone. He considered the Belgian Mastiff type to be well suited to the task, being thick set, with deep chests and muscular limbs.

Although dog carting did not receive outright bans on the Continent, as it had in Britain, there were nevertheless regulations to ensure more humane treatment. Officials might inspect a dog's feet, check for chafing from the harness and generally assess an animal's condition. They would ask to see a drinking bowl and water supply and all carts had to carry a strip of soft mat for the dogs to lie on when resting. When set up correctly, the harness of a two-wheeled cart enables a dog to lie down and rest between the shafts without incurring any weight burden from the vehicle. When carts were left unattended, dogs were usually unhitched from their traces altogether and tethered with a simple leash. However this was not for the dogs' comfort. It was to give them the freedom to act as guard dogs, ensuring the safekeeping of their master's wares. By the late nineteenth century, the ability of these dogs to guard effectively was compromised by city ordinances, requiring them to wear muzzles. Dogs could bite people and they could also bite other dogs. The greatest concern, indeed panic of the age, was the spread of rabies.

On the Waterfront

Newfoundland dogs are covered in greater detail in the chapter on water dogs, but these versatile giants were ubiquitous and arguably one of the most popular breeds in the nineteenth century. Among their many attributes is a willingness and an ability to pull a cart. In their Canadian homeland they were used in vast numbers to haul the catch from the harbour's edge to the salting warehouses. They would pull carts carrying 2–300 lbs of fish and it has been estimated that there were as many as 2,000 Newfoundlands doing this work in St Johns at the peak of the industry there. During World War II, they hauled provisions and ammunition for the US armed forces in the Aleutian Islands (off the coast of Alaska). These islands had been invaded by the Japanese and were considered strategically vital by the US, who feared that control of this area would give the Japanese a base from which to launch air attacks on the West Coast of the US mainland. The dogs slogged faithfully over harsh terrain, through blizzards, snowstorms and icy conditions to bring these vital supplies to remote outposts. Today the Newfoundland is used extensively in the USA to compete in carting trials.

The Calamity

The efforts of the RSPCA had begun as a genuine, and necessary, crusade to promote animal welfare. There can be nothing but the highest praise for laws that resulted in prosecution for the ill-treatment of dogs. The Dog Cart Nuisance Law passed in 1839 was less clear in its motives. Laws against animal cruelty already existed and some contended that, while these laws should be upheld, it was unnecessary to discriminate further against lawful dog-carting folk. Others argued that a ban should be put in place because dog-carts interfered with the smooth flow of traffic. Whilst debating a proposed extension to the bill in 1841, Sir James East reminded parliament that 'only within the last few months, the Lynn coach had been overturned by a dog-cart and much mischief was the result'.

Hailing from Lynn (King's Lynn), as I do, I have always found this little detail of particular fascination – I can almost imagine where the incident happened. A further impetus, that had nothing to do with canine welfare, was concern by country landowners (and their gamekeepers) that the nation's dog population was too great and too many dogs in the hands of poor folk could lead to an increase in poaching. Banning dog-carts would reduce dog ownership among the poor. Gradually the laws were expanded to prohibit the use of dog-carts in more and more areas. Then, in 1854, hysteria entered the argument.

Lord Brougham was a chief proponent of an erroneous theory that the use of dogs to pull carts actually caused the onset of rabies. His reasoning, if one may call it that, was that when dogs are over-exerted they foam at the mouth; similarly when a dog has rabies it foams at the mouth. Bad owners did work their dogs too hard, so it was not uncommon to see frothing animals in the streets. To an unscientific public, the association rang true. There was tremendous public anxiety about this horrible disease, for which there was no known cure. In 1854 an amendment to the 1849 Prevention of Cruelty to Animals Act was passed. It was nick-named the 'Dog Cart Act' and it placed a complete, nationwide ban on the use of dogs as draught animals. Within a few weeks of the ban in excess of 20,000 dogs were destroyed in London and the River Thames was polluted with the carcasses of drowned dogs. In Cambridge there were sickening piles of dead dogs, which had either been strangled or clubbed to death. Magistrates had to order their disposal, as they were a threat to public health. The cities of Birmingham and Liverpool each had over a thousand dogs put down in the space of a week. According to Stanley Coren (*The Pawprints of History*, 2003) between 150,000 and 250,000 dogs were put to death following the new laws. Many more were simply abandoned.

Dog Carts in War

Although the use of dog-carts had been banned in Britain, they remained ubiquitous in Northern France, Flanders and other parts of Europe throughout World War I. Local vendors used them as they plied their trade along the columns of British troops who had disembarked at Boulogne, Calais and Dunkirk. Between 1914 and 1916, around 1,700,000 British soldiers landed at Boulogne alone. These tradesmen's dog-carts carried a range of wares such as postcards, socks, soap and shaving gear, medicines, matches and cigarettes – the latter always in demand, despite the fact that cigarettes were issued as part of standard rations. For the most part, the dogs employed for this work were a motley assortment of mongrels but distinct types were bred for the work and most had elements of the 'Belgian mastiff' about them.

Convoy of supply dog-carts in the Hungarian army during World War I. Dog teams were used extensively by European armies to supply food, fuel and ammunition to the front lines. (Wikicommons)

The French and Belgian armies, as well as the opposing German and Austro-Hungarian armies, all used dog-powered vehicles to deliver essential supplies to the front line. Dog-carts were less conspicuous than horse-drawn vehicles and considerably less expensive. According to W. E. Mason's *Dogs of All Nations* in 1915:

> The price of a pack-horse is not less than £40, and his daily forage may be reckoned to cost about 1/4½ a day without taking into consideration the construction and upkeep of his stable. The pack-saddle costs about £15, whereas dog harness can be purchased for the pair of dogs for something less than £4. A male dog costs £4, and his food per day amounts to about 4½d*.

Small four-wheeled wagons, pulled by two- or three-dog teams, were most common, carrying a soldier's most crucial needs: rations, mail and ammunition. In some cases trenches were wide enough for these dog transports to operate along their length. Dog-carts were an exceptionally efficient distribution system for the topography. Wounded men were loaded onto dog-carts for transfer back to field hospitals and, occasionally, dog-carts were used for personal transportation by officers. In the aftermath of both world

* In British imperial currency (until Feb 1971) 1/4½ = 1 shilling, 4½ pence; 4d = 4 pence. 12 pence made a shilling, 20 shillings a pound.

wars, refugees trudged the roads of Europe with their most precious possessions laden onto dog-carts. However, the most extraordinary, and really very clever, use of draught dogs was during World War I. The Belgian army deployed brigades of Belgian Mastiffs hauling cart-mounted machine-guns.

Machine-gun dogs

Germany declared war on France on 1 August 1914 and launched a flanking manoeuvre through Belgium. The idea was to attack France on its border with Belgium at the same time as striking across the German/French border. During the first few months of the war, Belgium put up a brave and determined resistance against this invasion. The Belgians slowed this advance considerably, giving the French extra time to organize. Their success in frustrating the German war machine was all the more remarkable because the Belgian army in 1914 was largely a nineteenth-century army, not ready for mechanized warfare. Nevertheless they did have machine guns.

A British-American inventor, Hiram Stevens Maxim, developed the Maxim gun in 1884. It utilized the recoil from the firing of each chamber to both eject the spent cartridge and to load a fresh one. Previous incarnations of repeating guns, such as the Gatling gun, required hand-cranking. The Maxim gun could fire 600 rounds per minute. It was water-cooled in order to prevent over-heating. Such performance came at a cost. Maxim guns were heavy, bulky and cumbersome, requiring a constant and copious supply of both ammunition and water. Over the years various improvements were made to the basic design – in Britain the same basic gun was re-incarnated as the Vickers gun and in Germany it became the MG 08. Nevertheless Maxim's essential design was recognizable in the machine guns of all World War I armies. Although it only required one soldier to operate the trigger, the Maxim gun necessitated a crew of six to eight men to lug it into position and mount it, as well as keeping it replenished with ammunition and water, commodities that it devoured with hot-tempered avarice.

The Belgian army had an ingenious solution to these problems. It mounted its Maxim guns onto two-wheeled carts, which were pulled by a brace of sturdy and highly-trained dogs. Water and ammunition were similarly transported by canine conveyance. Not only did the system minimize manpower and speed-up deployment; it had the additional advantage of stealth. The carts were furnished with pneumatic tyres and, unlike iron-shod horses or hob-nailed men, dog paws are silent. These rigs were also low to the ground and when it came to fighting in flat pastureland, hedge-lined fields, gently undulating sand dunes or the marshy terrain of the polders, there was no better set-up for concealed machine-gun placement. In these topographies, dog-power was optimal. There is archive film, which shows machine-gun dogs working entirely to hand signals. The dogs wait off at a distance, while a human observer crawls to a forward position. He then waves the dogs on, and they trot forward with their gun carriage. The dogs are both silent and hidden by the slightest rise. Once in position, the dog team is unhitched and they fall back to take cover, lying down away from the action.

The type of dog used by the Belgian army was the Belgian Mastiff. Sadly these dogs became extinct during the 1960s but in 2002 a careful breeding programme,

In 2014, for the centenary commemorations of the outbreak of World War I, organized by the Belgian Royal Military Museum in Brussels, pairs of Belgian Mastiffs were trained to operate with authentically recreated machine-gun and ammunition carts. They were harnessed with superb, well-fitting tack made by Roger Louage. The dogs, who appear eager for the work, were bred and trained by the Belgian Mastiff Association. (*Photograph courtesy of Pascal Mathieu*)

A column of Belgian soldiers, with machine-gun dogs, retreating to Antwerp in 1914 (Chronicle / Alamy Stock Photo)

undertaken by enthusiasts, produced the first in the line of what is now recognized as a 'reconstructed breed'. Belgian Mastiffs are large, powerful dogs, with a double coat that protects them against the wind, wet and mud of a Belgian winter. They have a docile nature, are calm under stress and not easily provoked into barking. Furthermore they possess immense stamina, a necessary requirement for long marches.

Like many before and after them, these dogs were dragged without option into man's wretched wars. War is always tragic and, though we may admire the courage of the dogs and the ingenuity of the system, we must take care not to romanticize the experience. In *Pierrot, A Dog of Belgium*, a fictional story written in 1915 by the American author Walter Alden Dyer, the eponymous Pierrot is a dog who transitions from a working life of pulling a milk cart and the tender care of a thoughtful owner, to being pressed into service in the front line, pulling a machine gun. Dyer paints a vivid picture of what the reality may have been like:

> There was no time to unharness the dogs, so they were turned about and were obliged to stand facing away from the tumult of battle as the machine guns began to rattle directly behind them. It was very hard to bear, and some of them might have broken and run but for a half-dozen men who had been told to squat by the dogs' heads and hold them steady... Two of the dogs started wildly off, their gun bumping and careening behind them...Just as they were turning a speeding bullet caught a spotted young dog that Pierrot had become acquainted with. He was trotting close by with his mate and their gun, and with a cry of pain and terror he leaped into the air and fell at Pierrot's feet... They were soon overwhelmed and the dogs who were harnessed were quickly bayonetted that they might not run off with the guns. Some of the other dogs fled and perhaps a few escaped, but there was little chance for them.

Immediately after WWI, ten Belgian machine-gun dogs were sent to America for a fund raising tour in 1919. They captured the hearts and imagination of the American people. There are photographs of them parading through major cities and a sketch of the parade order still exists in the museum in Brussels. We see not only the names and positioning of the soldiers in the parade but also the names of the dogs. It somehow makes it all more real, more immediate, more poignant that we know the names of the dogs. Among them were Marc and Bonot, Katie and Sarah, Baron and Bamboula. Like Pierrot, they too may have once pulled a wagon of milk churns and been cared for by a kindly milkmaid; conscripted from civilian life into the army.

Just like Pierrot's friend, the spotted dog, not all machine-gun dogs were pure Belgian Mastiffs. These were simply a preferred type who had been bred for the work. It is a theme of this book that certain dog types were bred for specialist work. However, when it came to hauling carts, either amid the depravations of war or in the poverty-stricken alleyways of the city, people were less discriminating and almost any mongrel would do. Even so, carting did have its specialists and to see a Belgian Mastiff, a Bernese, a Newfoundland or a Rottweiler between the shafts is to see a dog that is both temperamentally and anatomically suited for the work.

Chapter 5

Carriage Dogs

*"A new coach dog [arrived] for the benefit of Madame Moose; her amorous fits
should therefore be attended to."*
—Letter from George Washington to his nephew, 1787

Dalmatian on duty at the rear of a carriage. (Photograph by the author)

Carriage dogs accompanied horse-drawn carriages, running either behind, or alongside or sometimes under the vehicle. Ostensibly their function was to guard the carriage against assaults from highway robbers on the open road or, if the carriage were left unoccupied, outside a tavern for instance, from petty thieves. Additionally they deterred other dogs, who might run out barking at and chasing the horses, while on the road. Many dogs retain an irresistible urge to run after moving vehicles. Such behaviour was a regular hazard in the age of horse-drawn transport, an age when many unregulated and stray dogs were at large. Space was at a premium in a carriage and so having a dog that had the stamina to keep up with the horses all day was a practical solution to maintaining a constant guarding presence. Traditionally this has been work associated with the Dalmatian.

Writing in *The American Book of the Dog* in 1891, Major T.J. Woodcock noted:

> A good coach dog has often saved his owners much valuable property by watching the carriage. It is a trick of thieves who work in pairs for one to engage the coachman in conversation while the other sneaks around in the rear and steals whatever robes and other valuables he can lay his hands on. I never lost an article while the dogs were in charge, but was continually losing when the coachman was in charge.

The basis of the carriage dog's dedication to its task was the bond it developed with the horse or horse team. Dogs intended for this job were lodged in the stables with the horses from an early age. Here they developed an enduring attachment and friendship with their equine companions. Not only did this instil in them the protective instincts to keep other dogs away from their charges and to not let strangers approach, it also resulted in a secondary, but no less important, security duty. Horse theft was an extremely common crime, especially from the stables of inns, where travellers would

Dalmatian with coach. Woodblock from Bewick's 'General History of Quadrupeds 1807. (Mary Evans Picture Library)

Tally and Jacko - inseparable friends. The key to a carriage dog's guarding instinct is the bond it forms with the horses in its care. This is established at an early age. (Photograph by the author)

lodge. A coachman without a dog was often obliged to string his hammock in the stall with his horses. However, with a dog to guard his team, he could take a room and a comfortable bed. Carriage dogs rendered further service in the stable by keeping down the vermin that infested these warm, grain-abundant, straw-strewn habitats and Dalmatians still have the reputation of being excellent ratters. A good carriage dog was also considered to have a calming effect on the horses. Hauling heavy carriages on long-distance journeys required teams of horses that had exceptional stamina and 'go'. Possessing such energy reserves often manifested in horses that were slightly highly-strung; the reassurance given them by a loyal carriage dog could reduce unnecessary agitation. Known variously as the English Coach Dog, the Carriage Dog, the Plum Pudding Dog and the Spotted Dick, spotted dogs seem to have been preferred for this service during the eighteenth and early nineteenth centuries, the Golden Age of coach travel.

Adventures with a Dalmatian
I contacted Alison Burgess through the British Carriage Dog Society and she invited me down to her lovely farmhouse home in East Sussex to meet her 5-year-old Dalmatian female, Tally. There was a great deal of barking when Tally first clapped eyes on me in the stable yard. However, after her initial alarm signal, she came running in and showered me with affection. Dalmatians really do have the softest, most velvety coats. This is of great advantage in shedding the dirt after

miles of jogging on muddy roads, a coat that needs no human maintenance, but it also makes for a dog that is irresistible to pet. However, in the age of coach travel, a carriage dog would not have been so friendly. Since their primary function was to act a guard dogs, they were once appropriately aggressive. Their bond was greater with the horses than it was with the people who owned them. They slept in the stables with the horses, followed the horses and interacted with a human only to beg or steal scraps for their subsistence. In the approximately ten or so dog-generations since a Dalmatian was called upon to perform its traditional guarding task in earnest, a gentler disposition has been bred into them. Today Dalmatians like Tally do double-duty as housedogs and family pets. Old guarding instincts linger insofar as they like to play games of possession and bark at strangers but they can no longer be considered aggressive animals. That has largely been bred out of them, partly by cross-breeding with pointers. Moreover, if Tally is anything to go by, the present-day Dalmatian is such an enthusiastically friendly animal that it is hard to reconcile it with the breed's former duties. The need to create an animal more compliant with national laws about aggressive dogs and the removal of its original function has undoubtedly influenced selective breeding towards a much gentler, and wonderfully affectionate, strain. Nevertheless some Dalmatians retain a curious, seemingly aggressive, behaviour known as the 'Dalmatian smile', in which the dog draws back its flews (the hanging, fleshy upper lip), furrowing its muzzle with deep quarrelsome creases, and thereby bares its teeth. It looks like a ferocious snarl to most people but Dalmatian owners recognize it as a passive, 'happy-to-see-you' face. Although the temperament of the modern Dalmatian has been softened, this motor response of bared teeth has remained in some as a disconnected reflex.

This Dalmatian has been guarding a modern carriage – a motor-car – and is greeting his owner on his return with what is known as a 'Dalmatian smile'. Modern Dalmatians have had the aggression bred out of them and they are delightfully affectionate dogs. The 'Dalmatian smile' is an inherited behaviour that exhibits the body language of aggression without its intent. Dalmatian owners recognize this as a friendly reception. (Photograph by Jeff Jones)

Road Dog

Those who travelled by coach or carriage were not the only travellers in need of a guarding dog. Both before and during the great age of coach travel many people still journeyed by horseback. When a companion dog attends a ridden horse, he/she is referred to as a 'road dog'. Whether stopping at a wayside inn or at tavern or tradesman in the city, there remained the risk of theft, either of the horse itself or of the contents of the saddlebags. I was introduced to Jacko, a steady old piebald cob. I mounted and walked him around a little before tightening the girths. Aware that we weren't yet going anywhere Tally pottered around the yard looking for food, as any dog would. Given that there was a stranger in the saddle, I wondered if Tally would follow me as readily as she would her owner. It seemed a good idea to encourage her and to this end I offered her some treats. She bounded up, stood on her hind legs, and rested her front paws against Jacko's side. It was extraordinary to see the trust and bond between the two of them. Most horses would have shied dramatically at a dog jumping up at them like that. Jacko was impervious to the activity, his stoic calm in stark contrast to Tally's effervescence. When walking on foot Tally could be called in, just like any other dog, with the command 'heel'. When I was seated on a horse, however, she responded to the instruction 'hock'. This brought her smartly in and alongside the on-side hindquarters; the appropriate zone for a road dog when going out on today's highways with motor traffic. Once there she was diligent

A 'Road Dog' is the name given to a dog that escorts and guards a traveller on horseback. Here Tally responds to the command 'hock' and tucks in to keep a steady pace by the horse's hindquarters. (Photograph by Gordon Summers)

There is such a bond of trust between horse and dog that, Jacko, the horse, remains nonchalant, even when Tilly, the dog, jumps up and rests against him in the quest for a treat from the author. (Photograph by Gordon Summers)

in her duties. There was not a hint of begging for more treats. She just stayed close and followed along, even though I'm sure she was deeply suspicious of the stranger on her pal's back.

An Excursion

At lunchtime we took Alison's modern, four-wheeled, cross-country competition vehicle and, with Jacko in the shafts, drove the several miles to the pub. It was May in England and it was a sunny day. Pale, translucent leaves, newly unfurled in the late spring, dappled the little lanes with coruscating light. I had lived in East Sussex many decades previously and have a great fondness for the area. On this occasion nostalgia

Tally wears a bell so that the carriage driver can hear if she is remaining close by. Carriage dogs are untethered and are potentially free to run off in search of the edible temptations that lurk within scenting distance of a country lane, as well as succumbing to sight-triggered pursuit of startled game. (Photograph by the author)

was complemented with the thrill of new experiences. The clopping of horse's hooves on the road, as we trotted along briskly, was a familiar sound but this was now mingled with the rumble and creak of the carriage and the sonorous chime of a bell on Tally's collar. It was the soundtrack from another age and it was glorious. Tally's bell did not annoy with a jarring clang but rather soothed with a melodic jangle. To what extent carriage dogs were furnished with a bell during the great age of coaching is uncertain but a bell clearly served a practical function in letting one know if the dog was still with you. Even when the sound faded, if she dropped back to answer a call of nature, it soon manifested again reassuringly.

I took the reins for half the journey but I much preferred my time spent on the groom's footplate at the rear of the carriage. Here I could observe Tally 'in the zone'. Her gaze was set on Jacko's hooves and she maintained a constant, consistently-paced jog for several miles. It was both beautiful and hypnotic to watch her and, entering a semi trance-like state myself, it's a wonder I didn't fall off. I have never seen a dog perform in this way before, with unremitting, rhythmic, exquisitely elegant movement for an extremely prolonged period. She looked so relaxed, 'right' and happy in her role and she gave the appearance that she could have kept it up all day. It was spellbinding and Tally had an expression and a body language, common to all dogs I have seen fulfilling their traditional roles, of self-assurance, capability and appetite for the task. She was doing what defined her and doing it with style and relish.

The command used to call a dog to attendance when driving a carriage is 'get under'. It is a familiar image in old prints to see Dalmatians running underneath a carriage; even today some dogs seem to stoop and get right under the axle, whether or not there is adequate clearance for them. Not only is this a potentially dangerous position, from the point of view of getting a paw run over by a wheel, but where the dog is having to crouch, it is very bad for them anatomically. In spite of these detriments the instinct to get under the carriage and as close to the horses as possible is very strong. The habit of getting fully under a vehicle, even if there is room, is not a sensible one and Alison discourages it. On the modern competition vehicle that we took to the pub, she has a rubber mat that falls, like a mud-guard, over the back of the footplate at the rear, creating a physical barrier. When out in her higher-axled nineteenth-century Clifton gig, she uses a water squirt when training young dogs to make sure that they don't 'get under' too much. The phrase 'intelligent disobedience' is often used in connection with Dalmatians. It conveys the idea that they have an intuitive awareness of hazards and although they will obediently go where instructed, they will nonetheless be aware constantly of hooves, wheels and other traffic and be quick to get out of the way without waiting to ask permission to go off station. Considerations of safety both for the dog and other road users in modern traffic make it essential that the dog stays tucked in closely behind the vehicle, though before the advent of motor cars, this was less important and carriage dogs might run alongside, in front or behind the vehicle they were attending.

On arrival at the pub, a picturesque establishment in a sleepy village, the usual practice was to let Jacko graze in the paddock that was situated behind the beer garden. There was a gate at the side of the pub that led directly to this. Unfortunately the gate was locked and the landlord, who had the key, was out. The barmaid suggested we take the horse through the beer-garden, which we did. It involved leading Jacko through an extremely narrow gateway with a pergola arch and then threading him past the tables of amused, and slightly concerned, patrons enjoying their lunches. Afterwards we headed back and then it was time to try my hand at driving a traditional carriage.

A carriage dog follows the horses, not the carriage. The vehicle is incidental. Note how Tally's gaze is locked onto the horse's hooves. (Photograph by Gordon Summers)

Alison maintains her nineteenth-century Clifton gig in immaculate condition. It is truly a thing of beauty and I felt very privileged to be allowed to drive it. Jacko seemed happy as the shafts were seated in their tugs; it was as if he knew this was the high-status vehicle he was supposed to be pulling. Tally, too, seemed excited. Wheeling out the Clifton gig obviously signalled to all an important occasion. Normally of course this would be true; the gig is what Alison uses when she competes in carriage dog trials. Today, however, they were simply going through their paces for a stranger. In deference to the punctilious preferences of carriage-driving folk, I donned a cap and driving gloves and Alison kindly lent me her antique holly driving-whip. One of her

The author taking the reins, with Tally 'on station', eager and ready to follow for as many miles as necessary. (Photograph by Gordon Summers)

neighbours had given permission for us to use one of their farm roads, a compacted gravel drive. Being neither modern tarmac nor a mud track it more closely resembled the sort of roads a carriage dog would have journeyed on in the eighteenth century. I bade Jacko 'Walk On' and commanded Tally to 'Get Under'. Both animals snapped to without hesitation and off we went. I clicked Jacko into a brisk trot and Tally tucked in for the duration, dropping her head, streamlining her tail and settling in to a rhythmic jog that kept her glued at a constant distance with her nose just between the wheels. The carriage creaked and squeaked as it should and the horse clopped on the hard road and Tally's bell jingled to let me know that she was still there.

In order to keep them at a level of fitness necessary to take part in carriage dog trials, Alison exercises Tally, and her other Dalmatians, on tarmac roads for around 10 miles every other day. Competitions require the dog to keep up a steady pace, staying in position on the carriage, for 25 miles. Dalmatians have paw-pads that are resistant to cracking or becoming sore, though this genetic predisposition is greatly assisted by steady conditioning and regular use on hard roads. Owners also report that their nails are exceptionally hard and require frequent cutting, even for dogs that are exercised regularly on hard roads – the nails simply don't wear down. Even so, the longer distance carriage dog trials are run on grass. My time with Jacko and Tally didn't require that level of endurance but it was a magnificent experience that gave me fresh insights. I could imagine what a wonderful sense of companionship, and indeed security, a carriage dog would give on a long journey.

Antiquity

Spotted dogs have been prized highly throughout history. They were valued by, among others, the Ancient Egyptians. However it would be far too tenuous to link these to the coach dog of the eighteenth century. Wherever he came from originally, the Dalmatian was and is, first and foremost, a hunting hound. The silhouette of the Dalmatian is the same as that of an athletic hound type. He has a conspicuously deep chest denoting a capacity for exceptional lung power; he has good scenting capability, keen eyes and impressive stamina. The Dalmatian's recruitment as a carriage dog came much later in his career. He remains versatile and still finds employment today as a pointer, a gundog, a general hunting hound or companion. In our present age, we are used to thinking of hunting hounds as either scenting hounds, that is dogs who run with their noses to the ground searching for and following a trail, or as sighthounds, dogs who sprint and catch their prey, stimulated by sight from a standing start. However, although they also used regular scenthounds and sighthounds, the ancient Greeks, the Romans and medieval Europeans valued another sort of pack hound for the pursuit of quarry such as deer: 'running sighthounds'. These were not quite the sprinters of the true desert sighthounds, like the Saluki, but dogs that nonetheless maintained visual contact with their quarry and hunted by pursuit over distance, triumphing ultimately with superior stamina. It was known as 'par force' hunting. These hounds hunted with their heads in the air and gave the hunters the exhilaration of an extended chase, whilst keeping the quarry in view. Dogs of this type could adapt readily to the demands of following horses for a day's journey.

Spotted hounds, with hints of an early Dalmatian type, appear on a number of frescoes in Tiryns, the Mycenaean city on the Greek mainland that flourished between 1400 and 1200 BC, the period of the Trojan Wars. They appear to be larger, more muscular versions of the desert sighthound, though still exhibiting the feathered tail of the Saluki. Intriguingly, these hounds are depicted as both white with black spots and white with liver spots; the two colourings that occur in Dalmatians today. The development of these sight-dominant pursuit hounds, hunted in packs and followed on horseback, continued throughout the Classical world. In the fourth century BC,

Xenophon observed that the basic hunting hound, known to him as the Cretan hound (with obvious allusions to a Minoan/Mycenaean heritage), occurred in three main varieties: 'Knossons', 'workers' and 'outrunners'. The Knossons were much prized and celebrated as the best type of scenthounds. He wrote that the workers hunted both by night and day but is otherwise enigmatic about them. The outrunners, he tells us, ran free. At first this seems a strange distinction to make unless it was the case that the other types were hunted on leashes, like Bloodhounds. These outrunners had scenting ability and could pick up a trail if visual contact were lost but their primary function was the steady pursuit by sight of either the four-horned antelope or the fallow deer. Aristotle, a contemporary of Xenophon, noted that the outrunners neither went ahead nor lagged behind but rather had an instinct to run beside the horses. It would be stretching credulity to imagine that there is an unbroken line of a Dalmatian-type dog dating back to antiquity. However we can note that the behaviour described by Aristotle is strikingly similar to that required of a carriage dog. All we can say with certainty is that there were spotted dogs in antiquity and that some hounds had a natural disposition to stick close to the horses in a chase. Genetic studies have linked Dalmatians to the pointer but that, in turn, simply links them back to a hound type, something that we can see just by looking at their physique. Hunting packs of sighting

Spotted dogs hunting wild boar, depicted on a Mycenaean fresco from Tiryns, Greece 1300–1200 BC. These heavy 'par force' hounds have distant echoes of Dalmatian types. (Ancient Art and Architecture/ Alamy Stock Photo)

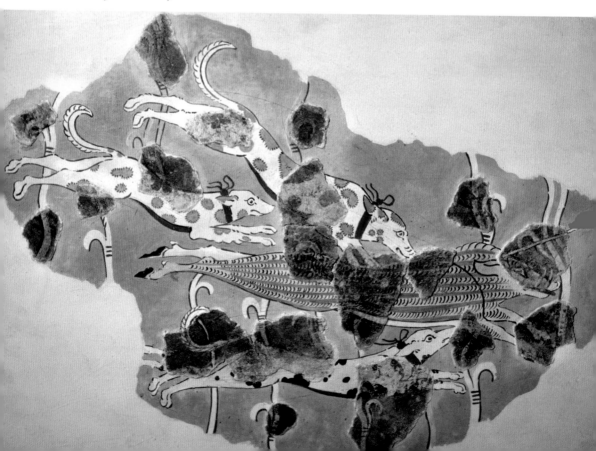

King John of England (1167-1216), hunting 'par force' with a spotted sighthound. From *De Rege Johanne*. MS Cott. Claud DII, folio 116, British Library. (Wikicommons)

dogs, who carried their noses in the air and pushed on with a steady pace in pursuit of distance runners like the fallow deer, remained popular in Europe during the middle ages. Medieval folk also had their packs of 'nose-down' scenthounds (*brachets*) for certain quarry but in a landscape that was as yet unfenced and unhedged, they enjoyed the long, endurance, galloping chases that were offered by the 'nose-up' hounds.

What's in a Name?
It is possible that the Dalmatian name derives from a combination of '*dama*' (Latin) meaning the fallow deer and '*chien*' (French) meaning dog, perhaps signifying that these dogs were used primarily to hunt fallow deer, as they were in Xenophon's time. Alternatively, because the fallow deer is distinctively spotted, '*dama-chien*' may have been a term, by association, for a 'spotted dog'. David Hancock (*Heritage of the Dog*, 1990) suggests that the medieval French expression '*de meute de chien*' is another contender for the name's origin. French was the everyday language of English nobility at the time. Modern French for a 'pack', when referring to hounds, is '*la meute*'. Since Dalmatians are of a pack-hound type, the link may be that simple, without

any reference to spots. However Hancock also notes that the word 'mote' means a blemish or spot. There are references in some documents to hounds that are 'de mota'. This may be an alternative rendering of '*meute*' or it may be that the term '*de mota chiens*' denoted spotted dogs. In the *Close Rolls* of King John for the year 1216, is an entry for thirty-one hounds '*de mota*'. On another occasion, his son Henry II referred to sixteen '*de mota chiens*' in a letter to the Sheriff of Oxford.

Whether or not they had spotted coats, we may imagine that like Aristotle's Outrunners, these pack-hounds stuck close to the horses. Moreover in order to have the stamina for the chase and the courage to bay their quarry, these would be big, strong dogs. It is a small leap of imagination to suppose that these would be exactly the type of dogs that a traveller would wish to accompany him for protection. Henry VIII's elder sister, who became Queen Margaret of Scotland, wife of James IV (r. 1488 – 1513), made a request in a letter for hounds that 'will ride behind me one hors back'. In 1524, the English diplomat Thomas Magnus, who was due to visit the Queen on Henry's business, and clearly fearful of travel through Scotland, referred to 'houndes of the beste kynde that woll [run] behynde men upon horseback'. Margaret's son, James V of Scotland (r. 1513 – 1542), in a letter to the Duke of Richmond, also asked for 'hounds, which could ride behind men on horseback'. The traveller's protection dog had arrived and there is little doubt that he was a hound and in the mould of the running sighthounds, so esteemed by Xenophon and Aristotle.

A century later, Gervase Markham in '*Countrey Contentments*' (1615) stated that the best hounds for hunting deer were 'the white hound, or the white with black spots or the white with some few liver spots'. Markham also signalled the last days of the sight-pursuit hound pack and made great store of the 'hunting cunning' required of the scenthound packs that were increasingly the fashionable way to hunt. A picture begins to emerge of travellers' protection dogs developing from hard-running deer-hounds in the Medieval period. Then, by the seventeenth century, the best of these were considered to be spotted dogs. At the same time their popularity on the hunting field was waning. Coach travel, though on the increase for a few, was still relatively rare, but we may imagine that many of these increasingly redundant spotted hunting dogs began to find new employment guarding travellers and their horses.

Major improvements in road-building methods ushered in the golden age of coach travel in the eighteenth century. It was at this period that the Grand Tour reached its zenith. The Grand Tour was a custom among well-to-do young gentlemen to complete their education by travelling through France, Italy and sometimes Greece, in a quest for cultural refinement and enlightenment. The main purpose of these patrician peregrinations was to see the art and to explore the roots of Western civilization. Dr Johnson considered that,

> A man who has not been in Italy is always conscious of an inferiority, from his not having seen what it is expected a man should see.
>
> (Quoted in Boswell's *Life of Samuel Johnson*, 1791)

Dalmatian or Coach Dogs.

Two Dalmatian coach dogs thundering in pursuit. These bruisers, appearing both more ferocious and muscular than their modern counterparts, are clearly dogs with a fearsome ability to guard. (Unattributed engraving in *Chatterbox*, 22, May 1886. Mary Evans Picture Library)

For many the tour stopped in Italy, with its twin splendours of Antiquity and the Renaissance. Those with deeper pockets extended their tour to Greece, usually travelling there by sea. It was a short ferry ride from Venice to Split, from where they could journey overland to Athens by coach. On their return, these modish and adventurous young men pioneered the fashionable craze for driving about town with an elegant Dalmatian in attendance. In doing so, they announced to the world that the driver of the carriage had been on this prestigious, intellectual and civilizing pilgrimage. Undoubtedly a fierce and loyal carriage dog would have been a great advantage when travelling through the Balkans, a territory renowned for its brigands. However, despite an association between Dalmatians and the Grand Tour, it is most probably apocryphal that travellers first encountered Dalmatians in the region of Dalmatia (a region of Croatia's Adriatic coast), though there could be some coincidence as spotted dogs were common throughout Europe. However, the first Croatian claim to these dogs, in the form of a tract from Bishop Peter Bakic, doesn't appear until 1719. By then, spotted dogs that fit the description are well-established and there is a plausible etymology of the name, connecting it to medieval French. It seems that the good bishop was merely the first of many to confuse the similarity of the name 'dama-chien' with that of his homeland and falsely claim that it was native to the region.

The Coachman's Dog
The Dalmatian's rugged paws, agile legs and powerful lungs enabled him to follow for extreme distances. There is a story about a famous Dalmatian owned by the ostler at the Newcastle Place stables just off the Edgware Road, London. His name has

not come down to us but his regular duty was to guard the London to Brighton coach, which, meandering via Leatherhead, Dorking, Horsham and Henfield, journeyed a distance of some 74 miles each way. This dog was reputed, on occasion, to have followed the coach for eight consecutive days. Although the dog was known for running beside the coach, he was also prone to taking little excursions en route, to indulge his ancestral hunting appetites. He had the reputation of being able to kill a goose, toss it over his back like a fox, and then continue to run in attendance to the coach for

This coachman looks down benignly at his trusty coach dog. Although the primary relationship was between dog and horses, coachmen also developed great affection for the dogs who accompanied them on arduous journeys in all weathers and who kept them safe. (Illustration from an unknown publication, 1828. Mary Evans Picture Library) many more miles. These farmyard forays understandably angered those who lived in striking distance of the coach's itinerary and who reared waterfowl for market. In order to placate their ire and to curb the dog's poaching tendencies, the coachman, who was very fond of the animal, placed him inside the coach. Needless to say, there were no passengers at the time. However, the coachman was soon surprised to see his dog running beside the coach again, in his proper position. The dog had jumped out of the window. On a fateful day in June 1851, the coachman set the dog on top of the coach. Tragically he jumped off at Henfield and fell between the wheels of the coach. He was killed. This game little fellow was just five years old. He was stuffed in 'an attitude of life' and displayed in the bar of a tavern in the Edgware Road. Sadly, this has long since disappeared.

George Washington

In one of George Washington's personal accounts ledgers (Ledger B, held at the Alderman Library in Virginia) is an entry recording that he paid fifteen shillings for a 'coach dog' that he had purchased in Philadelphia. Although this entry is recorded on 14 August 1787, it seems probable that it is the same dog he referred to in a letter to his nephew William Augustine Washington, which was dated two days earlier. Washington wrote:

> At your aunt's request, a <u>coach dog</u> has been purchased and sent for the convenience of Madame Moose, her amorous fits should therefore be attended to, that the end for which he is sent may not be defeated by the acceptance of the services of any other dog.

George Washington maintained a kennel of over two dozen hounds and Madame Moose was a clear favourite. She had presumably come into heat and Martha Washington, the aunt referred to in the letter, had suggested a new sire be found for her. Washington was a passionate fox hunter and keen to develop a new breed of hound – the American Foxhound. He had previously imported very large hounds from France (Madame Moose may have been one of these) in his quest for bigger, stronger hounds. These French dogs were reportedly so fierce that Washington assigned a servant to supervise them throughout their meals, since they were apt to tear each other apart in fighting over food.

The choice of a coach dog for a sire is interesting. Washington may have thought its stamina was just the thing to invigorate his new breed. Hounds need to have the ability to run all day in pursuit of their quarry and none excelled the staying power of a coach dog. Moreover he probably knew that coach dogs were originally hunting dogs in their own right. There is no mention as to whether or not the Philadelphia dog was spotted. Either way his mention of the term 'coach dog' highlights that the practice of using dogs for this task was well-established in the newly formed United States of America by the late eighteenth century. The need for the traveller, whether on horseback or in a carriage, to have a protection dog is obvious and a number of different dogs must have fulfilled the role over the centuries. However it is the Dalmatian who has come down to us today as the quintessential specialist.

The Firehouse Dog

Dalmatians are perhaps best known in the United States as 'Firehouse Dogs' and continue to be kept as much loved mascots by many fire stations. Originally they provided a valuable practical function. Early fire engines were horse-drawn and the Dalmatian served in the same way as it had as a protection dog for travelling carriages.

A fire engine galloped through the streets to a fire at breakneck speed. They used fine, spirited horses for these teams for obvious reasons – speed was of the essence. Running ahead, it was the duty of the Dalmatian to be a visual announcement of the impending arrival of this hurtling juggernaut just before it rounded a street corner. People may hear the bell but it was when you saw the Dalmatian coming round the bend that you knew the engine was heading your way and you'd better get to one side of the street.

As with coaches and carriages, fire engine horse teams were prone to be chased and annoyed by other dogs. If a pack of town

THE WHITEFRIARS FIRE ENGINE AND ITS FAMOUS DOG "BARON."

Baron, the Whitefriars fire-engine dog. Although this is not a traditional looking Dalmatian, he clearly did the job and earned a reputation. He has a dappled liver coat. The horses are pulling a 'steam pumper' engine. These first appeared in 1840 and were in service until around 1920, by which time internal combustion engines had replaced the horses. This image was painted in 1900. The artist has drawn one of the horses turning to look towards Baron, perhaps seeking reassurance. (Mary Evans Picture Library) mongrels started in nuisance pursuit, the firehouse Dalmatian would chase them off. He was an intimidating dog. Some fire services would have two or more dogs. Once at the scene of the fire, Dalmatians guarded the equipment on the truck, while the firemen attended to their duties. Hoses, buckets, axes and other tools, as well as the horses themselves, were valuable and useful commodities in nineteenth-century pioneer America and vulnerable to theft from opportunistic thieves. Once back at base the Dalmatian guarded the firehouse, particularly the horses, and offered his companionship to both horses and firefighters alike. When the internal combustion engine replaced the horses, the Dalmatian lost a lot of his function but, by then, he was so much a part of fire service culture that he was kept on as a symbol, mascot and friend.

The Budweiser Dalmatian

When prohibition ended in the United States in 1933, the Busch brewery (makers of Budweiser beer) commemorated the occasion by sending a team of Clydesdale horses, hauling a wagon of beer, to New York. It was greeted by enthusiastic crowds. This and

The Budweiser beer wagon, pulled by Clydesdale horses and guarded ceremonially by their Dalmatian mascot, parading along Peachtree Street, Atlanta, Georgia. (Photo-IStock: Credit BluIz60)

another horse-drawn wagon went on to tour much of the Northeast and Midwest of America, including making a symbolic delivery of beer to President Roosevelt at the White House. The Budweiser dray became an established emblem of the brewing dynasty and, in March 1950, a Dalmatian was added to the team as a mascot. Now a Dalmatian travels with each of the dozens of Budweiser drays throughout America. Although the Budweiser Dalmatians travel on board, rather than running alongside, they still represent that tradition of the carriage dog guarding its master's property and one might imagine that an unattended wagon of beer might need quite a bit of guarding!

Chapter 6

Water Dogs

'The water dog is a creature of such general use, and so frequent amongst us here in England, that it is needless to make any large description of him: the rather since not any among us is so simple that he cannot say when he sees him: "This is a water dog".'

—Gervase Markham, 1621

The author with a Standard Poodle. (Photograph by Angie Louter)

Labradors have webbed feet, Newfoundlands have webbed feet, Irish Water Spaniels have webbed feet and Standard Poodles have webbed feet. The possession of webbed feet is a very strong clue to a breed's intended purpose. Poodles were once highly sought-after working dogs whose specialty was swimming. They were used to hunt, flush and retrieve ducks. In line with this function, Poodles may also be described as a variety of 'water spaniel'. The difference between the terms 'water spaniel' and 'water dog' is nuanced. 'Water dog' may be used as a general collective for all dogs that work in and around water. However when used in a specific context, it refers to dogs such as the Portuguese Water Dog or the Labrador (originally the St John's Water Dog) whose first occupation was to work as fisherman's dogs, on boats and in the sea, predominantly as retrievers. 'Water spaniels', on the other hand, are dogs that work around rivers, lakes and marshes, partly as retrievers but primarily as finders and flushers of game. Of course any well-trained Labrador is more than capable for such assignments but it was not the original purpose of his breed. Dr Caius (1576) was specific about a water spaniel's function, explaining that:

> This kinde dogge is properly called Aquaticus, a water spaniel, because he frequenteth and hath usual recourse to the water where all his game lyeth, namely, waterfowl, ducks and drakes, whereupon he is likewise named a dog for the duck, because in that quality he is excellent.

The essence of a spaniel is that it excels at finding hidden game and Caius elaborated on the particular difficulty of locating ducks:

> Although the duck otherwise notably deceives both the dog and the master by diving under the water, and also by natural subtlety... For when they have an inkling that they are espied, they hide themselves under turfs or sedges, wherewith they cover and shroud themselves so closely and craftily, that... there they will harbour without harm, except the water spaniel by quick smelling discover their deceits.

There are many surviving breeds of water spaniel, among them: the Irish Water Spaniel, the Curly-coated Retriever, the Dutch Wetterhoun, the Barbet, the Barbone and the American Water Spaniel. The English Water Spaniel became extinct in the first decades of the twentieth century. Each of these has its own distinguishing characteristics, some stand taller, some broader, some are this, some are that; they are not all exactly the same but they are nonetheless all of a similar sort. Dr Caius characterized them as follows:

> Of the Dog called the water spaniell...This sort is somewhat big, and of a measurable greatness, having long, rough, and curled hair

It is a description that fits the Standard Poodle as much as any other of the types.

American Water Spaniels, established in the early nineteenth century, were bred from a mixture of land spaniel and water spaniel types, including the Poodle.

Irish Water Spaniel – a close relative of the Poodle. Although larger and heavier set, the similarity to the Poodle is unmistakable. (Radomir Rezny/Shutterstock.com)

Two American Water Spaniels. This breed was first developed in the nineteenth century and their kinship with the Poodle is clearly apparent. (Juniors Bildarchiv GmbH/ Alamy Stock Photo)

Although a relatively modern breed, they look and behave like the sort of dog described by sixteenth and seventeenth-century writers. There would have been any number of variations of the broader type but a Frenchman seeing such dogs would probably have called them '*barbets*', an Englishman have dubbed them water spaniels and a German described them as '*Pudels*'. The German word '*puddle*' is an archaic term for 'splash' (hence we have the English word 'puddle') and the term '*Pudelhund*' applied to a range of water spaniel type dogs. Canine historians generally consider the Barbet to be the closest ancestor to the Poodle but since strict breed standards didn't apply in earlier centuries, it is a moot point. Undoubtedly there have been some 'refinements' to the Poodle breed since the inception of Kennel Club regulations in the nineteenth century but I suspect that a Standard Poodle (not the Miniature or the Toy) would be recognized for what it is by countrymen in Shakespeare's England. Shakespeare himself referred to these types as 'water rugs' (Macbeth, act III, sc 1), an appellation that I find both apt and endearing. At some stage the word 'poodle' changed from being a generic description of type to being the designation of a specific breed. It is difficult to say exactly when that was but there can be little doubt that the Standard Poodle of today descends from an ancient line of aquatic working dogs.

Water Spaniels at Work in the Sixteenth Century

John Caius was born in 1510, in Norwich in the English county of Norfolk and so would have grown up wildfowling on the nearby Norfolk Broads, vast tracts of open water circumvallated by dense reed beds, the perfect haven for all manner of duck. Later in life, at Cambridge University, he would have had similar opportunities to hunt the plentiful wildfowl in the reeds and sedges of the watery fens. These swampy expanses were also the landscape of my childhood and they still thrive with anatidaean abundance. The principal method of hunting for duck at the time was with a crossbow. It is not easy to hit a duck with a crossbow and a missed bolt (the proper name for a crossbow arrow) would be impossible to find in a marshy morass. Compared to a lead ball for a musket, crossbow bolts were of elaborate construction and therefore valuable ammunition. Dr Caius tells us:

> We use them [water spaniels] also to bring us our bolts and arrows out of the water (missing our mark) whereat we directed our level, which otherwise we should hardly recover, and oftentimes they restore to us our shafts which we thought never to see, touch, or handle again after they were lost: for which circumstances they are called *Inquistitores*, searchers, and finders.

Images of canines retrieving a huntsman's bolts appear occasionally in art. In 1530 an inventory of the Cardinal of York's household lists, among other items, a tapestry of hunting scenes, noting that one of these scenes featured 'a dog carrying a bolt out of the water' (*Letters and Papers, Foreign and Domestic*, Henry VIII, Volume 4, 1524-1530).

By the later sixteenth century, some hunters were experimenting with the new matchlock arquebus but these early black-powder guns were sensitive to damp

A pair of Standard Poodles, Cooper and Reba, hold steady and watch intently as the author aims a crossbow at a mark on the water. (Photograph by Angie Louter)

environments, not greatly accurate, and the flash from the priming pan usually alerted a bird to take flight, long before the main charge detonated. A crossbow was more reliable. It also had the advantage over a longbow in that it could be spanned and loaded and held ready to take the shot when the optimum moment presented. Longbows could only be drawn at the last moment before shooting and the movements of the archer could set the birds in flight. For hunting ducks, blunt heads were favoured because they stunned the bird without damaging the meat, which was destined for elegant presentation at table. Using horn-capped wooden blunts had the secondary advantage that, without metal heads, bolts did not sink and so could be retrieved by a dog. To summarize Dr Caius, a water spaniel should be an all-round bird dog able to hunt and find game, to be able to retrieve it, be a good swimmer and be able to bring back a hunter's arrows if he missed. Does such a dog still exist today? I wondered.

My Adventure with Hunting Poodles
About an hour's drive from Atlanta airport is the kennels of Louter Creek Hunting Poodles. Set in unspoiled acres of beautiful Georgia countryside – shimmering grasslands girdled by broad swathes of mixed woodland and speckled with small lakes and ponds – the kennels is run by Rich and Angie Louter, pioneers in re-introducing Standard Poodles to their ancestral task. It all began when Rich, a keen gun dog and duck-hunting man, decided to marry Angie. She was allergic to most dogs. However some dogs, Poodles for instance, are hypoallergenic, and Angie was fine with Poodles;

in fact she owned one. Rich had heard that Poodles were once considered good hunting dogs and so he set out to train one to hunt ducks. First he had to find a suitable candidate for the job and at the time nobody was breeding working Poodles, only show dogs. Fortunately the breed criteria for Standard Poodles has meant that the right physical characteristics for the job have been preserved. Their form has been preserved to be consistent with their original function. What was less certain was temperament and game-sense. Fortunately, Rich found Cooper. Cooper was a show dog but he took to the work as if he was made for it (which of course he was) and he has become the first Poodle to win 'hunt test' and 'working field' titles. He won his first at fourteen months and holds all three upper-level Master Hunter Titles in AKC, UKC and NAHRA. Cooper is a Poodle with punch. He is also the founder of a dynasty, having sired numerous litters. Most of his progeny have gone on to be successful hunting dogs. The Louters breed hunting poodles. They also train them. Louter Creek possess a state-of-the art gun dog training facility and Rich diligently pursues rigorous daily regimens both with his own Poodles and with those sent to him by others. I visited in early March to see the dogs in action.

Although primarily water dogs, Poodles are equally at home finding, flushing and retrieving upland birds, as they are waterfowl. I was first introduced to Layla, a five-year-old bitch. Layla and I took to each other right away. Rich showed her off quartering in the long grasses with cartographic precision. She took direction flawlessly, responding to every whistle and hand signal that bade her stop, turn and hunt. She had an elegant lope when quartering and a speedy gallop both for the recall and when sent out. This was a very well put-together and athletic dog. I had never before seen a Poodle worked in this way – like a spaniel. I was also struck by how she suited her environment, not only the camouflage of her wheat-coloured coat against the tawny grasses, but how that distinctive high head-carriage of the poodle lent itself to being able to see in the tall pasture. Even so, in the longer grasses, she could disappear from view. Then she would re-appear springing, as much like a deer as a spaniel, and keeping her eyes fixed firmly on her handler. It was a delight to watch – a sporty, nimble, energetic dog, perfectly suited to the work. Poodles are predominantly air-scenting dogs but when left to her own devices, while we humans chatted for a moment, Layla dropped her nose, lured by the whiff of something or other, and followed a trail. These versatile dogs are also capable trackers and known to be excellent truffle-hunters.

Cooper was a little more stand-offish. He was well-mannered and obedient to a fault, but very much his own man. His plush, dense coat was dark red. Both the Egyptians and the Greeks admired red coats on their hunting dogs; it was believed to indicate strong scenting prowess. First I wanted to test Cooper retrieving a crossbow bolt, just as Dr Caius had prescribed. Both he and Reba, a four-year-old female of a similar red hue, sat calmly and alert by my side as I levelled a replica of a sixteenth-century crossbow. Today, in America, duck-hunters use duck calls to lure the ducks and then they are shot in the air as they fly in. However, in the sixteenth-century, when the primary hunting weapon was a crossbow, it was more usual to shoot them as they paddled along or simply floated on the surface. It was possible to shoot them

Layla – a Standard Poodle working a beat in the manner of a Spaniel and under the command of a whistle. She is head up and air-scenting. She worked fast and with precision. (Photograph by the author)

Layla running. She showed both tremendous enthusiasm and admirable athleticism, having energy and drive that countered the modern Poodle stereotype. (Photograph by the author)

in the air but that was significantly more challenging than shooting them as 'sitting ducks'. Accordingly I aimed at an imaginary mark on the surface about 35 yards out. The bolt made a dramatic splash and then came to rest, floating. Both dogs sat steady at my side. Even after several shots, when they already knew the association between the twang of the crossbow and an imminent water retrieve, they sat stock still until bidden. Cooper was sent; he went determinedly and he powered through the water. He had marked the point of splashdown and his gaze never left the spot where the bolt sat bobbing. Undistracted by anything else, such as other sticks on the water, he went unswervingly for the stick with the feathers; he took it and came straight back to the shore, pushing through the vegetation at the water's edge to bring it directly to my hand. On command he yielded it gently and there was not so much as a tooth mark on the shaft or a feather ruffled. It was a good game and we did it again and again.

The obedience, the focus, the marking ability, the swimming ability, the flawless retrieve and delivery were all exemplary. Naturally I also wanted to see a Poodle

Cooper on the return trip, having swum out to find and retrieve the crossbow bolt (Photograph by the author)

Cooper swimming ashore with the retrieved bolt. He holds it securely but with a soft mouth; there was not so much as a scratch on the shaft. (Photograph by the author)

carry a duck. It was outside the hunting season so a previously shot mallard, one that had been liberated from the freezer earlier that day, was brought into service. Rich threw the bird out, giving a retrieve of about 30 yards. This time Reba was sent. She swam with drive and purpose, stretching her neck forward in keen anticipation of reaching the retrieve. Once there she took the bird in a controlled and gentle manner and turned for the shore, where she brought it to hand without fuss. She delivered it softly, with finesse. The bird was in perfect, undamaged condition. At the handover she looked me straight in the eyes. She was clearly proud of her achievement and also a little puzzled by this stranger to whom she had to relinquish her prize. I have owned two Labradors and I count a number of spaniels amongst my friends – I know that slightly manipulative, adoring look a dog can give you. This was not that. Reba's eyes revealed a thoughtful intelligence. It was as if she was reasoning the slightly unfamiliar situation thus: 'That is what you wanted, wasn't it? If so I'm happy to have been of service. Is there anything else I can do for you?' It wasn't a demand to do it again for her own pleasure but it was an expression that she relished the work and an offer to do it again was on the table. I know that is a lot of anthropomorphic guesswork to put into a glance but I definitely got a sense, from both her and Cooper, that they had professional pride. Those who know the breed often remark upon the Poodle's intelligence and although Border Collies usually top the table for canine intellect, Poodles are frequently a close second. It is generally thought that they have an ability to understand a wider range of human vocabulary than other breeds.

Reba returning to shore to deliver the retrieved duck. It was outside hunting season and the duck had been taken from the freezer earlier that day. She delivered it to hand undamaged. ((Photograph by the author)

No words were required to indicate that the dogs were beginning to get a little chilly. Although crisp and bright, it was a cold day and for the dogs in the water it was even colder. Enough was enough and we called it a day. Angie Louter wrote to me after my visit and said: 'The dogs took to you like they have always known you'. I felt the same way about the dogs. Although I had never had anything to do with Poodles previously, I felt completely in tune with and bonded to these magnificent, noble animals and watching them go through their paces – hunting, running, swimming, retrieving – they demonstrated that they had a tremendous natural aptitude for the work. Not only that but they were clearly happy dogs – engaged in what they had been bred for.

The Poodle Clip

Dr Caius alluded to the peculiar haircuts we associate with poodles today, when telling us that the water spaniel was 'powled and notted from the shoulders to the hindermost legs, and to the end of his tail'. His 'powled and notted' translates into modern English as shaved and clipped. A little over fifty years later, Gervase Markham offered a similar description of 'cutting and shaving him from the navill downward'.

These descriptions are recognizable as the 'Poodle clip', albeit without the silly pompoms that have become a feature of modern parlour style. Both writers perceived the benefit in removing excess hair was to improve speed in water, with Caius explaining that, being as it were made somewhat bare and naked, by shearing off such superfluity of hair, they might achieve the more lightness and swiftness, and be less hindered in swimming, so troublesome and needless a burden being shaken off.

The traditional view is that by shaving the body, both drag and weight were minimized. However, the theory goes, leaving the hair full around the chest and shoulders protected the heart and lungs from the shock of icy waters and pom-poms were left to cozy the kidneys and around the joints for similar thermal advantage. Left unattended a Poodle's coat will continue to grow. It can become absurdly long and dense – a characteristic that has led to the worst excesses of Poodle coiffeur. Undoubtedly an over-abundant coat would be a disadvantage when swimming, so some sort of haircut was necessary. Rich Louter gives his dogs an all-over short trim every six weeks or so. It is functional and it looks good to modern tastes. The dogs appear noble and athletic, which of course they are. However, unlike genuinely water-repelling coats - that of the Labrador for instance – Poodle hair absorbs water and so the practice of leaving a thick coat of hair over the chest and shoulders is unlikely to have the desired effect of defending this area from the cold; in fact it more probably has the opposite effect. It may nonetheless be true that people believed that thickets of hair covering vulnerable areas were bulwarks against the cold and so it may still be true that the genesis of the 'pom-pom Poodle' did derive from considerations in the hunting field, albeit these considerations were based on a false assumption.

As for the coloured ribbons that are often tied in the show poodle's hair to give it a 'cutesy' top-knot, popular mythology has it that these too originated in the field. It is said that different colours were used to distinguish different dogs. As someone who, at a pheasant shoot, once put the wrong Labrador in his car, I have to admit there could be some benefit to such a system. In that instance my own dog was indifferent to my error but the purloined dog's owner was quick to spot the mistake! However, I have not seen references to such identifying ribbons in either art or books, so this may be pure invention from the frillier side of Poodle culture. Another instance of poodle chic, one that owes everything to fashion and nothing to function, is the creation of the corded coat. If left uncut a poodle's coat will continue to grow; if left unwashed it will matt and clog and curl into cords, akin to dreadlocks. For a working Poodle that is required to swim, these weighty ropes of hair would be a great impediment and have no practical value. The decorative excesses of the Poodle parlour – the form-distorting cuts, the fluffing, the primping, the blow-drying and the rainbow dyeing – have given Poodles an effete image and a reputation for being no more than fashion accessories. For Miniature and Toy Poodles, there is some truth to this opinion. Like all toy and miniature breeds they have been selectively bred as companion dogs and have lost much of their inherent working ability in the process. For instance, not all Toy and Miniature Poodles have webbed feet. However, for anyone to deny the vigour, alertness, intelligence and hunting ability of the Standard Poodle, is both unjustifiably disparaging and extremely short-sighted.

Standard Poodles with a 'continental clip'. The constantly growing coat of a Poodle creates opportunity for all manner of shape-distorting haircuts. This has had an equally distorting effect on the Poodle's popular image. (a = Photo: iStock. Credit eAlisa) (b = Eudyptula / Shutterstock.com)

The French Connection

In previous centuries Poodles and other water spaniels were held in far higher esteem as hunting dogs than they are today. The Barbet (the French water spaniel), now a rare breed, was to all intents and purposes the same 'type' of dog as the poodle. Historical references to 'barbets' and 'poodles' may be no more than regionally different words applied to the same dog. The archived *Letters and Papers (Foreign and Domestic), Henry VIII, Vol. 15*, contain correspondence that supports this idea. Honor Grenville, Viscountess Lisle, was the wife of Henry VIII's Lord Deputy of Calais, England's last French possession. She was stationed there for seven years. In February 1540 her friend Anne Rouaud, Madame du Bours, wrote to her, letting her know that 'Monmorancy has written that he is sending the bearer to ask you to help him to obtain some poodles (barbetz) for the crossbow'. In her subsequent reply, Lady Lisle employed the same phrasing that indicated an understanding that Poodles and Barbets were one and the same:

> I will send to England for poodles (barbetz) for I can get none in this town, except one, which I send to your son. He is very good at retrieving the head or bolt of a crossbow both on water and on land and will fetch a tennis ball or a glove put on the end of a stick and other tricks.

Here we also find another mention of an aptitude for retrieving crossbow bolts. I am not entirely certain why retrieving a tennis ball (albeit the heavier type used at the time for 'real tennis') or a glove constitutes a 'trick'. It sounds like a simple game of 'fetch' and a further endorsement of these dogs' retrieving talent. I presume that the stick was used as a mechanical means for improving the throw of the glove and it is rather a clever idea, akin to those plastic ball throwers we see today.

The Barbet. This French water spaniel is another close relative of the Poodle. During the Tudor period, the names were interchangeable. A principal difference in the breeds today is that the Barbet grows a profusion of hair on its muzzle. These dogs are the epitome of what Shakespeare called 'water rugs'. (Photo: iStock. Credit ysbrandcosijn)

I do not suggest that everyone who owns a Standard Poodle should take it duck-hunting but I do recommend that their owners should be more mindful of their dog's inherent traits. Poodles love to swim and should be given the opportunity, whatever consequences that may have for the maintenance of a fashionable urban coiffure. They also love to hunt. When walking cross-country, on our way to the water, Cooper and Reba hunted every fence line and hedgerow assiduously. They became especially animated at an old woodpile, sniffing around it and scrambling over it like spaniels. Poodles need regular visits to proper countryside, to be off-leash with all manner of game smells, where they can exercise their noses, even if that means getting dirty like the other dogs. Poodles are also natural retrievers – throw something for them once in a while.

Poodles on the Battlefield

One seventeenth-century poodle was said to jump for joy whenever he heard the name of the King – 'Charles'. The poodle's name was Boye and he belonged to Prince Rupert of the Rhine, nephew of King Charles I of England and commander of the Royalist cavalry during the English Civil War (1642-46). Prince Rupert cut his soldier's teeth during a bitter conflict between Catholics and Protestants in Europe, known as the Thirty Years War (1618-48). In 1638 the 19-year-old Rupert was imprisoned in the fortress at Linz, in Austria, for three years. Charles I's ambassador in Vienna, the Duke of Arundel, anxious for the young man's welfare, sent him Boye, a white Poodle, so that he might have a companion while he languished in jail. As well as being valued for their hunting and retrieving abilities, Poodles have also been highly thought of as loyal companion dogs and Boye proved worthy of his assignment. Prince Rupert enjoyed privileges denied to the average prisoner and his captivity was not as bleak, nor as lonely, as we may imagine. Whilst incarcerated, the suave prince managed to carry on an affair with the governor's daughter! In the end, efforts by his uncle, the King, led to his release and he, and Boye, set sail for London.

Almost exactly a year from the date of his arrival on English soil, Prince Rupert was leading the mad-dash, pell-mell, helter-skelter cavalry charge that was the dramatic overture to the Battle of Edgehill (23 October 1642), the first major battle of the English Civil War. Boye, as always, was at his side and the dog's celebrity as a military mascot was established. Known for his swagger as well as his bravery, Prince Rupert personified the debonair, reckless, cavalier esprit of the Royalist camp and he became the frequent focus of character-assassinating propaganda in satirical pamphlets distributed by the Parliamentarian side. Boye came in for equal approbation and was accused of having malevolent supernatural powers, of being the devil in disguise and being a witch's familiar. This last was a condemnation usually reserved for cats and perhaps the leonine silhouette created by certain poodle-clips reinforced such feline associations. Boye was said to be able to catch bullets shot at his master in his teeth and to have cocked his leg at every mention of John Pym, a principal architect of the Parliamentarian cause. Reviled by his master's enemies, Boye was equally celebrated by those on his side and was given the rank of sergeant major general. The Battle of Marston Moor (2 July 1644) was fought on a flat plain a few miles outside the

Prince Rupert's Poodle, Boye. He was a celebrity in his own right, vilified by the Parliamentarian forces and lauded by the Royalist cause. Boye was the subject of many satirical pamphlets and propaganda sheets. Here he is portrayed alongside his master in battle, sporting a Poodle-clip. However a portrait of Boye, painted by Prince Rupert's sister, Louise, shows him with a full, unclipped coat. (Wikicommons)

city of York. It was a turning point in the English Civil War and a defining moment in the career of Prince Rupert's nemesis, the Parliamentarian cavalry general, Oliver Cromwell. Boye had been tethered in the Royalist camp before the battle but he escaped to seek out his master on the battlefield. Whilst running to-and-fro on his quest, Boye was shot by an enemy musketeer. Although the Royalist forces suffered a crippling defeat, Prince Rupert escaped and fled south. What became of the body of Sergeant Major General Boye is unknown.

Poodles were especially popular amongst military men during the late eighteenth and early nineteenth centuries and there are numerous mentions of their loyalty and bravery. One story concerns a black Poodle called Moustache who was attached to a company of French grenadiers during the Austrian campaign. At the Battle of Austerlitz (2 December 1805) Moustache braved the thick of the fighting when he rushed to the aid of a mortally wounded soldier. The soldier was the regiment's colour ensign and although the dog could do nothing for his dying comrade, he retrieved the flag, despite his leg being broken in the process. Moustache was awarded a medal for gallantry and is reported to have drawn full rations and pay. Some accounts say that Moustache was presented to the Emperor Napoleon and that he was trained to lift his leg at the mention of the Emperor's enemies. Similarities with the legend of Boye are immediately apparent and it is possible that this crude trick was commonly taught in times of war. Moustache is said to have been with his regiment at the Siege of Badajoz (March/April 1812), where he was killed by a cannonball. He was buried where he fell and the words '*Ci gît le brave Moustache*' inscribed on his headstone. It was a Poodle also that Napoleon is said to have encountered many years earlier, when walking the battlefield after the Battle of Bassano (8 September 1796) during the French Revolutionary Wars. Napoleon discovered the dog guarding and mourning the corpse of his master. He later described the scene:

> This soldier, I realized, must have had friends at home and in his regiment; yet he lay there deserted by all except his dog. I looked on, unmoved, at battles which decided the future of nations. Tearless, I had given orders which brought death to thousands. Yet here I was stirred, profoundly stirred, stirred to tears. And by what? By the grief of one dog.

Newfoundland Dogs

On 26 February 1815, Napoleon had cause to be grateful to a dog, indeed to owe him his life. After three hundred days in exile on the Italian island of Elba, the deposed Emperor planned to escape and return to France. His banishment on Elba had been a fairly grand affair, maintaining a large personal staff as well as a guard of several hundred soldiers. Though mindful of British ships patrolling in the area, his departure was not stealthy. A large crowd turned out on the shore to cheer him on. The French frigate *Inconstant* lay a few hundred yards off the coast. As he was rowed towards her aboard a small skiff, Napoleon stood in the prow, despite squally weather and a heavy sea swell. A small flotilla of local fishing boats had been attracted by all the ballyhoo and were witness to Napoleon being swept unceremoniously overboard. First to reach him was a fisherman's dog. The Emperor, who at best was a poor swimmer, took hold of the dog and was kept afloat until he could be rescued. That dog was a Newfoundland Dog. Newfoundlands, or 'Newfies' as they are called affectionately, are water dogs. Above all else, they are water-rescue dogs. Current practice is for them to swim to a victim with a flotation device that is attached to a harness on the dog. The person in difficulty grabs onto

A Newfoundland Dog. These masters of the sea are exceptionally strong swimmers. Note the patch of white on this dog's chest. It recalls his heritage from the St John's Water Dog (TheHighestQualityImages / Shutterstock.com)

A Newfoundland dog practicing a traditional rescue. When the victim is able to float on their back, the dog just takes a hand or arm gently in its mouth and swims the person to shore. These dogs have an impressively secure but soft grip with their mouths, even under the duress of being buffeted by waves. Modern rescue techniques fit a harness to the dog, which a person can hang on to for a tow. Traditionally though, the dog did it all, either in the manner shown here or by ducking its head under an armpit and lifting the victim's head from the water line. (Kathy Wright / Alamy Stock Photo)

the lifebelt and is towed to safety. The Italian coastguard has trained Newfoundland Dogs with this equipment, to jump into the sea directly from a low-flying helicopter! In Napoleon's time, however, a Newfoundland Dog would turn a drowning person onto their back by using their nose and then take their upper arm gently between their jaws to swim them ashore or to a nearby boat.

Seaman

Newfoundland Dogs are seldom seen today. Once, though, they were as popular and beloved as their close cousin, the Labrador Retriever. President James Buchanan, the only bachelor president of the United States, had a Newfoundland called Lara. The composer Richard Wagner had a Newfoundland; in fact he once escaped from Russia and fled to London with it. The dog in Peter Pan, Nana, is a Newfoundland. Lord Byron's dog, Boatswain, was a Newfoundland dog. However, perhaps the most famous Newfoundland of all was a dog called Seaman. He belonged to Captain Meriwether Lewis. Seaman travelled with Captain Lewis and his co-explorer Captain William Clark on their 4,000 mile journey from the Atlantic coast to the Pacific coast of America, which began in May 1804 and concluded in September 1806. During

the expedition Seaman was a popular companion to all. He caught squirrels, rescued expedition members from drowning whilst crossing rivers and protected them from buffalo and bears that marauded their camps. In researching this book, I encountered a lady and her Newfoundland dog at a carting meet. She told me that she and her dog had once been in the woods, when a brown bear approached in anger. Her enormous, and it turns out courageous, dog faced off the bruin by rearing up onto his hind legs and the bear turned tail and fled. On one occasion Lewis and Clark had to perform

Bronze statue of Meriwether Lewis, William Clark and Lewis's Newfoundland Dog, Seaman, in Frontier Park, St Charles, Missouri, USA (Malachi Jacobs/ Shutterstock.com)

surgery on one of Seaman's hind legs. An artery had been severed by a bite from a wounded beaver. When Seaman was stolen by Native American tribesmen in 1806, Captain Lewis threatened to send three men to kill those responsible. The dog was returned. The Corps of Discovery, as the expedition was known, had several periods of challenging survival. At times they had to resort to eating dogs. Seaman, I am happy to report, was spared.

Exactly what happened to Seaman is not known but there is a clue in a book by Timothy Alden published in 1814. In *A Collection of American Epitaphs and Inscription's*, Mr Alden records seeing a dog collar in a museum in Alexandria, Virginia, which read:

> The greatest traveler of my species. My name is SEAMAN, the dog of Captain Meriwether Lewis, whom I accompanied to the Pacific Ocean through the interior of the continent of North America.

This implies that Seaman enjoyed some celebrity after the voyage and was shown off at public events. We may expect that he would have been. Of course it is equally possible that the collar belonged to some fairground fraudster, who passed off another Newfoundland as Seaman. However Alden supplements his information about the collar with a note:

> After the melancholy exit of gov. Lewis, his dog would not depart for a moment from his lifeless remains; and when they were deposited in the earth no gentle means could draw him from the spot of interment. He refused to take every kind of food, which was offered him, and actually pined away and died with grief upon his master's grave.

This note was written less than five years after Captain Lewis's death. The story of Seaman's loyal vigil and broken heart is likely to have been well known at the time and so it seems probable that Mr Alden's account is true. The collar and most of the museum's records were lost in a fire in 1871 and with them any certainty about Seaman's fate.

The Fisherman's Dog

Fishermen must always have had some sort of powerful swimming dog to help them with their nets, taking rope lines from one boat to another and to rescue those who fall overboard. As with most breeds, the precise details of the origins of the Newfoundland Dog are a little murky. Some suggest that there was a 'black bear' type dog brought to Newfoundland by the Vikings around 1000 AD. Certainly Newfoundland, on the Canadian coast, was a place of settlement for Vikings at this period and significant archaeological evidence has been found at L'Anse aux Meadows in present-day Newfoundland. The idea of Viking settlement in North America is further supported by detailed accounts in Norse sagas, which tell of explorations to a land, Vinland, to the west of Greenland. However, at present, we do not have any evidence for these 'black bear' dogs. In 1497, the Italian explorer John Cabot (Zuan Chabotto), on an

Pêche à la morue sur le grand banc de Terre-Neuve. — Dessin de Le Breton.

A fishing fleet on the Grand Banks. Larger vessels decanted dozens of small boats, called dories. These were flat-bottomed, which offered a broader hopper for the catch. It was gruelling work in heavy seas. Dogs could assist by stringing lines of nets between the boats. They would swim carrying floats attached to ropes, which in turn were connected to the nets. The low-sided dories were accessible to the dogs. (Chronicle / Alamy Stock Photo)

expedition funded by England's King Henry VII, set sail from Bristol in his ship, *The Matthew* and landed on what he described as a 'new found land'. Acknowledging the earlier Norse settlement, we now know that it was re-discovered rather than newly found. However more significant, at the time, than this rediscovery of the North American mainland was the discovery, just offshore, of the richest fisheries the world had known. John Cabot's crew reported that 'the sea there is full of fish that can be taken not only with nets but [also] with fishing-baskets'.

The Grand Banks became a vital source of food supply for expanding European populations and seasonal fishing fleets soon made their way there in great numbers. Even so it was another century before the landmass of Newfoundland was, once again, colonized with settlers. They were fishermen from various parts of Europe, who had jumped ship and made a permanent base there to harvest the great shoals of cod for their own profit. These fishermen were aided in their work by dogs of a type, now extinct, known to history as the St John's Dog. St John's is the capital of Newfoundland. The St John's Dog is the common ancestor of both the Newfoundland

A Newfoundland-type St John's Dog being hauled aboard a ship, showing one method for deploying these dogs from large vessels. (From *Dog Breaking* by W.N. Hutchinson 1920. Photograph by the author)

Dog and the Labrador Retriever. In time, two strains emerged: the Labrador remaining similar in size and function to the original St John's Dog and the Newfoundland, who developed into a larger and more powerful version. This was achieved by cross-breeding St John's Dogs with European flock guardian types. Basque fishermen were prolific on the Grand Banks and their Pyrenean Mountain Dogs seem likely candidates. Whatever the precise genetic cocktail, this 'new' dog had the stamina and strength to power-swim though crashing waves. His mass and his might, his lungpower and his buoyancy, made him perfectly adapted for rescuing fishermen who had fallen into the sea. It was once extremely common for fishermen not to be able to swim and Newfoundland dogs were a common feature of fishing fleets. Newfoundland dogs became ever more ubiquitous on sailing vessels. It is one thing for them to be hauled aboard by their ample scruffs, when working from a low-sided rowing boat for fishing but how did these dogs get aboard a ship when at sea? There may be a clue in an account given by General W.N. Hutchinson in his book *Dog Breaking* (1920). He recounts a tale of a ship's Newfoundland dog that used to:

> jump overboard the instant the anchor was dropped, swim ashore, and return, after an hour or two's lark, to his own ship…He would then bark anxiously, until the bight of a rope was hove to him. Into this he would contrive to get his fore-legs, and, on his seizing it firmly with his teeth, the sailors, who were much attached to him, would hoist him on board.

St John's Dogs

A renowned nineteenth-century writer on country matters, Colonel Peter Hawker, travelled to Newfoundland in 1814. He wrote:

> The St. John's breed of these dogs is chiefly used on their native coast by fishermen. Their sense of smelling is scarcely to be credited. Their discrimination of scent ... appears almost impossible ... For finding wounded game of every description, there is not his equal in the canine race; and he is a *sine qua non* in the general pursuit of waterfowl.

Characteristically they had a white 'tuxedo' blaze on the chest, which still shows up occasionally in modern Labradors or Newfoundlands. St John's Dogs were used by the fishermen to help haul in nets and were adept at rounding up and catching

Above left: Nell – A St John's Water Dog belonging to the Earl of Home (1799 – 1881). The image was taken in 1867, when Nell was eleven years old. This is the earliest known photograph of the breed, which is now extinct, but which is the foundation stock for all Labrador Retrievers and Newfoundland dogs. She has the distinguishing white markings on paws and muzzle and the beginning of some white on her chest can just about be discerned. St John's Dogs typically had either a small white 'T' or a full tuxedo marking on the chest. (ART Collection / Alamy Stock Photo)

Above right: St John's Water Dog. This is Lassie, one of the two last remaining St John's Dog's found at Grand Bruit, an outpost on Newfoundland's south coast, in 1981. Despite the name, Lassie was a male. He was thirteen years old at the time of the photograph and his brother was fifteen. They were the last two survivors of the breed. (Photograph by Richard Wolters) those fish who tried to jump free. As well as nets, lines of hooks were used and the St John's dog would help set these by swimming away from the boat with a float until the line was fully extended. When the line was reeled in, he would be ever watchful for a fish wriggling off the hook and as often as not would catch it before it was able to swim away. In his book, *Excursions In and About Newfoundland During the Years 1839 and 1840*, Joseph Jukes describes a St John's Dog trying to catch fish at the water's edge:

> I observed he once or twice put his foot in the water and paddled it about. This foot was white, and Harvey said he did it to 'toil' or entice the fish. The whole proceeding struck me as remarkable, more especially as they said he had never been taught anything of the kind.

Their appetite for fish was also mentioned by the naturalist John Guille Millais, who visited Newfoundland in 1907:

> The dogs, which seem to be well nigh amphibious, rush barking through the pools, and at low water search the shores for discarded cod-heads.

Millais, however, was to play a dark role in the history of the indigenous St John's Dog. In the late nineteenth century sheep farming was introduced to the area. In order to encourage this boost to the local economy, the Newfoundland government (though still a British colony, it was administered autonomously) issued the Sheep Protection Act in 1885, which levied massive dog-licensing fees for all non-sheepdog breeds and in many cases banned dog ownership altogether. It was the custom for fishermen to let their dogs roam free when not in work and it would seem that packs of these temporarily feral dogs were responsible for a great deal of sheep predation. Millais advocated stern measures:

> the shooting of ownerless dogs, and stringent laws would have to be enacted that the owners of dogs must keep their dogs in check and under proper supervision. A man who allows his dog to stray should be heavily fined. At present these half-wild 'Labrador' dogs roam the country in spring and autumn, searching for anything they can kill.

A great many dogs were killed as a result of such harsh attitudes. Although the St John's Water Dog didn't finally became extinct until the 1970s, the adoption of sheep rearing had been a tragic death sentence on an extraordinary and exceptional breed. Physically similar to the more active-looking black-coated Labradors of today, the St John's Dog was distinguished by a blaze of white on his chest. Modern breed purists looking at a Labrador with a white patch on its chest, a legacy of his St John's heritage, might consider it a fault. If I were lucky enough to own such a dog, I would consider it a real prize!

The Labrador Retriever

We get our first real glimpse of the versatility of the proto-Labrador in an account written in 1662 by W. E. Cormack, a resident of St John's, Newfoundland. In describing the local water dogs he noted that they were:

> admirably trained as retrievers in fowling and are otherwise useful...the smooth or shorthaired dog is preferred because in frosty weather, the long haired kind become encumbered with ice on coming out off the water.

Here, with the reference to the long-haired and short-haired types is a clue that the split in the breed had already begun with the long-haired dogs being what we today would call Newfoundlands, though I suspect the major disparity in size was not yet fully apparent.

Although the St John's Water Dog was primarily a fisherman's dog, his ability to also be a useful retriever for the fowler was a great boon to those who lived in this remote land, and who wanted to supplement their larder of salted fish with freshly caught waterfowl. In his youth, my own Labrador, Crockett, had quite a knack with waterfowl. I lived in Scotland at the time and before he was fully a year old, he was retrieving shot birds from the icy waters of the Solway, astonishing everyone with his power in

The author's dog Crockett demonstrating a Labrador's innate ability to retrieve fish. The image was staged but there was never any hesitation on Crockett's part. His instinctive ties to the traditional tasks of the St John's Dog were alive and well. (Photograph by Kim Hawkins)

Crockett. Sadly he is no longer with us. This photograph was taken in his old age but he still retained an athletic build and a spark in his eye. As he aged he went grey around the muzzle in a pattern exactly as one would expect a St John's Dog to be white. (Photograph by Kim Hawkins)

the water, swimming with apparent ease against strong currents. He competed in local gun dog trials and was a regular at the local shoots. His most spectacular moment came when picking-up on his first duck drive. No shot ducks fell nearby but he was alerted to the ducks returning to the pond, as they do, diving straight underwater on arrival. Crockett, without soliciting my approval, dived in after one and retrieved it under water. As he came up another duck circled in and broke the surface as it sought sub-aquatic refuge. Crockett plunged again. He came up with the second duck in his mouth and made for the bank. Both ducks were delivered softly, completely unharmed and undamaged. Even the seasoned old gamekeeper was amazed.

My Scottish years were spent close to Drumlanrig Castle, the ancestral home of the Dukes of Buccleuch, who are famed for a strain of Labradors that have an unbroken line dating back to dogs imported into Britain from Newfoundland in the 1830s. This foundation stock was crossed at an early stage with St John's Water Dogs from the Duke of Malmesbury's kennels. The dukes had met at a shooting party and discovered their shared passion for these wonderful, but at the time esoteric, dogs. Although not directly from the Buccleuch kennel, Crockett had a lot of Buccleuch blood in his pedigree and his fine features were reminiscent not only of other Buccleuch dogs today but they also mirrored the looks, seen in old photographs, of the St John's Dog. Even in his old age, Crockett preserved an enviably athletic body and has the distinctive Buccleuch head shape, which is more refined than the rather hefty, square crania sported by many modern Labradors. I am biased of course but I think he was exceptionally handsome. Like all Labradors he had webbed feet, a water-repelling double coat and a great rudder of an otter tail.

The Labrador Retriever in its natural element, powering through the water. (Photo: iStock/Tom Meaker)

A Labrador Retriever, equally at home on the moor as in the water. (Photo: iStock/ Beth Bellamy)

The Dukes of Buccleuch and Malmesbury were not the only architects of Labrador Retrievers. In 1855 Major C.J. Radclyffe of Hyde in Dorset originated a third strain of 'British Labradors'. Radclyffe had purchased some dogs of the St John's type from a Portuguese fishing vessel that had docked in Poole harbour on its way home from an expedition to the Grand Banks and he developed his variety from this stock along similar lines to the ducal strains. In all cases the dogs were black. However, when his dog Foxendon Neptune was mated to Duchess, another black Labrador belonging to a Mr Tapper, the litter contained a yellow pup. All yellow Labradors can trace their lineage to this single dog, whose name was Ben. The yellow gene was lurking somewhere in the St John's Dog ancestry. Indeed it was not uncommon, before the mid-nineteenth century, for Newfoundland dogs to be yellow also.

What's in a Name
Newfoundland and Labrador are two halves of the same region, separated by a stretch of sea. Labrador is named after João Fernandez Lavrador who mapped its coastline in 1499. '*Labradore*' is also the Portuguese word for 'worker'. The Portuguese fishing fleet was even more active in fishing the Grand Banks than were

Cao de Castro Laboreiro – the Portuguese Cattle Dog. These dogs bear a strong resemblance to Labrador Retrievers and it seems probable that they shared a common ancestor. (Dorling Kindersley ltd/ Alamy Stock Photo)

ships from Britain and the dogs who assisted them might quite naturally be called 'worker dogs'; that is, '*labradors*'. To add to the confusion, there is a village in Portugal called Castro Laboreiro and the local landrace of dogs bear an uncanny resemblance to the modern day Labrador. Called the Cão de Castro Laboreiro, these are much taller dogs that worked originally as livestock guardians with cattle. Their origins are lost in time but their striking similarity to the Labrador suggests they may be the true ancestors of the St John's Dog. Castro Laboreiros are known in English as Portuguese Cattle Dogs. Speculatively, varieties of this regional type were bred to create dogs that also performed well as water retrievers to assist on the fishing boats and which were subsequently taken to the Newfoundland/Labrador region by the Portuguese fishing ships. If so, then perhaps the name Laboreiro was carried there with them. Whichever of these antecedents inspired the name, they all have a resonance. However when first encountered by Englishmen, the dogs from the Canadian seaboard were known either as the Lesser Newfoundland Dog or the St John's Dog.

Technological Change

Despite the passions of its advocates, the Labrador Retriever remained a rare sight in the nineteenth-century shooting field, where pointers and setters were the norm. These dogs were better suited to working with muzzle-loading guns. They would hold the game in position while the shooters took time to ready their finicky firearms and then got themselves into a viable position to shoot. Only then was the command given to flush the birds. It was called 'walked-up' shooting. However, at the Great Exhibition held at the Crystal Palace in 1851, Monsieur Casimir Lafaucheux displayed an invention that was destined to change the manner of game shooting forever. He had developed a breech-loading gun, with hinged barrels (it wasn't the first of its kind but it was the first to function with reliability and ease). Lafaucheux's version was used with a new type of paper cartridge that contained the shot, the black powder (propellant) and had a percussion cap (detonator) attached as an integral part. A few more improvements were made over the next several years, including the development of centre-fire cartridges. The modern sporting shotgun had arrived. It revolutionized game shooting. Reloading became much, much faster than before and this led to the introduction of 'driven game', a system in which dogs and beaters stretched out in a line and, in walking forward, moved the birds slowly, still hidden by the ground cover, towards a line of guns. Once they had pushed the birds to within range, they sent the dogs forward to flush them. The birds then took flight up and over the guns. Birds were flushed in large numbers, against which the guns could discharge successive volleys. It was high-speed shooting. Dozens and dozens of birds could fall in a single drive and this required rapid response retrieving dogs to bring in the bag and to ensure that any wounded were quickly recovered for humane despatch. There was none faster and none better than the water dogs, dedicated retrievers, that had been developed from the St John's Dog. First in line of these new young breeds was not the Labrador Retriever however

An example of a Flat Coated Retriever (formerly the Wavy Coated Retriever). Both St John's Dog and setter ancestry is evident and, although black is a more usual colour for these dogs, his red hue shows a gene that may have been passed to Golden Retrievers. (Photo: iStock/ BiancaGrueneberg)

but rather his close cousin the Wavy Coated Retriever, now more usually called the Flat Coated Retriever. He was broadly similar, but had British setter blood mixed in with the St John's line. The Wavy Coated/Flat Coated Retriever was once called the 'gamekeeper's dog' because he was so common on country estates.

There is a painting by William Henry Davis (1786-1865) that shows a Wavy Coated Retriever at work. It hangs at Plas Newydd on the Isle of Anglesey and portrays Sir Henry Paget, the 1st Marquess of Angelsey shooting grouse on Cannock Chase in 1830. Fifteen years earlier, as Lord Uxbridge, Paget was struck in the leg by a cannonball at the Battle of Waterloo. At the time he was on his horse standing alongside his commander, the Duke of Wellington. He exclaimed famously, 'By God, sir, I've lost my leg!' to which Wellington replied drily: 'By God, sir, so you have'. As a consequence his leg was amputated and replaced with an artificial limb. In the painting he is shown shooting from the saddle of his horse. It is a tribute not only to his phlegmatic resistance to allowing an inconvenience like a missing limb interfere with his sporting pleasure but also to the trust he has placed in his loyal dog to work so independently. In using such a 'new-fangled' dog, the peg-legged Marquess showed himself to be quite ahead of his time. The artist's description of the painting includes the name of the dog. He was called Nep. An abbreviation of 'Neptune', Nep was an extremely popular name for all St John's Dog derivatives; they were all 'gods of the

The Labrador Retriever in his natural element. A downy layer of hair next to the skin helps to retain body heat; whilst a second coat of longer and stiffer hairs is an aid to repelling water and in assisting the process of shedding water with a brisk shake. (Photo: iStock/AdamBagshaw)

sea', even when they worked on dry land. It took a while for old breed loyalties to fade but Wavy Coated Retrievers gradually replaced the pointers and setters. However, it wasn't until the middle decades of the twentieth century that the rise of the Labrador Retriever, to both ubiquity and supremacy, became unstoppable.

The Dog From Brighton

During the first half of the nineteenth century, owing to the patronage of the Prince Regent, who subsequently became George IV, the small fishing village of Brighton was elevated to an immensely fashionable seaside resort. On a visit to this elegant retreat at some point during the late 1850s, Sir Dudley Majoribanks noticed a medium-sized, yellow dog being taken for a walk. The dog took his fancy. He approached the owner and bought it on the spot. Sir Dudley was an eminent Liberal politician, country sportsman and dog breeder who subsequently became Lord Tweedmouth with substantial shooting estates in Berwickshire. The dog was a yellow Wavy Coated Retriever by the name of Nous. Like both Labradors and Newfoundlands, this scion of the St John's Dog family, though customarily black, also produced the occasional yellow pup. Black was the fashionable choice, so yellows were usually discarded, but in the case of Nous, a different fate awaited. He was to sire an entirely new breed: Golden Retrievers. Nous was crossed with a Tweed Water Spaniel called Belle. Tweed Water Spaniels became extinct by the end of the nineteenth century but it is thought that they, too, may have developed from the St John's Dog, crossed with local water dogs. From art we discern that they had a similarly textured coat to the Curly-coated Retriever, which has Poodle-like tight curls. Belle was supposedly (no evidence exists) of similar colouring to Nous. What is certain is that she produced a litter of four golden pups: Ada, Cowslip, Crocus and Primrose. All Golden Retrievers can be traced back to this line. There were subsequent outcrosses. Counter-intuitively these were mostly with black retriever types (both Wavy Coated and Labrador); in all cases the yellow factor was retained in the offspring. There was also a dash of Bloodhound to improve scenting ability.

A Curly-coated Retriever. The Poodle-like, tightly-curled coat is believed to be similar to that of the, now extinct, Tweed Water Spaniel, one of the foundation breeds for the Golden Retriever. (Photo: iStock / CaptureLight)

A Golden Retriever doing what it does best – swimming. Although this breed was only developed around 150 years ago, it has become a firm favourite both as a working dog and as a family pet. (Photo: iStock/ Capuski)

Like Poodles, Flat Coated Retrievers and Labrador Retrievers, Golden Retrievers are excellent at scenting, finding, flushing and retrieving, whether in woodland, on moorland or on pasture. Of course, they are all at their most impressive when powering through water or working the reed beds at the water's edge. They are all water dogs, all working dogs and all, at various points in history, have also been a top fashionable choice as pets and companions; they have the most wonderful temperaments. Labradors have touched my heart like no other dogs I have owned and Golden Retrievers remain one of the most popular family pets of all time. The appearance of these water dogs may differ but when it comes to function, they are of the same tribe.

Chapter 7

Game Finders: Spaniels, Setters, Pointers and Tollers

'How necessary a thing a Spaniel is to falconry'
—(Nicholas Cox, *The Gentleman's Recreation*, 1697)

The author with a falcon and Brittany Spaniel (Elizabeth Keates Photography)

Spaniels

Historically 'spaniel' was a loose descriptor, referring to dogs that hunted and flushed birds, as well as small game such as rabbits. Moreover, spaniels and setters can be thought of as variations of the same basic type; they were bred for similar work. It has long been a common belief that the word 'spaniel' derives from '*Espagnol*', with the implication that this large and diverse group of dogs were originally native to Spain. However the pre-eminent dog-breed historian of our time, Colonel David Hancock, suggests instead that the word may come from the Old French '*espanir*', which means to crouch or flatten. These are actions that we would associate with a setter. Similarities in coat, head shape, ears and overall conformation between breeds of spaniel and setter are evident and their common ancestry is obvious. William Youatt in his book *The Dog* (1854) wrote 'the setter is evidently the large spaniel improved to his particular size and beauty'.

In *The Master of Game* (15th century*)* Edward of Norwich classified spaniels as 'hounds for the hawk' and noted, in accordance with the thinking at the time, that 'their kind cometh from Spain'. He described them as, 'going before their master, running and wagging their tail, to raise or start fowl' – an image that brings to mind the energetic pulse of today's working spaniels like the Springer and the Cocker, fizzy go-getters who barge in and put the birds up without waiting for an invitation. However, he also identified a distinctly different style of Spaniel behaviour. Continuing, he wrote, 'when they be taught to be couchers, they be good to take partridges and quail with a net'.

It seems clear that he too considered spaniels and setters to be the same class of dog, with couching (setting) a skill that could be trained. By couching (crouching or lying down) a setting spaniel held the quarry steady and in position, ready for the hunter to make his move. The suggestion that the spaniel was of Spanish origin occurs again in Dr Caius' book *Of English Dogges* (1576) where he states that spaniels are 'called in Latin *Hispaniolus*'. Since he probably got the idea from reading *The Master of Game*, he may be perpetuating an old myth here. Caius goes on to say that spaniels are a group of dogs that 'serve for fowling', which is an altogether more helpful definition. He is telling us that the working types are bird dogs. However he makes a distinction between these and what he calls 'spaniels gentle', which were strains of toy spaniel. These were miniature versions of their working cousins, with an equally long ancestry. Bred solely as companions, spaniels gentle are discussed separately in Chapter 12.

'Bird dog', used predominantly in the USA, is a useful collective term, encompassing, as it does, spaniels, setters, pointers and tollers. In Britain we are more apt to include these types in a disparate group called 'gundogs'. Here they are lumped together with Labradors and Golden Retrievers. This is too broad a brush. It relates only to the relatively recent use of guns for shooting birds and obscures earlier origins for the springing, setting and pointing breeds, who were required to work with either falcons or nets. Ground-nesting birds such as grouse, quail, pheasant and partridge, react to the nearness of a dog, provided that it approaches slowly, by clamping down to the ground and slowing the heartbeat, thus minimizing the amount of scent emitted.

Cody, a black-and-white Brittany Spaniel. No amount of American Kennel Club regulation, which does not recognize this colouring, can change the fact that this is a fine example of a classic type, worthy of the name. (Elizabeth Keates Photography)

A Brittany Spaniel with the 'approved' orange-and-white coat. (Radomir Rezny / Shutterstock.com)

In this way they hope to remain undetected. Pointing and setting dogs exploit this behaviour by stalking from upwind and then, once the quarry bird has been scented, they both signal its precise location and hold it in place, by freezing in a rigid posture until ordered to flush by the hunter. All fall silent. From the perfect stillness, a powerful energy is emitted as the dog mesmerizes its quarry into a hypnotic trance. The tension of the moment is palpable and thrilling; human heartbeats accelerate in inverse proportion to the slowed rhythms of the animal actors. Any breed has it in them to point occasionally but only the specialists do it reliably, consistently and with such aplomb. These are the spaniels required by the falconer and the netsman. Today's working breeds of setters, spaniels and to a lesser degree pointers, developed from historical strains of land spaniel. Dr Caius marks a difference between 'land spaniels' and 'water spaniels'. Land spaniels occurred in different forms depending on whether they were setting spaniels, springing spaniels or pointing spaniels. A useful illustration of the blurred lines that existed between these designations is the Brittany Spaniel. I went to meet one.

Adventure with a Brittany Spaniel

Despite it being called a 'Brittany Spaniel' for as long as I can remember, some present-day aficionados now insist that it should more properly be called the 'Brittany Pointer'. Others prefer to rename it simply as the 'Brittany'. Their rationale is that, although this dog looks like a spaniel, it behaves like a pointer. It holds game in place by the action of pointing. *L'epeugnal Breton*, to give it its French name, is probably the most akin to a historical type – a type that would have been known as a spaniel (*epeugnal*). With its distinctively small head, it brings to mind the spaniel-type dogs represented in art from the sixteenth to the nineteenth centuries depicting falconry scenes. Today it remains a favourite amongst falconers and is a good example of a 'pointing spaniel'. Although these dogs have earned a good reputation in the modern shooting field, they were, and are, first and foremost dogs for the falconer.

'Ah – he's a black and white', I exclaimed, with a hint of disappointment, when a lively little Brittany called Cody came bounding up to me in a Hertfordshire field. 'Oh dear', sighed my photographer friend Liz. I had promised her it wouldn't be a black dog. Black dogs are notoriously difficult to photograph because, unless you know what you are doing, the features can disappear into an un-delineated blob of dark pigment. It is one reason why black dogs remain in rescue centres far longer than other colours; their photographs are less appealing. Brittanys are usually orange-and-white or liver-and-white, occasionally a tri-colour, so when I first enquired about the dog on the telephone I didn't think to ask about his markings. I just assumed he would be the more familiar orange-and-white. Will Duncan, Cody's affable and knowledgeable owner, smiled and said, 'If we were following American Kennel Club rules, Cody would probably have been euthanized at birth, but he's a Brittany all right'. Cody's spaniel-style head, his overall size and shape, the texture of his coat, his running action, all confirmed that Cody was indeed a Brittany Spaniel. Then to underline that conclusion, he stood rigidly on point in a classic stance. Fortunately the

Cody on point. Although his shape is unmistakably spaniel in character, here he marks the scent with the rigid body and raised paw of a pointer. He is representative of an old type of pointing spaniel. (Elizabeth Keates Photography)

absurd colour regulations of the American Kennel Club do not apply in the land of his origin; the French Kennel Club accepts black-and-white as a legitimate coat for these superb dogs. It is equally absurd that the modern Brittany has been stripped of his historical title 'spaniel'. These dogs are spaniels – pointing spaniels. Pointing spaniels were used originally for falconry and Will had also brought along his male goshawk. Dog and bird made a handsome pair, each turned out in striking, *en suite* black-and-white livery. Long before guns were used to shoot flying birds, they were taken with hawks and falcons. Falconry was an art that demanded the services of this type of spaniel; it was an equal collaboration of man, dog and bird.

A spaniel's first job is to find the birds, whether they are in woodland thickets or hedgerows or lying out in the open in heather or grassland. This process begins with quartering, whereby the ground is scanned for scent systematically. Man and dog stand downwind and directed by the handler's whistle (one peep means stop and two peeps means change direction) the dog is sent out to one side ahead of his human and then, peep-peep, he changes direction and hunts out to the other side. Given that I was a total stranger, Cody responded extremely well to my whistle commands, though he retained a weather eye on Will. First out to the left, then out to the right, advancing the zig-zag only a couple of feet forward with each run; all the while getting further and further away from the handler. This was dog-control at a distance. Cody covered the ground with exhilarating speed but I had no doubt that he was scenting diligently. Will had brought along a pigeon, which he had placed in a small cage and hidden in the long grass earlier, so that Cody had live scent to react to. After half-a-dozen beats to left and right, Cody, head aloft and scenting the air, reacted to the whiff of proximate

Cody quartering the ground under the direction of the whistle. He performed with speed, style and zest, locking-on quickly to an air scent. (Elizabeth Keates Photography)

pigeon and slowed his pace, stalking towards the quarry with careful, silent stealth. Then he froze rigidly on point, his front paw raised. The moment was dramatic and charged. If we had been hunting, this would have been the time to ready the hawk for its flight. A hunting bird knows the dog it hunts with and recognizes when that dog is on point. In response it will stretch its wings and rouse; raising all the feathers on its body for a vigorous shake, then lay them flat and sleek in readiness for the chase. From a standing start off the glove, this will be a sprint and these avian athletes need to be primed to reach their top speed as quickly as possible. However, since we were not hunting, we simply took photographs of dog and bird and then released the pigeon, which flew away unharmed. The necessity for a pointing spaniel is that a hunting bird requires preparation time, not only for its own stretching regimen and for the falconer's fussing with its equipment, but also so that the falconer can walk up and position himself with the bird, before commanding the dog to flush the quarry. The spaniel's usefulness to men with guns came later, and with it, changes to the type of spaniel that were favoured.

Falconry and Hawking

Although both falconry and hawking can be considered under the umbrella term 'falconry', there is a technical difference between the two activities. Falcons are long-winged birds that hunt by spiralling into position high in the sky and waiting. When they see their prey flying below, they close their wings, dropping like meteorites to

Cody on point. At the scent of game – in this case a pigeon in a cage that was later released unharmed – he freezes, raises a paw and points with his nose and body-line towards the target prey. In response to a dog's proximity, birds will also freeze. Both bird and dog remain fixed in place until the dog is signalled to flush by its handler. This gives a falconer time to prepare his predator bird and get into an advantageous wind position before triggering the dog and flying the hawk. Dogs like this are essential partners for the falconer. (Elizabeth Keates Photography)

strike from above. It is spectacular to behold and often results in breathtaking aerobatics from both the hunter and the hunted. A falcon does not always succeed on the first strike and she may then have to give chase like a jet fighter. Such a pursuit could go quite a distance. Aristocratic followers were most usually mounted on horseback so that they could gallop after the flight and get as close a view of the action as possible. They also required their horses to travel the many miles to the hunting ground in the first instance. Falconry was a high status, aristocratic sport organized with great ritual and pageantry.

Hawking, on the other hand, was less elitist and took place on foot, though it too attracted a following amongst kings and nobles. Hawks are distinguished from falcons by having shorter, broader wings. They fly after game directly from the falconer's fist and can operate in woodland equally well as they can in open fields. In formal terminology hawks are flown by an 'austringer' but 'falconer' is the more common generic term for those who fly either hawks or falcons. Acceleration is the key for hawks as they seek to overtake their quarry in a straight cross-country pursuit from a standing start or banking deftly through the trees in wooded country or hugging the ground, like dare-devil, low-flying aircraft, when in pursuit of a bolted rabbit. Esteemed above all other hawks was the goshawk. No other bird of prey had quite the same fierce intensity, quite the same call-of-the-wild or quite the same menace. Goshawks are notoriously the most difficult of all birds of prey to train, or 'man' as falconers describe the process.

Matilda – a female peregrine falcon. All falcons are known also as 'long-wings'. They hunt by spiralling up to a colossal height and then closing their wings to drop (stoop) onto their quarry from above. Here the falcon has come out of a stoop for a lure and is banking before attacking it again. These birds are capable of thrilling aerial manouevres. Note the telemetry device attached to the falcon's back. This enables the falconer to find her if she goes down and stays put in cover. Before these electronic devices, falcons were located by the bells that they wore. (Photograph by Andy Collins)

A male goshawk. All hawks are known as 'broad-wings'. They often hunt by straight pursuit, even in wooded country and are capable of impressive acceleration. The goshawk is considered to be the most challenging to train but it rewards by being the most spectacular to fly. (Elizabeth Keates Photography)

Hawking was especially popular in Medieval and Tudor England and Henry VIII was a passionate devotee. Once the dog had flushed a bird and the hawk had given chase, the followers had to run to keep up, whether the ground be rough, smooth, hard, soft, hilly or flat. Not only did they wish to maintain hawk and quarry in sight to observe the action, they also needed to know where their hawk would eventually settle so that they might retrieve her. These days the use of a tiny electronic telemetry gizmo attached to the hawk's back results in fewer lost birds. Prior to this technology, the falconer had to rely on hearing the distinctive sound of small bells. For falcons these are attached to the legs, while for hawks a single bell is attached to the tail. Hawks are more likely to take their prey to ground in rough undergrowth and a tail-bell is less prone to becoming entangled. Racing cross-country, to stay within the sound of the bells, was all part of the sport and an all-terrain dash was exhilarating exercise. Before the days of pumping stations, land drainage depended considerably more on systems of ditches and dykes than it does today. For a hawking party hurrying pell-mell over the fields these could present significant obstacles. The answer was to vault across using poles. In certain parts of Europe like the fen country in England or parts of the Netherlands, there remains a tradition of 'pole-dykeing' and competitions are held in which people leap over astonishing distances. For the spaniel man, out with a hawking party, skill with a dykeing-pole would have been an essential part of his field repertoire.

A King's Misfortune

The suddenness of the loud, whip-crack snap of the pole must have sent shockwaves of fear through courtiers and hunt servants alike. Fortunately for the king, the swift actions of one of these attendants saved his life. Henry VIII had been out hawking, near Hitchin in Hertfordshire, when the pole he was using to vault across a dyke broke.

Tim Dow demonstrating the technique for clearing a dyke with a pole. For everyday use in the hawking field, only relatively modest distances were necessary. An average drainage dyke was seldom more than 6 feet from bank to bank – often less. In some country, it would not be so much the distance of the jumps but rather their frequency that proved exhausting. It is a convenient mode of traversing rough land that has been lost to the countryman today. (Photograph by Corin Ashleigh Brown)

Agosto

Partenza per la caccia

Image of hunt servants with dykeing-poles from the 15th-century Grimani Breviary by an unknown artist. The original purpose of pole-vaulting was to jump for convenient distance rather than for height. Gaining height assists in reaching distance but it would be impractical to carry overlong poles into the hunting field. Medieval art portrays hunters porting modest staves between 8 and 10 feet in length. These poles have a slight taper towards the top, to give them spring. They also have a wide circular flange at the base, so that when placed on a soft, muddy riverbed, there is some resistance and the pole doesn't drive in like a nail into custard. (Lebrecht Music & Arts / Alamy)

An account of the incident in *Hall's Chronicles* for the year 1526 reports that the king plunged headfirst into the deep ooze and then lay helpless at the bottom of a watery ditch. Hall attributes the king's survival to one Edmund Moody, who managed to instantly grab the muddied monarch by his heels and drag him out. Naturally such a tale plays into humorous stereotypes of Henry's corpulence but he was only 34-years-old at the time, and although a big man, he was not yet the overweight glutton he was to become. In fact this was only a couple of years after he was famously injured in a joust with Charles Brandon the Duke of Suffolk. Henry was still in his prime and he was active. This younger Henry was renowned for his physical prowess, he was a vigorous sportsman and hawking was one of his favourite pursuits. I have little doubt that the spaniels that accompanied the king that day would have been remarkably similar to Brittanys.

Setters and Netters
Spaniels for hawking and falconry were the prized possessions of Roman patrician, Medieval lord and Renaissance prince alike. War was their profession but falconry

Dancy, a Llewellin Setter, scenting game and dropping low to set. A 'set' is the same as a 'point', in that it has the effect of freezing game birds. A pointer drops a little but remains standing, raising a paw; a setter traditionally set flat to the ground. Here Dancy is not quite creeping forward 'like a worm', as Dr Caius described, but she is nonetheless crouching. (Photograph by Kim Hawkins)

was their passion. However falconry was not an efficient method for procuring numbers of birds for the table. Other methods were used to harvest birds in quantity. One abominable practice, called 'liming', used twigs coated with an adhesive, so that the birds' feet stuck to it instantly upon landing. A common blend in Europe was made from fermented holly bark mixed with nut oil. Traps of all manner of cruel ingenuity were also employed. Stocking the larder with large quotas of birds could also be achieved by netting. There were various techniques for netting and these required the services of a different type of spaniel – the 'setting spaniel', or 'setter'. When a setter crouched low on the approach to game, freezing it like a pointer, it allowed a net to be drawn over both the dog and the birds under his spell. These days, setters are more likely to work for the gun, and although a few still instinctively crouch flat on their bellies, others stand more in the manner of a pointer. It is all that is now required of them and they have been bred accordingly. Traditionally, however, they assumed a fully prostrate position. In 1576 our old friend Dr Caius wrote of setting dogs:

> When he hath found the bird, he keepeth sure and fast silence, he stayeth his steps and will proceed no further; and with a close, covert and watching eye, layeth his belly to the ground, and so creepeth forward like a worm…whereby it is supposed that this kind of dog is called Index, 'Setter'.

Another Elizabethan who makes a brief appearance in the setter's story is Sir Robert Dudley (1574-1649). This Robert Dudley was the illegitimate son, by Lady Sheffield, of Robert Dudley the first Earl of Leicester (1532 – 1588). The first Earl was courtier, confidante and very nearly husband to Queen Elizabeth I. His son, Sir Robert, was a man of astonishing accomplishments, as well as having a reputation for being dashing. He led expeditions to the West Indies, he was knighted for his role in the capture of Cadiz (1596), he was a navigator and a cartographer (designing the first maritime atlas to cover the whole world), he was an engineer, a shipbuilder, a skilled mathematician and, according to the Oxford scholar Anthony Wood (1632 – 1695), he was also 'noted for riding the great horse, for tilting and for his being first of all that taught a dog to sit to catch partridges'.

The meaning here is not that Sir Robert Dudley was the innovator of the method (setting dogs had been used to take game from earlier times) but rather that he was the 'best' at training a good setter. That such an accolade was worthy of mention in describing such a high-status figure points to the regard in which hunting partridge with a setting dog was held. It also indicates the value placed on the ability to train such a dog. Setting dogs have to work at a significant distance from their handler; that is their purpose. They also need a fair amount of independence and initiative so that they may respond appropriately to what they can smell but their handler cannot see. Being able to maintain control of such a dog from afar – he must hunt but not run amok – required a rare finesse and a great deal of training. Evidently the gallant Sir Robert was something of a dog-whisperer.

Bowie, a Llewellin Setter, quartering. In order to find game, setters first quarter the ground, working into the wind, running from left to right of their handler, sometime as much as 50 yards to each side on a pass. Having longer legs than other spaniel types, there is considerable reach to their stride. They work quickly with a rangy movement that covers a lot of ground. A setter may get 100 yards or more ahead of its handler. This requires dogs of exceptional temperament and intelligence. (Photograph by Kim Hawkins)

Nicholas Cox's *The Gentleman's Recreation* (1674) described working with setting dogs in revealing detail. He wrote:

> There is no art of taking partridges so excellent and pleasant as by the help of a setting dog…a certain lusty land-spaniel…running the fields over with such alacrity and nimbleness, as if there was no limit to his fury and desire, and yet by art under such excellent command, that in the very height of his career by a Hem or sound of his Master's voice he shall stand, gaze about him, look in his Master's face, and observe his directions, whether to proceed, stand still, or retire: nay, when he is even just upon his Prey, that he may even take it up in his mouth, yet his obedience is so framed by Art, that presently he shall either stand still, or fall down flat on his belly, without daring either to make any noise or motion till his Master come to him, and then he will proceed in all things to follow his directions.

Cox's words are a testimonial to both the quality of breeding and standard of training that was expected of a setter to be worked with the net. That some of today's setter strains have the reputation of being scatterbrained and hyperactive is ironic considering the absolute steadiness and restraint once required of the working setter in the field. Such can be the price of breeding for looks rather than function. Cox tells us that once the dog has halted because he has sensed game, the hunter should go into him and urge him ever closer. If the dog sets firmly, as if to say 'here they are under my nose', then the hunter should walk to the side in a broad arc until level with the dog's nose, where he should be able to see the partridges. Finally he explains:

> Then commanding the dog to lie still, draw forth your net and prick one end to the ground and spread your net all open, and so cover as many partridges as you can; which done, make in with a noise, and spring up the partridges;

which shall no sooner rise, but they will be entangled in the net. And if you let go the old cock and hen, it will not only be an act like a gentleman, but a means to increase your pastime.

Although Cox's endorsement makes it plain that this was a gentlemanly sport, the net was also the silent arm of the poacher. In listing a number of game laws pertaining at the time, he records that:

None shall kill or take any pheasants or partridges with any net or engine in the night-time on pain to forfeit for every pheasant 20s and for every partridge 10s.

Such hefty fines indicate the premium that was placed on 'gentleman's sport'. It wasn't just nocturnal netting that could land you into trouble. If your legal status (i.e. ownership of the requisite amount of land or annual income) did not permit you to hunt, it was an offence to own a setting dog. Cox cautioned:

If any person keep bows, greyhounds, setting dogs, ferrets, tumbler, hays, snares etc, he shall be subject to the same penalties as the person who shall be found to have any, hare, partridge, pheasant, fish, fowl or other game in his house.

An Encounter with Setters and Nets

Not wishing to incur such penalties, I first checked with the US Department of Fish and Game about the legality of taking birds with a net, with the proviso that I wanted to take them on a 'catch-and-release' basis, not to kill them. I was assured it was fine, provided the birds were from reared stock. For wild birds 'netting' is not on the list of proscribed 'take methods', so although I could blast away at them with a gun, the more humane act of drawing a soft net over them and then releasing them would not have been allowed. However this restriction did not apply to reared birds and every year, reared birds are released by the tens of thousands for hunters to shoot. Birds reared for shooting are not bred in the disgraceful, cruel conditions of the farmed poultry that supply our supermarket shelves but are raised in their natural environment. They are enclosed in a wide area with soft netting, not so much to keep them in but to keep predators out. In this way there is a high survival rate of young 'poults', which are then much better able to fend for themselves, and survive, when they are finally released at around a year old. I was to carry out this experiment in California, where I live, and the Department of Fish and Game also told me that I would need a California Hunter's Licence, even though I intended to release the birds unharmed. There is online study and there is a course one must attend in person and there is an examination. For an Englishman brought up with one particular set of rural customs, it was an 'education' on many levels. It is nonetheless very thorough and the scheme is to be applauded, focusing on safety issues, wildlife and habitat conservation and codes of behaviour.

The author with bags and bundles of nets and Bowie, the Llewellin Setter, ready to experiment with the traditional way of using these dogs. (Photograph by Kim Hawkins)

The most important party in this enterprise is, of course, the dog. I wanted a good historical looking type and I wanted a dog that would crouch low, in the way that the old writers had described. Llewellin Setters are a particularly handsome line of English setters established in the 1860s by Mr R. Purcell Llewellin of South Wales, with a high reputation for being a good working strain. I contacted Scott Moore of San Joachim Llewellins, based in Clovis, California. He told me that his ten-year-old dog Bowie often got very low, inching forward on his belly, especially when he was 'honouring' the set of another dog. Worked as pairs, both setters and pointers mirror each other by both setting or pointing when game is found. So, to stand a better chance of getting a low set with Bowie, we would need to work two dogs. Scott would invite his friend, Debbie Mahnke, to come along and bring her Llewellin, a nine-year-old female called

Bowie – making light work of the rough ground. Setters are high-energy dogs, capable of traversing an immense area in a day's outing. (Photograph by Kim Hawkins)

Dancy. Unfortunately, the second Dancy sprang from Debbie's truck to rendezvous with Bowie, it became apparent that she was coming into heat. It was therefore not going to be possible to work them as a pair. This meant lowering our expectations for a belly-crawling low set. However both dogs were capable of being worked separately and my enthusiasm for the day remained undiminished. I believe we were probably the first people to attempt netting over setters in a very long time.

The San Joachim valley is a vast flat upland area that lies beneath the high sierras to the east. It is farm country and it provides excellent habitat for partridges. Unfortunately the golden grasslands are speckled with thorn bushes and tumbleweed, features that, as I was soon to discover, are great obstacles to the use of the net! These were most definitely not the gentle, scythed stubble-fields of Staffordshire, Shropshire or Sussex. Netting was hopeless when a partridge took cover beneath net-snagging brambles but there were also dense patches of tall grasses and, in a couple of places we assembled some piles of loose brush, which served as enticing cover. Both Bowie and Dancy showed style, dashing to-and-fro to catch any scent, an action known as 'winding'. This was challenging because it was an exceptionally still day with no discernible wind direction. They took turns and both dogs performed well, finding and setting birds over a wide area. When quartering the ground and making sudden changes of direction, their long, feathered tails helped to balance the dogs. Tireless athletes, they made light work of the brush. Disappointingly there were only a few moments when they 'dropped fully between their shoulders' and made that classic setter prowl, low to the ground like stalking panthers, or for that matter Border Collies, creeping up on their prey. I could see that the anatomy was there and that they had the instinct. I could see how ideal it would be for the netsman to slip a net over such a posture but sadly such moments were brief, largely eluding the camera and certainly not tarrying for the net. A potential snag for the modern netsman is that modern breeders, wanting their setters to signal to shooters from dense bush or from a long distance, favour upright, flag-waving tails, rather than a low set, with the tail snaking behind on the ground.

Scott decided to stay 100 per cent focused on his dog, delegating the duties of being my companion netsman to his young apprentice. Despite the upright stance of the dogs and their erect tails, Dominic and I were able to lay the net softly, sweeping the tail down and to the side without disturbing the set. It was then an easy matter to draw the net over dog and bird. Each time we netted a bird, we released it unharmed. The setter stare is intense and it is extraordinary how unperturbed the dogs were by the action of netting. A distinguishing feature of netting, in sharp contrast to the shooting field, is the silence of the activity; it has stealth and serenity. We were in the field for several hours with barely a word spoken or a sound made. A red-tailed hawk circled constantly as we went about our business. Its presence helped to deter the partridges

The author and assistant walk the net in slowly to where the Setter has indicated the partridges are concealed. (Photograph by Kim Hawkins)

A hand-coloured engraving from Richard Blome's '*The Gentleman's Recreation*' (1686). It illustrates the method of netting that the author attempted to recreate. In the background a stalking-horse is being used to drive birds into a tunnel net. (Wikicommons)

from taking flight. In fact, in the days when netting was a mainstream activity, a falcon was sometimes taken to the field and tied to a perch on a high pole for exactly that purpose. On other occasions, a netting party might fly a kite on a string, to give the impression that a raptor was present.

Richard Blome's *Gentleman's Recreation* (1686) catalogues an array of different nets that were used in the taking of game. Among them are the tunnel net, the broad net, the clap net, the draught net and the bramble net. I wished that I had known

Softly, softly the net is drawn over the dog and then over the pile of brushwood that holds the birds. (Photograph by Kim Hawkins)

the specifications for the 'bramble net' but alas it is only alluded to by name. In an illustration of two men drawing a net over a covey, the man in the foreground carries a slender peg. Similar wooden skewers appear in other images of netting, so I equipped myself with a pair. I had realized that they would be for staking the net but hadn't thought this was of much significance. However the instant I had drawn the net over both setter and partridge, I intuitively deployed them as swiftly as possible. I sensed an urgent need to secure the net as a barrier between dog and bird before the dog broke its set and snatched the bird between its jaws. 'Pegging' is a term used in the modern shooting field to describe the action of a dog that seizes a bird before it has been able to get airborne; it is a cardinal sin for the dog handler. At that moment it occurred to me that this procedure of pegging the net, now no longer practised, was the derivation of the expression 'pegged' as used by today's shooters.

We worked with a draw net, a long net and also a throw net, having considerable success with all three. The draw net was a two–person operation but the long net could be worked by a solitary operative. I also experimented, with success, using a throw net. Netting over well-disciplined, trained dogs may offer a humane system for a number of scientific and wildlife management tasks and suggests that this old working-dog skill has a future.

By the 1830s the art of netting was already an outmoded curiosity but an account of netting over setters was set out in an article published in *The Sporting Magazine* in 1837. Writing under the pseudonym 'Nimrod', Charles Apperley reported on a

As soon as the net is over the partridges, wooden pegs are driven into the ground, pinning the net in such a way that the Setter cannot dart forward and snatch the birds. (Photograph by Kim Hawkins)

The author using the long net. Once Bowie had set the bird, the nets-man drives a wooden stake into the ground behind the dog. Then, taking a wide arc so as not to disturb the quarry, the net is unfurled and deployed to the upwind side. It is drawn forward slowly and carefully. Dog and birds stayed put throughout the procedure. (Photograph by Kim Hawkins)

Although not mentioned in historical accounts, it works equally well to use a throw net over a setting dog. Nets like this, with a weighted perimeter, have been in use since ancient times, mostly by fishermen. They are the type of net used by the *retiarius* in the gladiator arena. Bowie remained staunchly on set when the net was thrown over him. (Photograph by Kim Hawkins)

system he had seen used by a Flintshire squire, Peter Davies of Boughton Hall, a gentleman who still took to the field not only with dogs and nets but also with horses.

> The old gentleman took the field in good style, being accompanied by a servant to hold his horse when he dismounted, and two mounted keepers in their green plush jackets and gold-laced hats. A leash of highly-bred red and white setters were let loose at a time, and beautifully did they range the fields, quartering the ground in obedience to the voice or whistle. On the game being found, every dog was down, with his belly close on the ground; and the net being unfurled, the keepers advanced on a gentle trot, at a certain distance from each other, and drew it over them and the covey at the same time. Choice was then made of the finest birds, which were carried home alive, and kept in a room till wanted, and occasionally all would be let fly again, on ascertaining their fitness for the spit. Modern sportsmen may consider this tame sport, and so in fact it is, compared with the excitement attending the gun; but still it has its advantages. It was the means of preserving game on an estate, by equalising the number of cock and hen birds – at least to an extent – and killing the old ones; no birds were destroyed but what were fit for eating; and such as were destroyed, were put to death at once, without the chance of lingering from the effects of a wound, which is a circumstance inseparable from shooting.

The Spinone Italiano, a methodical worker, with considerable stamina. This HPR designated breed crouches low like a setter. (Photo iStock / Credit. whitneyartgirl)

The sentiments expressed are remarkable for their time, recognizing both the benefits to game management and considerations of a humane kill that can be attributed to netting.

An alternative etymological explanation for the word 'spaniel', suggested by Colonel Hancock (*Gundogs*, 2013), derives from an old Italian word, '*spaniare*', which meant to 'get out of a trap or net'. The Italian Spinone clearly owes his name to this and although designated today in the HPR (Hunt, Point, Retrieve) group, he is really just another setting spaniel, albeit with a coarser coat and a walrus moustache. Spinone adherents claim great antiquity for this breed; writers in Ancient Greece allude to a rough-coated dog that would point hares. Compared to other, more exuberant spaniel types, the modern Spinone is a rather deliberate fellow, though he has the reputation of being able to work all day without tiring. Perhaps the Romans had sprightlier versions to help them fill their nets.

Springing Spaniels

Netting over setters was only one method of taking birds by means of a net. Another approach was to spring the game into pole nets, large nets suspended between upright poles. For this 'springing spaniels' were required. The nets would be set up vertically, anchored at intervals on poles, and dogs and men would drive the birds towards them. It was an efficient way of farming a moor to put food on the table. Both English and Welsh Springer Spaniels readily reveal their origins in their name. Today these are breed appellations but previously 'springer' simply described function. In her book *The Truth About Sporting Dogs* (1972), C. Bede Maxwell cites the tale of a breeder whose famous stud dog, Corrin of Gerwin, was first registered

A Springer Spaniel, called
Peggy. This familiar breed
is used today to flush game
for the gun. Originally,
Springing Spaniels were
used to spring birds into
pole-nets. (Photograph by
Andy Collins)

A Cocker Spaniel called
Pepsi. These fizzy
workers were developed
as specialists at flushing
woodcock (hence their
name), especially from
the dense Rhododendron
plantations in Ireland.
They are now used as
all-round gundogs.
(Photograph by Andy
Collins)

The noble head and well-proportioned ears of a working Cocker Spaniel named Teal. (Photo: iStock/ shugsfishing)

A Cocker Spaniel with over-exaggerated ears that are a parody of the original type. (Photo: iStock/ Konstanttin)

as a Welsh Cocker Spaniel but then subsequently re-registered as a Welsh Springer Spaniel and whose son, Guy of Gerwin, was registered as an English Springer Spaniel. Such inter-breed mobility highlights that these dogs are all variants of the same basic type. Cocker Spaniels are really just compact versions of Springer Spaniels. Known also in the nineteenth century as 'Cocking Spaniels', their specialty was getting into the sort of underbrush that was favoured by woodcock; hence their name. One of their distinguishing features is their long, 'judge's wig' ears. It is a characteristic that initially had some functional benefit; the swinging flaps helping to funnel poor scent towards the nose. However in recent decades the ears of show Cocker Spaniels often seem excessively over-exaggerated, much to the breed's detriment. Nevertheless a good working Cocker Spaniel is a dog to be greatly admired. They have tremendous drive. No thicket is too tangled, no shrub too dense and no bramble too thorny. The courageous Cocker will dive in, wriggle and writhe, in the ever-hopeful search for scent. Even when a Cocker is hunting out of sight, deep in vegetation, his activity is plain to see. Rippling waves ebb and flow over oceans of bracken and elsewhere, individual bushes may appear to be alive as they gyrate in interpretative dance. The tireless enthusiasm of a Cocker Spaniel energizes all around. Similarly the Springer Spaniel bustles and bounces effervescently, flushing game without a moment's pause for eager guns to test their reactions. However such vim and verve had limited use before the invention of rapid-firing, rapid-loading firearms. Spaniels for the net or hawk didn't require the same urgency, nor even did the spaniels for the early guns. In fact the first shooters required an altogether steadier dog.

Spaniels for the Gun

Hand-held firearms were developed for the battlefield before the end of the fourteenth century. They were short-barrelled with limited range, poorly balanced, imprecise when aimed; they were slow to load and fiddly to shoot, requiring a piece of match-cord (rope soaked in saltpetre) held in one hand to introduce fire into the breech. Hence 'firing' a gun (note that bows are shot, never fired!). Such arms were not useful to the needs of field sportsmen. In the ensuing century, barrels became longer, stocks improved to balance the gun and with the matchlock, a basic trigger mechanism evolved. These were all improvements that assisted the gun's inexorable rise to pre-eminence in war but were of little use for hunting. Matchlock muskets were slow to load and required preparations to shoot – blowing on the match, fixing the match, opening the pan – movements which alerted wary quarry. There was also a considerable delay between the flash of the priming powder and the detonation of the main charge; during which time the birds had flown. During the sixteenth century the wheel lock mechanism offered some advantages to the hunter. It could be loaded well in advance and the mechanism spanned, ready for an instant shot. Thus the hunter with a wheel lock musket could lie in wait for the optimum moment to take his shot, as had the crossbowman in previous ages. When it worked, which was by no means always, the wheel lock was a viable hunting arm, though too expensive and unreliable for widespread use on the battlefield. Flintlock fowling pieces made their appearance

Shooting from horseback with flintlock muskets. A great many springing spaniels have been set to flush as many birds as possible. From Richard Blome's 'The *Gentleman's Recreation*' (1686) (author's collection)

in the seventeenth century. The mechanism was altogether more reliable and although there was a perceptible delay between the flint striking and the charge going off, it was much less than with the matchlock. Barrels had become longer, offering both greater accuracy and range. Consequently the flintlock became a viable hunter's weapon. To the extent that they were used at all, these early firearms were shot at static game and to the extent they required canine assistance, it was with setting spaniels that could hold the game steady while the hunter prepared his shot.

Writing in 1621, Gervase Markham doesn't mention shooting flying birds, nor does his plagiarist Nicholas Cox in 1674. Possibly the first mention we have in an English text comes from Richard Blome in 1686. His *Gentleman's Recreation* features a plate depicting two men on horses, shooting their flintlock muskets from the saddle at flying birds. There is a pack of at least half-a-dozen springing spaniels dashing around with great excitement to put the birds up. It foreshadows the whirlwind flushes of the modern shooting field. Even so, the flintlock, like its predecessors, had a significant drawback. It was a muzzle-loading weapon. The loading procedure took an age between shots, during which time game vacated the vicinity. It wasn't until the breech-loading gun, which came to maturity in the nineteenth century, that successive shooting and loading became a quick operation. It changed everything. Henceforward birds were hunted predominantly with the gun. For the 'battue' style, a line of shooters stand by designated pegs, while dogs and beaters drive the birds towards them. This is modern spaniel work. Steadiness is required for the dogs not to get ahead of the birds. If it is taken slowly, pheasants, partridge or grouse stay grounded and scuttle forward from the beating line, threading their way between bracken stalks or heather clumps, beneath bramble or under cover of leafy crops, until brought before the guns. Then the spaniels are ordered to flush and the birds become airborne, accelerating overhead of the waiting guns. In 'walked up' or 'rough' shooting, the hunter works his dog a short way ahead of him, poking in hedgerows and bushes, combing pastures and rummaging through woodland. Springing birds, one at a time, as he comes to them, the rough-shooter's dog demands a shooter with rapid reactions. The requirements of these modern shooting methods, together with the concurrent decline of falconry and netting, had a major effect on the types of working spaniel it became fashionable to breed. In an earlier era, when walked-up game was shot with slower, flintlock fowling pieces, setting and pointing dogs were the order of the day. They had to hold the game until the marksman was ready.

Pointers

Closely allied with spaniels are the pointers. This chapter began with the Brittany, a pointing spaniel. However there is a group of smooth-coated pointing dogs that are so distinctly different in appearance from this wider spaniel family, that they must be considered separately, even though they do more or less the same job. In France they are called *braques*, in Italy *braccos*. These are a more muscular version of the spaniel, one that has been infused with hound bloodlines to give greater range, stamina and scenting ability. In addition to having a smooth coat, both head and body

An English Pointer on point on the grouse moors of West Yorkshire. This classic breed has the length of leg, the muscle, the drive and the stamina to make it a tireless worker over the exhausting terrain of a heather moor. Although, if trained from puppyhood, English Pointers can retrieve, it is not their strong suite and they are mostly employed as specialist game-finders, while other dogs, such as Labradors or Golden Retrievers gather any shot birds. (FLPA / Alamy Stock Photo)

German Wire-haired Pointer. Having the coat of wire-haired hounds, these tough pointers are grouped together with similar types under the collective name of Griffons. (Photo:iStock/PavelRodimov)

are distinctively hound-like, with a large chest cavity and tucked-up loins – one might even describe them as pointing hounds. The Braque Français is thought to have existed since the fifteenth century and a Spanish version, the Perdiguero de Burgos, occurs in the sixteenth century. English Pointers, which drew on these bloodlines, together with further additions of Foxhound, Bloodhound and Greyhound lines, began to develop in the seventeenth century. '*Braque*', according to the ever-reliable Colonel Hancock, derives from an Old French verb '*braquer*', which meant to aim. Pointing, like setting, is a natural behaviour that occurs from time to time with virtually every breed and one that has been observed with wolves in the wild. There can be no other canine moment to rival the intense energy of a pointer standing rigidly on point; it is thrilling. The clean, sleek lines of smooth-coated pointers accentuate muscle tone, revealing the active effort required to stand so perfectly still. It is literally spellbinding. This new type of elegant, pointing bird-dog soon became popular for early black-powder shooters, sportsmen whose guns required time to prepare for the shot. A pointer could hold the game before flushing on the marksman's signal. Of course this was little more than the old job of the setting spaniel but during the eighteenth century the English Pointer ascended as the fashionable choice. With its high head-carriage, the pointer was an air-scenting dog par excellence and with its longer limbs and light build, it could range effortlessly over a wide area of demanding terrain.

HPR – Hunt, Point, Retrieve

HPR is an abbreviation of 'Hunt, Point and Retrieve'. The HPR breed-group is a variant of the 'pure' pointer type. Although some well-trained English Pointers do retrieve, they are generally regarded as mediocre at the task. HPRs began to be developed on the European mainland towards the end of the nineteenth century and beginning of the twentieth century. The 'all-rounder' approach catered to the needs of the solo shooting man who had a single dog. These types were formulated for 'rough shooting' or 'walked-up' game, whereby the shooter, or small party of just a few guns, has a single dog to do all the work of hunting to locate, holding and flushing, and finally finding and retrieving shot game. British servicemen, stationed in Europe after World War II, discovered these superlative dogs, which soon became popular in Britain. The Brittany Spaniel (now classed as an HPR) and his ilk were performing these tasks long before the HPR designation was coined. Similarly the HPR role is little different to that of a good setter. Spaniel skills (game-finding and flushing) are at the heart of the business, with the different breeds exhibiting differences of style and approach. Some examples that parade under the HPR banner could equally well be called setters. For instance the German Long-haired Pointer and both the large and small varieties of the Münsterländer are, from their phenotype, unmistakably setter in origin. Griffons, a Continental term for a group of HPR dogs that have a coarse, wiry coat, are also broadly similar to spaniel types. The Italian Spinone is a Griffon, as is the German Wire-Haired Pointer and the Dutch equivalent, the Wire-Haired Pointing Griffon. All fall under the HPR umbrella. Smooth-haired members of the HPR group include three widely popular breeds: the Vizla, the Weimaraner and the German Shorthaired Pointer.

An HPR type – the Hungarian Vizsla. In the 1880s it was fashionable for Hungarian nobility to employ English gamekeepers, who brought their own preferred breeds with them. As a consequence of these imports, the native Viszla bird-dog was crossed with both Irish Setters and English Setters to produce the all-rounder HPR dog we know today. (Eve Photography/Shutterstock.com)

When I lived in Scotland during the 1990s I owned a German Shorthaired Pointer (GSP). His name was Keeper and he was an exceptionally affectionate and magical creature, who I miss deeply to this day. Training Keeper was an all-consuming and challenging experience that opened my eyes to a level of dog-training that I hadn't experienced previously. It takes time and patience to fully train a GSP, as they are highly intelligent and the masters of more than one task. Introducing the concept of remote control, for working at distance from the handler, has to be done in small incremental steps. I used a very long line when teaching Keeper to quarter and to sit at a distance. Fortunately a childhood that had involved a lot of fishing gave me both

A Large Münsterländer. This popular German dog is classified as an HPR breed, yet from his appearance it is plain that he is a type of Setter. (Photo: iStock /CaptureLight)

A German Shorthaired Pointer, on point. These are the quintessential HPR breed. (Ricantimages / Shutterstock.com)

forbearance and an elementary skill in untangling! There are other methods but, no matter how you get there, it is immensely rewarding to develop a level of connection in which a dog, in the midst of following his most basic hunting instincts, continues to collaborate fully with his human handler even when he is far away. That sense of being part of a team with one's dog is priceless and, one hopes, it may be equally gratifying for the canine.

All dogs have the capacity and the instinct to retrieve. Throwing a stick or ball for your dog is a universal experience for dog owners and one in which virtually all dogs delight; though not necessarily excel. However, retrieving freshly shot game without chomping on it and delivering it gently and immediately to hand is a far greater test than picking up rubber balls in the park. Indeed, if the bird has only been wounded and is still moving, it is all the more demanding a task. The dog must bring it gently to hand without mangling it. It is for the human to dispatch it humanely. That is a lot to ask of a dog. All the HPR breeds and all spaniels have game-retrieving capabilities, though some are better than others. As noted, this wider range of skills was developed for the gun (although HPR breeds in general are also able companions to the falconer). Originally bird dogs came into being to assist in hunting with either nets or birds of prey; retrieving was not a desirable quality for either of these activities. You certainly don't want your dog trying to wrestle the quarry from your falcon. Although pointing and setting spaniels had been considered perfectly adequate for the falconer for centuries, from the eighteenth century onwards the new smooth-coated pointer breeds, now mixed with hound blood, began to eclipse them for hunting with long-wings. Compared to broad-winged hawks, falcons offered more spectacular flights in open country – on vast heaths and moors - and English pointer types had the exceptional stamina for quartering and finding game on these wide expanses, often covering over 100-miles as they track back and forth on their beats during a day's hunting. Pointers have a running ability and staying power like no other game-finding breed.

Adventure with an English Pointer

I visited Karl Jennings, a falconer who flies peregrine falcons over English Pointers. Both peregrines and Pointers are animal athletes without equal and have an exhilarating style in the way they go about their work. We met in a field in Shropshire. It was November and from that field we could see many other fields, crisscrossed with neatly laid hedges of thorn. The fields were populated here and there with sheep and everywhere with trees and bushes outfitted in their finest shades of autumn gold. Field after field undulated into the distance in an unspoiled landscape. The large skies held a painterly mixture of strato–cumulus clouds, broad layered streaks with accenting wisps and distant clumps of cotton-wool cumulus. They appeared in a subtly blended range of hues, in greys, whites and purples. In places they parted to reveal the vivid blue of the firmament. There was a light wind. It was a beautiful crisp day, ideal for scenting dogs and flying birds.

Karl's 6-year-old female English Pointer, Summer, was a joy to behold as she flowed effortlessly over the rough pasture, responding to the twin blasts on his whistle to

The author with Matilda, the peregrine falcon and Summer, the English Pointer. With falcons, the female is significantly larger than the male, whereas this female Pointer is smaller than her male counterparts. (Photograph by Chrissy Stone)

change the direction of her beat as she came to the field's edges. She got out ahead a very long way before going on point and stayed there steadfastly until we could all walk up. In addition to Karl and myself, our party included the photographers Andy Collins and Crissy Stone; Steve Cross of Shropshire Falconry, who had brought along his Cocker Spaniel, Pepsi; and Jamie and Helen Cureton who were with their

Springer Spaniel, Peggy. I was carrying one of Karl's magnificent peregrines, whose presence must have signalled to Summer that she had a collaborator in her project. We were quite the circus but Summer held her point assiduously until we arrived. Photographs were taken. If we had been hunting, this is where I would have readied the bird and put her up. Since we were not, Karl commanded Summer to flush and a very fine cock pheasant flew off unharmed. In a hunting situation the falconer seeks to set up his falcon in the optimum position for a thrilling performance, factoring in considerations such as wind direction and speed, as well as adjacent refuges such as woodland. This is his art. Falcons, unlike hawks, do not fly at game straight from the falconer's glove. They first have to be given time to fly, in steeply ascending spirals, to a high point in the sky. Up and up and up until they are a mere speck. It is from this vantage point that they are ready to strike. Then the dog is signalled to flush the quarry and the aerial pursuit is underway. Pointers need to be able to hold their charges in situ for a considerable amount of time and despite distractions. They have to wait until the falconer arrives. The approach must be relatively stealthy, so even when the hunting party was mounted (the common practice during the Middle Ages), it is done quietly and slowly. Pointers must continue to wait while the bird is prepared and until she has flown and climbed to her starting point in the clouds. Falcons take longer to prepare than hawks. First the falconer removes the leash and swivel, which connect to the 'jesses'. These are the leather straps that attach to the bird's ankle and by which the falconer holds the bird on the glove. Jesses have a slit at one end, by which they fit to the swivel. This would be a hazard to a falcon landing in a tree, as the slit could snag. Consequently they are replaced with hunting jesses that have no aperture at all. Finally the falconer must remove the bird's leather hood, which it wears to keep it calm and quiet – the optical equivalent to earplugs. Hawks are seldom furnished with a hood but for falcons it is essential. Only once the hood has been removed and she has roused is a falcon ready to fly.

Karl had several birds with him; they were all hooded and on perches in the back of his truck. In order to demonstrate the power of a peregrine at full throttle, Karl took the controls of a drone, which trailed behind it a small piece of meat on a lure. Meanwhile I took the controls of Matilda, Karl's magnificent female peregrine. While the drone was climbing to a good height, I began the preparations of switching her tackle and removing her hood. Matilda roused herself ready to fly. Once the drone and its lure were in position, I cast her off. Up she went and Karl put on a deftly acrobatic show with his drone, which Matilda pursued with exhilarating panache. He landed the drone at our feet and Matilda, from a great height, closed her wings and dropped like a thunderbolt until she was just above our heads. Only at this last moment did her superbly muscular body apply the brakes to pull out of the dive and in a few whooshing turns slow to drop surely onto her reward on the ground. It was a heart-stopping display of raw power and a rare privilege to witness it that closely.

All game-finding dogs, pointers, setters and spaniels, work closely with a single human partner, spending all day in the field in common pursuit. The human/dog

Matilda on the author's fist. On her legs are leather straps called 'jesses', which the falconer pinches between thumb and forefinger. Held securely under control in this way, the bird is 'under the thumb'. Attached to the jesses, via a metal swivel, is the leash. For added security, the falconer has this 'wrapped round his little finger'. A falcon has highly developed eyesight and being carried into the hullabaloo of the hunting field can cause it to become over-stimulated and agitated. For this reason they wear a hood, to 'hoodwink' them into believing it is dark and they respond by being quiet and calm. These hoods, custom made to fit individual falcons, have an ingenious set of leather braces, which allow the hood to be loosened or tightened by pulling either one set to open (the shorter ones with buttoned ends) or the other set to close (the longer ones with tapered ends). The falconer, who carries the bird on his fist, achieves this by grasping one brace in his teeth and pulling the other with his right hand. (Photograph by Chrissy Stone)

Summer on point. She held this steadfastly despite the distraction of the author and the rest of the party making their way over to her. (Photograph by Andy Collins)

bond is especially close and these breeds are known to be exceptionally affectionate. It is little wonder that, as well as being working dogs, they are immensely popular as pets and companions. Spaniel-type dogs were of equal service to the hunter with bow, crossbow, musket or shotgun, as to the falconer or those who hunted with nets.

Tollers

There is one other branch to this spaniel tree – tolling dogs. Dr Caius gives a vivid description of the behaviour of such dogs, indicating that they were in use at least as early as the sixteenth century. He called them 'tumblers', noting that they achieved everything 'by craftes, fraudes, subtelties and deceipts…in hunting they turn and tumble, winding their bodies about in circle wise'.

Tolling dogs were portrayed often in the art of Rembrandt and Jan Steen during the seventeenth century and their popularity endured into the eighteenth and early nineteenth centuries. Eccentric cousins to the spaniel, tollers are decoy dogs. Rather than 'finding' birds, the toller entices them to find him. More specifically, tollers have the ability to attract wildfowl. Their comical antics of dancing, jumping, general cavorting and energetic tail waving have the effect of luring curious birds to witness their artistic gyrations at close quarters. For some reason ducks seem particularly susceptible to this form of Vaudeville entertainment. The decoy dog most represented by the Dutch Masters was the Kooikerhondje, a red and white dog with a striking resemblance to a Brittany. It is evident that both shared a common spaniel ancestry. Kooikerhondjes were used to lure ducks into a system of pipes that were constructed by means of bent arches of willow covered in fine netting. Starting as wide as 12 feet high and 20 feet wide, these pipes could narrow to as little as 2 feet high and 2 feet wide. Once crowded into this tight catchment area, the decoy-man could easily take his catch by means of a side opening. This was a commercial harvest for a country's kitchens. Records at the Hale Duck Decoy, near Halton in Cheshire, which date to the seventeenth century, show that a catch of 400 ducks per year was usual and that in 1875, a record number of 1,162 were taken. Visitors to St James' Park, adjacent to Buckingham Palace in London, will be aware of the abundance of wildfowl there. Its waterways were constructed as a duck decoy system for Charles II in 1665.

Tolling dogs are still used today, serving the needs of the wildfowler, a hardy fellow who spends long days in cold and wet estuaries and marshlands waiting for the chance to take a shot at duck with his gun. The Nova Scotia Duck Tolling Retriever, as the name implies, is adept at calling in the many species of duck that flock to the 5,400 lakes that speckle this Canadian peninsular. Known also as the Little River Dog, these tollers were first developed in the nineteenth century. Hunters had noticed that foxes had this trick of luring ducks with similar frolicsome capers and they bred a dog to exploit this glitch in a duck's artistic discernment. It is no coincidence that the Nova Scotia Duck Tolling Retriever sports a gleaming,

The Nova Scotia Duck Tolling Retriever. This classic decoy dog has a thick double coat, insulating it from the icy waters when retrieving waterfowl in its homeland. (Photo: iStock / yes_please)

fox-red coat. Having enticed their prey to within range of the guns, tollers function equally well as other spaniel-types in locating shot game and retrieving it to hand. There is resemblance, and perhaps connection, between the Nova Scotia Toller and the Golden Retriever. Interbreeding for function frequently confounds our best efforts to put all types neatly in certain boxes. In fact Golden Retrievers, popular and versatile water dogs, are not only good retrievers, they too have also been used effectively as decoy dogs.

Chapter 8

Sighthounds

'He is a gentleman – he grew up with a Saluki.'

—Arab proverb

A Saluki, with henna on his legs, ready to run in the desert. The author is set to follow him on a camel. (Photograph by Kim Hawkins)

The canine racing machines, known variously as sighthounds, gazehounds, running dogs or long dogs are built for speed. They hunt predominantly, though not exclusively, by sight. The various breeds – Salukis, Greyhounds, Borzois, Afghan Hounds, Scottish Deerhounds, among them – have adapted their coats according to climate and their size according to their prey but they are all derivative breeds from a basic type of desert dog. It is a tall, deep-chested, narrow-headed dog that has a unique metabolism and stamina. It also has long legs, a long flexible spine and the explosive running action of a cheetah. Sighthounds are among the oldest type of domesticated dog and records of their use trace back to the earliest known civilizations. Prince among them is the Saluki, arguably the oldest identifiable breed of dog still in existence, whose form has remained unchanged for at least five millennia. He is the dog of the Bedouin.

Adventures with a Saluki

The Saluki is the flop-eared sighthound of the Arabian deserts. He carries his long tail high and curled and his delicately featured head sits proud and aloof on a long slender neck. His penetrating, mystical gaze is ever watchful. He is ancient. There are regional differences such as the length of coat and the amount of feathering. Some Salukis are smooth coated. Most however have distinctively fringed and feathered ears, legs and tails. My quest to see a Saluki in action in its traditional environment began in Jordan's famous Wadi Rum Desert. Wadi Rum means 'large canyon'. Its vast

Profile of a Saluki's aristocratic head. The eyes are ever watchful, scanning the horizon for the slightest movement. (Photograph by Kim Hawkins)

Sabbah waits, concealed against the rocks and scanning for opportunity. He wears a traditional cloth belt called a '*cir*' and his legs have been coated in henna paste. Salukis appear in a variety of colours: golden, cream, fawn, red, grey, black and tan, black and white. These once indicated the dog's area of origin. Traditionally, they were bred to blend with the local terrain. (Photograph by Kim Hawkins)

expanse is speckled with the sculptural splendour of wind-chiselled rock formations floating on an ocean of sand. Here the light drapes the landscape with a gossamer glaze that softens everything to a shimmering mirage. Home to Bedouin tribesmen, who continue to live a traditional nomadic life, Wadi Rum is also famous in recent times as the location for the film *Lawrence of Arabia* (1962). As a work of history the film rather exaggerates the role played by T.E. Lawrence during the 1916 Arab Revolt against Ottoman occupation and underplays the role of the Arab leaders. Nevertheless its cinematography captures both the mysticism and the majesty of this timeless, enchanted land. I was only there for a short while but there is something about it that enters your soul. My wife Kim and I were taken into Wadi Rum in a 4x4 driven by our guide Adeeb. He was an adventurous driver and it was an exciting off-road ride, a good deal of it airborne! We camped in the desert overnight and the following day Adeeb took us to rendezvous with some Bedouin. After arriving at their isolated tent, we were greeted warmly. I was garbed ceremoniously with a '*shemagh*' – the signature red and white keffiyeh (cloth headdress) of Jordan. I was honoured to wear it and it was also immensely practical for the searing heat. We were invited in and served glasses of sweet tea; a traditional gesture of hospitality. Bedouin tents are ingeniously woven from a yarn spun from the hair of black goats. If it rains or is damp, the fibres contract rapidly to create a waterproof, windproof fabric. However in the heat of the summer, the fibres open, allowing gentle breezes to blow through, whilst still providing shade. With rugs on the floor and cushions for seats it was a still, peaceful and airy refuge.

It was in the privileged domain of the tent that I met Sabbah, an eighteen-month-old male Saluki. He belonged to Fayad, a quiet man with the watchful eyes of a hunter, who was both knowledgeable and passionate about Salukis. Given that we were about to run Sabbah, it was not the time to feed him but seeing him at home within the sanctuary of the tent was enough to endorse his standing. In Islam, dogs in general are considered unclean. They are used by those who need them for tasks like herding and guarding but they are not kept otherwise and certainly not in the house. An exception to this rule is the Saluki. He is known also as '*al-hur*' (noble one) and considered quite differently from the common '*kalb*' (dog). Salukis alone among canines are permitted, indeed welcomed, into the living quarters of the home. Among their traditional and poetic nicknames are 'wind-drinker', 'son-of-the-desert' and 'daughter-of-the-tent'. They enjoy a privileged status, not only sleeping in their masters' tents but also being hand-fed food from his table. This high status is in deference to the Saluki's recognition in the Koran. In Islam only certain foods are considered '*halal*' (lawful) to eat. For instance it is well known that Muslims do not eat pork. The Koran also lays down regulations for the manner in which animals must be slaughtered in order to be *halal*. The butcher must be a Muslim and the name of Allah invoked at the time of the killing. Furthermore the animal must be slaughtered by means of cutting the throat with a sharp knife. However the Koran specifically exempts meat caught by a Saluki from these rigid laws. Traditionally Salukis were used to hunt for fresh, wild game – a vital source of additional protein for the desert-dweller – and the Koran declares meat from an animal that has been hunted and caught by a Saluki lawful. Even so, Salukis are most usually trained to catch their prey, to hold it but not to kill it, until the hunter has arrived and can dispatch it with a knife and the appropriate holy words. Young pups are sometimes brought up with live rabbits, which they fetch and carry but do not harm.

Desert-bred Salukis are the most highly prized for hunting. Sabbah is from a Jordanian mother and Saudi father. To the Western eye, especially compared to their plumper cousins in the show ring, desert dogs can appear rangy but to the Bedouin hunter they look to be in peak athletic condition. Fayed told how Sabbah had recently disappeared for three months! During that time he managed to survive on what he could catch – mostly hares and jerboas – which is a pretty good testament to the vitality of his constitution and his hunting skills; though it did mean that he was

Sabbah watches intently as the author drinks tea and is introduced to a falcon. Salukis are alone amongst dogs in Islam that are permitted inside the dwelling. (Photograph by Kim Hawkins)

looking even leaner than usual, when I met him. The build of a Saluki also varies according to the type of prey it was bred to chase. Once they were used to bring down onagers and oryx and that took a heavier, stronger dog than one needed for either gazelle or hares. Gazelle hounds need the most stamina and salukis bred to course hares require an impressive sprint as well as the ability to reach out with a long neck and seize the hare as it turns. Sabbah's light frame and delicate features suggested that he was a harrier. Personally, I find the Saluki both aesthetically and athletically appealing. Others, oblivious to the engineering brilliance of their slight build, have not been so kind. One correspondent to *Blackwood's Magazine* in January 1924 described them as 'slim, mincing and disdainful'. By contrast, a ringing endorsement of their hardiness had been recorded earlier by Lady Anne Blunt in her account of Arab culture, *A Pilgrimage to Njad* (1881). She reported that Salukis 'have been seen to course hares over ground that would have broken every bone in an English greyhound without hurting themselves'.

Henna and Cir
Even so Fayad wasn't taking any chances. He applied a henna paste to Sabbah's legs and paws. When running a dog on harder ground, the Bedouin use henna to protect and strengthen its legs. The sands of Wadi Rum are ever shifting and in places they form only a thin layer over hard rock. A dog hunting in Wadi Rum may run over both soft and hard ground. Henna is reputed to have anti-inflammatory and anti-spasmodic properties. Adeeb informed me that it was also an analgesic and that it was common among older Bedouin to use henna for the relief of cracked or painful feet. Henna also has antifungal, antiseptic and antibacterial properties, so there would be less chance of infection occurring in the event the dog suffered a cut or puncture wound during the chase. Henna's medical use is controversial in the United States and the FDA only approves its use as a hair product, not for direct use on skin. I doubt they are right to

dismiss such an ancient remedy. Squeezing globules of the blood-coloured paste from a tube, Fayed applied the henna to each of Sabbah's legs, rubbing it in evenly with his fingers. During the process Sabbah lay still, with a far-away look in his eyes that demonstrated he was well-accustomed to having such attention lavished upon him. He received the slow, methodical massage as if being anointed in an age-old, solemn ritual. The procedure took time and it built anticipation.

Sabbah looked resplendent in his crimson socks. They stood out in shocking and vivid contrast to his pale, honey-coloured coat; he was dressed to kill. Of course we weren't actually going to kill anything. I simply wanted to meet all the players that would have been involved in the complex ritual of a traditional Bedouin hunt. Within the tent I had met a saker falcon called Tarrad and later on I was introduced to a camel named Sharaar. Together with the Saluki, this unlikely trinity once formed a hunting cadre who, in partnership with man, collaborated to hunt the various species of small gazelle that once inhabited the deserts of Arabia. Gazelle no longer roam in Wadi Rum even though Jordan today, to its credit, has very strict conservation and hunting laws to protect its wildlife. The idea was to simulate key aspects of the experience and, most importantly, to witness Sabbah swim across the desert sands – '*sabbah*' is

Before running in the hard desert, Sabbah's feet and legs are coated with henna paste. Henna is a traditional liniment that has anti-spasmodic, anti-inflammatory and analgesic properties. These help to protect the dog's legs from the harsh concussion of running on desert rock. It also has anti-fungal, antiseptic and antibacterial properties, which guard against infection in the event of the dog's feet getting cut or punctured during the chase. (Photograph by Kim Hawkins)

Arabic for 'swimmer'. The historical method for hunting gazelle used to involve the hunter, together with dog and falcon, riding out on a camel in search of a herd. This may be a journey of some days and at times the Saluki would also ride, sitting on the hunter's lap to save its legs for the chase. The falcon was carried on the hunter's fist. When a likely location was found, the falcon would be flown. It would wind up high into the sky until it was no more than a speck. With its superior eyesight and high vantage point it could see game that neither man nor dog could perceive. Then, like a thunderbolt, it would stoop, hurtling down towards its prey at tremendous speed. As the speck became larger, it would catch the keen eyesight of the Saluki and the chase was on. The Saluki headed towards the action at a flat-out pace and the hunter did his best to keep all in view, galloping after on his camel. A falcon is not large enough to take a gazelle on its own. It depended on the Saluki to do that. It served merely as a marker and to confuse and slow the flight of the prey animal. Falcons were trained to bind onto a gazelle's head. This was achieved by feeding them the eyes as part of their regular diet. Once the Saluki had the prey in sight, it was more than capable of outrunning it and bringing it down. I had no wish to participate in such a cruel system of hunting, nor would it have been legal to do so. However I was able to experience the intricacies of handling a bird, a dog and a camel in their natural environment.

Although the accolade of fastest dog is generally given to the Greyhound, it is a crown disputed by Saluki fanciers. Greyhounds can only maintain their maximum speed for a very short distance, whereas the Saluki can run at full speed for 2 miles or more and keep going for even further. One of the problems in collecting data for the Saluki's top speed is that it is an extremely intelligent dog, reluctant to follow an electric hare around a greyhound track. In such artificial environments Salukis tend to work out what is happening, anticipate, calculate and cut across. Even when coursing live game they constantly gauge their tactics during the pursuit, going fast enough to stay in touch with their prey but pacing themselves to be able to sustain the chase for longer if necessary. Ultimately they vanquish creatures of superior speed, like the gazelle, by beating them on endurance. Propelled forward by powerful kicks from its long hind legs, a Saluki flies through the air gaining about 12 feet with every stride. Its elongated, flexible spine, much like that of a cheetah, is capable of remarkably tight turns, turns that can put great strain on such a long back. Both the spine and the core abdominal muscles that support it are further taxed by the rapidly repeating explosive action of the Saluki's running pattern – a double-suspension gallop. Between each stride it draws its back legs up to its front legs, contracting the stomach muscles fully before slamming down its hindmost pads and lifting the whole front end to kick forward again in a great straining, stretching reach into full extension.

Fayad produced a length of folded cloth, which he tied around Sabbah's waist. He called it a '*cir*', a belt, and told me that it was a traditional accouterment when coursing these high-performance dogs. It may have some function, similar to a weightlifter's belt, to protect the abdomen from strain and hernia - a Saluki running is an explosive event – but it was principally used as a means to help with lifting these long dogs. One hand grasped the scruff, while the other grabbed the *cir* to hoist the dog into the passenger seat on a camel. In the days of hunting live game, it was also used to assist

pulling the Saluki off its prey. Very often, though not exclusively, Saluki type dogs are hunted today in their native deserts without collars. This is quite different to the images we encounter from Ancient Egypt, where we see all sighthounds wearing broad collars. As a precursor to the buckle these are secured with an elaborate knot but it is clear from the art that the collar remains on the dog during the chase and the dog is slipped from a leash. Sabbah was leashed with an old bit of rope

In the traditional Bedouin gazelle hunt (no longer legal in Jordan) the Saluki would be carried on his master's lap as he rode, sometimes for days on end, in search of a herd to course. This saved the Saluki's legs and stamina for the chase. (Photograph by Kim Hawkins)

First introductions: The camel was frightened of the falcon, the falcon was frightened of the Saluki and the Saluki was frightened of the camel. The author had insufficient hands. (Photograph by Kim Hawkins)

from which he could be slipped. However this was a temporary precaution prompted by Sabbah's recent escapology and in anticipation of meeting strangers. It was soon dispensed with.

The Team

Salukis possess legendary speed, stamina and intelligence. Throughout history they have been used for hunting solo, in pairs and sometimes in larger groups, depending on both quarry and custom. For the hunting of desert gazelle however, the traditional partnership is between Saluki and falcon. The falcon, like the Saluki, is also known as '*el hor*' ('the noble one'). Sabbah had not met a falcon before. Traditionally dogs and birds trained to hunt this way are fed together as soon as they are old enough but that had not been Sabbah's purpose. Hammed, the falconer, whose eyes were clear and piercing as those of the bird he carried, had brought Tarrad along to meet me but Sabbah was equally fascinated by this flapping creature in the tent. Tarrad was a tiercel (a male) and male falcons are significantly smaller than their female counterparts. Sabbah had been shy of me at first but soon came round to being friendly and was happy to be stroked. Now he lay by my feet looking up at Tarrad on my fist. It was time to introduce Tarrad to the dog. I asked permission first and then, using teeth and the fingers of my right hand, I drew apart the two leather strips that fasten the falcon's hood and slipped it off. Tarrad baited at the sight of the dog – that is he flew off the fist and hung upside down. I gently lifted him back onto the glove and soothed him by stroking his breast gently. Gradually he settled to being around Sabbah. We were set – it was time to go and find a camel.

We drove across the desert for another half hour before finding Ismael and his camel under a very attractive arch of rock. Although I am an experienced horse rider, I hadn't ridden a camel before. I was excited to do so and clambered aboard eagerly. The right leg is wrapped over and around the front horn of the saddle and then hooked securely into place by the left leg. As the camel rises from his fully prone position there is a dramatic series of extreme angles that lurch the rider rearwards and forwards alternately. Camels first get up onto their front knees, then onto their back knees, before then extending their back legs into the fully upright position. Finally they stand up onto their front legs. It is quite a shock the first time but I quickly got in tune with the rhythm and was able to go up and down on camelback with some degree of decorum. Steering was more problematic. A rope halter around the camel's head connects to the rider via a single rope rein, which passes on the left-hand side of the camel's neck. Pulling this to get the animal to turn left worked reasonably well but it is the stick you carry which is the principal aid for direction. Tapped on the right side of the camel's neck it augments the rein command for a left-hand turn but a right-hand turn is solely dependent on signals from the stick. Compliance to my directional wishes was both intermittent and reluctant. Even so, camels have a majestic walking pace, very easy to sit to, and the views of the desert from that height are superb. Trotting was more challenging but great fun so long as the animal maintained a consistent pace. My camel, Sharaar, was an uncooperative and cantankerous beast. His owner, Ismael, I'm happy to report, was of an entirely opposite disposition. When Ismael smiled, which he did a lot, he exposed an unusually wide gap in his front teeth, a dental landscape that mirrored the outcrops of rock in Wadi Rum itself. His smile broke into broad laughter when I fell off!

After an amount of practice, I had become reasonably proficient at turning and trotting but try as I might, and I really tried, I could not get the idle creature to gallop. My efforts were very enthusiastic and there was a great deal of whooping and hollering, all to no avail. With horses it can sometimes be easier for a novice rider to get them to change pace more easily when turning a corner. I thought I'd try this with Sharaar. Trotting very, very fast soon becomes quite difficult and when you add a turn into that mix – disaster! It is a very long way to fall and it hurt. However, unlike horses, camels, after depositing you, have the decency not to run off; they simply drop

The simulated hunting party, ready to set off. (Photograph by Kim Hawkins)

to their resting posture on their knees, looking disdainful. Ismael's bright smile and helping hand got me back on my feet and back on the camel but me riding in pursuit of Sabbah's run no longer seemed an option.

The Chase

I got into the 4 x 4. Kim, as chief photographer, had prime position sitting in the tailgate and alongside her was Fayed with a lure. Adeeb was driving. I knelt on the back seat. All was set and off we went, rapidly accelerating to a fair lick. Foolishly, I was so engrossed watching Sabbah run that I forgot to take the opportunity to look at the speedometer or even to ask. No matter, it was spectacular sight. Sabbah sprinted after us with purpose. Each bound forward was a leap of staggering length. He soared over the sands as if he was flying – a mirage made all the more believable by the clouds of dust that shimmered and shrouded his progress like a jet stream. It was an even stride and right from the start he found his rhythm. This was the style of an endurance athlete. I hadn't noticed before quite the extent to which the forelegs are raised at the beginning of each pouncing bound. Salukis rear up to a surprising height before reaching forward to make maximum length with each driving advance. Now, viewed from head-on, this dramatic elevation was plain to see. Adeeb drove straight for a while but then began a curve to keep the chase going without getting too far from base. Sabbah read the action and subtly slowed and cut the corner. This was a very smart dog. On the first run alone, we far exceeded the distance one would expect an English Greyhound to stay in touch. We did three runs like this with only relatively short rests in between. Sabbah looked fine and Fayed assured us he was. Kim and I got out and stationed ourselves strategically to photograph the run in profile. Adeeb stepped on the throttle and, with Sabbah in pursuit, drove back and forth across our field of view. I've seen sighthounds at a flat-out gallop before and it never ceases to

Sabbah with all four legs in suspension and the core muscles in full retraction, like a coiled spring. A Saluki at full speed is a spectacular succession of flying leaps (Photograph by Kim Hawkins)

Sabbah reaching out in extension and releasing the explosive power of the contracted phase. He devours the landscape with massive forward strides. (Photograph by Kim Hawkins)

Up on his hind-legs like a kangaroo, Sabbah about to throw his front legs forward for maximum reach. (Photograph by Kim Hawkins)

Taking a break in the shade. The fire boils water for cups of tea. It was a timeless scene. (Photograph by Kim Hawkins)

delight but seeing it happen across the mystical sands of Wadi Rum was both a thrill and a moment of astonishing beauty. The antiquity of the experience was spellbinding and with eyes transfixed by Sabbah's power, I didn't even notice the jeep.

At the end of it all we retreated to the shade of an overhanging rock and a few precious sprigs of dried scrub were spared to build a small fire in order to boil water for the necessary glasses of tea. Only Adeeb was fluent in both languages. He had once lived in Glasgow for a while and, although he normally spoke with a standard English accent, he had an unnerving ability to imitate a Glaswegian accent with great authenticity. However, sitting there with my new Bedouin friends and the hunting menagerie, language seemed largely superfluous. We all felt the connection of shared experience.

Saluki heritage

Saluki is the anglicized version of the Arabic word '*saluqi*'. He has also been called the Gazelle Hound, the Oriental Hound and the Persian Greyhound. In Iran (Persia) he is known as the Tazi, which means 'the Arabian', suggesting that they at least consider him to be a dog from the deserts to their west. To muddy the waters further, the terms *slughi* and *sloughi* have both been used in equal measure in the past to describe the same dog. Modern Kennel Clubs will tell you that there is a separate breed called the Sloughi, deriving from North Africa, which is a smooth-coated dog, without the Saluki's distinctive feathering. Such a fine distinction did not register with people writing about these dogs in earlier centuries. The terms were all interchangeable and referred to the same broad landrace of dogs that were bred throughout the desert regions of the Middle East. You could have a smooth-haired Saluki or a feathered

Sloughi; it was a question of vernacular, not an absolute breed distinction. Such rigid taxonomies can sometimes interfere with common sense groupings that would provide a larger gene pool of type.

Oriental Greyhound, Assyrian Greyhound and Nubian Greyhound are yet more appellations that were given to the same dog by nineteenth-century commentators. One of these was Howard Carter, the archeologist who famously discovered the tomb of Tutankhamun in 1922. Although Carter had no particular personal interest in dogs, other than the fact that they were central to Ancient Egyptian culture, he corresponded about them to Lady Florence Amherst, a passionate aficionado and early historian of the Saluki. Howard Carter was the son of a jobbing portrait artist living near Swaffham in rural Norfolk. Both he and his father had received patronage from the Amherst family, who were the local lords of the manor. Lord Amherst was a keen Egyptologist and in particular had encouraged and supported the young Carter in his early career. Known for his exquisite draughtsmanship, Carter soon became established in Egypt, drawing and recording tombs and their contents. At the time these were being discovered on an almost daily basis. Owing much to the Amhersts, and before his fortuitous patronage from Lord Carnarvon, Carter was happy to indulge Lady Amherst with her insatiable quest to find out as much as she could about Saluki history. In his correspondence, he referred to these dogs either as Nubian Greyhounds or as Slughis. Swaffham, the little town where he grew up, until he left for Egypt at the age of seventeen, is very close to where I was raised and I am very familiar with the strong local accent. It is probable that Howard Carter spoke somewhat in this manner and if one says 'Saluki' in a Swaffham accent, it sounds very much like the phonetically rendered 'Slughi'.

Regional Variations

There is a mummified dog from the 18th Dynasty (1550-1292 BC), now in the Cairo Museum, that resembles a modern Saluki and lop-eared, Saluki-type dogs appear often in Egyptian art. Sharing with the Welsh an apparent disdain for vowels, the Ancient Egyptians called this dog the '*tsm* (pronounced 'tesem'). It is a word that has echoes of the Persian 'Tazi'. Iran's neighbour, Afghanistan, is also famous for its local sighthound. The Afghan Hound is a taller, more muscular version of the Saluki and known for its much longer and heavier coat. However, the over-exaggerated, ultra-long 'fashion' coats of the show ring have been a relatively recent manifestation and the result of selective breeding in Europe and the US to produce an 'Afghan look'. For hunting in their mountainous homeland, Afghan Hounds were not only bred with a more modest coat but these coats were also stripped for the chase. Traditionally, Afghan Hounds looked like what they were: long-haired Salukis. In Iran both the Afghan Hound and the Saluki are called the Tazi; it is the same dog. Sadly, in the West, the excessively long-coated variety, bred for the whims of European fashion, has now eclipsed the older type entirely.

Also among the sighthound types to be seen in the art of ancient Egypt are those that have prick ears. The desert dog was a pan-regional type that occurred in two main strains – the lop-eared and the prick-eared. A cluster of modern

An Afghan Hound. Despite the disguise of its over-exaggerated coat, the familiar desert-dog silhouette can be discerned in this modern representation of the breed. Traditionally, although these dogs had a relatively long coat to protect them from the harsher mountain weather of their region, it was nowhere as long as this. (I-Stock images: Massonstock)

sighthounds are also of the prick-eared variety. They are found throughout the Mediterranean, predominantly in areas of rocky terrain. The Ibizan Hound, the Portuguese Podengo, the Pharaoh Hound, the Cretan Hound and others, are all distinctive for their extremely tall ears, more like radar dishes than regular auditory organs. In other respects they are the same 'dog of the desert', though generally of smaller size. Their aficionados have long claimed that these breeds have direct lineage to the dogs of ancient Egypt, taken to the islands by the Phoenician traders, and that they qualify as the oldest type of canine in existence. Contradicting this theory, David Hancock (*Sighthounds* 2012) cites an enquiry published in the journal *Science* in 2004, which concluded that these breeds are relatively recent reconstructions of the type and that none of them have ancient genes. Even so, their similarity to the dogs in Egyptian art is remarkable. They are all rabbit dogs, like Whippets, with a distinctive manner of hunting. Above all they are fleet-footed sighthounds, detecting the slightest flicker of movement and locking onto a fleeing rabbit with laser vision throughout the chase. However, hunting as they do in boulder-strewn terrain or tall grassland, they rely equally on their noses and their highly developed hearing for initial detection. Ibizan Hounds are distinctive in having an astonishing ability for high vertical jumps. Not only do these caprine leaps make light work of challenging landscapes, but they also offer a momentary aerial advantage to scan hidden horizons. Whether or not they entertained Egyptian huntsmen with these spectacular pogo antics can only be a matter for speculation but their similarity in appearance is indisputable. Another aerial artist is the Basenji (best known for having no bark, though it can make some sounds). Aficionados claim that this is the breed represented on Egyptian reliefs. Certainly it has the same prick ears and curled tail but this little dog barely stands any taller than a large Jack Russell Terrier, not quite what was required to hunt large antelope such as oryx. Although sighthounds in Egyptian art vary, they generally appear as larger specimens. Packs of feral dogs that frequent Egypt's ancient sites to this day, a form of pariah dog, have a strikingly similar silhouette to the prick-eared hounds depicted on tomb walls, other than that they are generally smaller than the great hunting dogs of the Pharaohs.

The Ibizan Hound. This is another version of the desert dog, which, with its characteristically large ears, is also reminiscent of dogs in Egyptian art. Ibizan Hounds exhibit a distinctive bounding gait when hunting, springing high to gain a line of sight over the tall grasses. (I-Stock images: Kristiinatammik)

The Gre(y)hound

Greyhounds are not all grey. They occur, and always have, in a wide variety of coat colours. Medieval authors mostly referred to them as 'gre-hounds' and the 'y' was inserted in subsequent eras, seeking to inform pronunciation. The poet Geoffrey Chaucer (1343 – 1400) rendered the word as 'greihounde'. '*Gré*' in Old French meant pleasing or agreeable and 'gre' in Middle English denoted rank and status. These esteemed canines could lay claim to either derivation. A 'gre-hound' signified a great or noble hound and referred to a fairly broad range of medieval sighthound types. King Cnut (r. 1018-35) made a proclamation that a gre-hound may not be kept by any person whose station was inferior to gentleman. Although today's sleek specimens have been slimmed down and elongated for the racetrack, they nonetheless remain recognizable in medieval art. Having said that, medieval hunting gre-hounds were

Hunting dog care from a fifteenth-century illustrated version of *Le Livre de la Chasse* by Gaston Phoebus, showing wounds and sprains incurred in the hunting field being attended to. Medieval gre-hound types are clearly represented to the right of the image. Note their broad collars and the ring for a slip leash. To the left of the picture are scenthounds, recognizably similar to modern foxhound types. In the centre is what may be some kind of water spaniel. Bibliotheque Nationale, Paris. (Photo © CCI/Bridgeman Images)

generally stockier and bolder. They were prized for their swiftness and keen sight but they also had nose. For hunting large game, such as the stag, gre-hounds were leashed (three or more together) and stationed in relays around the perimeter of the area to be hunted. If the stag got away from the pursuing pack of scenthounds ('brachets'), then the relays of gre-hounds were slipped to keep up the chase and hopefully turn the animal back towards the main pack.

The word 'gre-hound' was applied to a group of dogs with similar morphology and function. Of slighter build, but within the broader group, were 'lebrels' or 'levriers', specialists at hunting the hare. These hounds were not only a match in a flat-out race but were equally adept at taking seemingly impossible tight turns at high velocity, a manoeuvre known as the 'wrench'. This style of hunting by high-speed pursuit is called 'coursing'. Coursing was also popular with the Ancient Greeks. Although they more often hunted hares by means of scenthounds, driving the prey into nets, the pure chase with sighthounds was extolled by both Xenophon and Arrian. It was standard practice to set a pair of hounds to chase a hare. They worked co-operatively to anticipate the zig-zags and doublings-back of this swift master of evasion. Arrian asserted that such hounds must 'stand long from head to tail...[because] you could not find any single mark of speed and breeding as accurate as the length of the body'. What is puzzling is that Arrian claims that the sighthounds he is referring to were Celtic hounds from Western Europe. It is curious because we might assume that, geographically, he would have been more familiar with Saluki-type dogs from the Middle East – a type that we know has a foundation in antiquity. If Arrian has reported correctly, there may be another branch to the sighthound family, originating in Europe but, as with anything regarding early dog history, it is very difficult to be certain of anything.

Whatever the genesis of the Greyhound, there is no dispute that he is an elite sprinter and, in common with other sighthounds, Greyhounds differ physiologically from other types of dog. They have a field of vision of 270 degrees. This compares to 180 degrees in humans. Sighthounds often sleep with their eyes open, on constant alert. In the first 7.5 seconds of a 30-second race, a Greyhound metabolizes high-energy creatine and glycogen stored in its muscles without the need for oxygen. At maximum acceleration, a Greyhound reaches a full speed of around 45mph within 30 yards or six strides. The only other land animal that can accelerate faster over a short distance is a cheetah. The muscles of a Greyhound generate 75-80 per cent of their power from unique anaerobic metabolic pathways. In distance races in excess of 40 seconds, 80 per cent of the total energy in the final half of the gallop is metabolized using oxygen. A Greyhound circulates its entire blood volume between four and five times during a 30-second gallop. An average 160lb human athlete has a heart size similar to a 65lb Greyhound, but the Greyhound's heart delivers blood at almost twice the rate (this data was assembled in an online article by Dr John Konkhe for the US charity Greyhound Pets Inc.). By any standards, the Greyhound is an extraordinarily impressive animal and as soft as they come around the house! Today's Greyhounds have been refined to be the ultimate racing machines. Their medieval hunting ancestors

These modern racing Greyhounds are muzzled to prevent them from nipping at each other in the competitive environment of a race. Their drive and speed is exceptional. However, the racing life of these dogs is short and they are discarded once they have no more profitable use. Greyhound shelters exist to rehome these beautiful animals, so that they may live the rest of their lives being cherished and cared for. (I-Stock images: magdaloubser)

had more muscle and bulk and for those that went after large or dangerous game, were most likely built along the lines of Deerhounds and Lurchers (all 'great hounds'). Medieval Greyhounds might be either smooth- or rough-coated. Today the dogs we call Greyhounds are all smooth-coated, although a closely related dog, the Spanish Galgo, continues to manifest in both smooth- and rough-coated varieties.

All sighthounds have dolichocephalic heads, meaning that they are long and slender. This gives them long, powerful, pincer jaws that are superb at snatching prey at speed and which align the eyes in such a way to maximize their capacity for long distance sight. A consequence of this is that the neck is as broad as the broadest part of the head. Sighthounds can therefore get out of standard collars quite easily and require extra broad collars to prevent them from doing so. When coursing in the desert, the Bedouin customarily use no collar but Ancient Egyptian sighthounds are always represented wearing collars throughout the chase. Xenophon (fourth century BC) described Greek hunters using a long leash that went through a ring on the collar. An identical arrangement can be seen in medieval art. The huntsman holds both ends of the cord; to slip the hound, he simply lets go of one end. Depictions of medieval huntsmen show them with half-a-dozen leashes tucked into their belt, indicating that one handler managed several hounds at once. Being able to slip Greyhounds instantly was crucial lest they lose valuable seconds in their pursuit.

Deerhounds and Wolfhounds

Beneath the shaggy exterior of a Scottish Deerhound is a desert dog – sharp-eyed, fleet-footed, with tucked-up loins and possessed of immense stamina. Coursing a powerful red deer stag across the crags and heather of the highlands was neither for the faint-hearted nor the lightly muscled. A Scottish Deerhound is a substantial dog. Irish Wolfhounds are built even more robustly. The first dog that I owned as a young adult was an Irish Wolfhound called Olly. He was truly a gentle giant. Olly, of course, never had to face such deadly odds as a snarling pack of wolves and was entirely content to lounge around after a daily run. The closest he came to danger was the day he jumped out of my car unbidden, while I was distracted in unloading some awkward object, and made a dash from the car park into the kitchen of a Chinese restaurant via its back entrance. I was first alerted by angry shouts in Cantonese, only to look up to see him, duck in mouth, being pursued by two Chinese chefs wielding large cleavers. Naturally I paid for the duck.

Today's Irish Wolfhounds were developed after wolves became extinct in Ireland and long after they ceased to exist in England, Wales and Scotland. In 1786, three years prior to becoming President of the United States, George Washington wrote a number of letters in the hope of procuring genuine Irish Wolfhound stock from Ireland but they proved impossible to find; the breed had already died out. When mastiffs were suggested as an alternative, Washington replied:

> Mastiffs, I conceive, will not answer the purposes for which the wolf dog is wanted…[the objective of wolfhounds] is to hunt and destroy wolves by pursuit, for which the mastiff is altogether unfit.
>
> (Letter to Col. Charles Carter 1786).

Almost a century later, a Scotsman, Captain George Graham, began the business of 'reconstituting' the breed. Mostly, it seems, he bred Scottish Deerhounds infused with some Great Dane blood in order to make the progeny more massive. To what extent these dogs resembled the original Irish strain is difficult to determine but Graham faced a great deal of doubting criticism from his contemporaries. Whatever a medieval wolfhound looked like, and images in art suggest both rough- and smooth-coated hounds, there is no doubt that these dogs faced a daunting and ferocious quarry in the wolf.

Wolves were a major predator of sheep throughout Europe during the Middle Ages, a time when wool was the staple of many economies. As King of the Franks (768 – 814) Charlemagne recruited a royal corps of '*Luparii*' to keep wolf populations under control and in 950 England's King Athelstan (r. 927 – 939) required Hywel Dda (King of Dyfed, Powys and Gwynedd 942 – 948) to pay an annual tribute of three hundred wolfskins. Edward I (r. 1272 – 1307) called for the extermination of wolves in several counties and wolves always carried a price on their head - a 'wolfshead' was a nickname for an outlaw in medieval England. Wolves finally became extinct in England during the reign of Henry VII (r. 1485-1507), though they survived longer in Scotland. Mary, Queen of Scots (r. 1542 – 1567), is known to have gone on wolf hunts. Throughout Europe bows, crossbows, snares and traps (and later on guns and poisons) all played their part in the slaughter but hunting the wolf par force, with hounds, was considered a worthy pursuit for the nobility in many countries. Gaston Phoebus describes an elaborate rigmarole in which wolves were first lured

A Scottish Deerhound noses ahead of an Irish Wolfhound in a chase across the snow. The sheer size and raw power of these burly athletes is probably similar to that of the larger, smooth-coated Greyhounds represented in medieval manuscripts. (I-Stock images: nemoris)

to a particular area of woodland adjacent to a large forest with baits of carrion. This was done for several days in order to encourage them to remain nearby during the day. One method of checking if the wolves had remained in the locale was to imitate their howl, prompting them to return the call. On the day of the hunt, a line of fires, a stone's throw apart, was lit around the perimeter of the wood at roughly two bowshot's distance from its edge. This dissuaded the wolves from breaking cover and seeking sanctuary in the vaster main forest. A small army of 'fewterers' (hunt servants who handled the greyhounds in a medieval hunt) was stationed downwind of the wolves, each with three or four leashes of greyhounds. These were probably more similar to today's Wolfhounds and Lurchers than they were to today's racing Greyhounds. A cavalcade of horsemen lined each side of the wood and then a pack of scent hounds were sent in to chase the wolves out towards the relays of wolfhounds/greyhounds. Camouflaged with foliage, the fewterers and their charges were set in a staggered formation. When a wolf broke cover towards the relays, the first remained hidden and let him pass, the second and third relays were slipped as the wolf drew level and, at the same time, the last relay was slipped to turn him back. In an instant the wolf was surrounded and the dogs set about their attack.

I am especially sentimental about wolves, not least because of their direct connection to dogs, so I find the idea of a wolf hunt horrific. Nevertheless it is important to understand that, at the time, the scale of wolf predation was significant, perceived to threaten human communities as well as the economic resource of livestock. For many centuries the woodman's axe bit ceaselessly into the trees of Western Europe, providing timber for ships and homes and to provide constant fuel to warm a chilly continent. By the same acts, land was cleared for agriculture, more people and more sheep. Wolves lost their natural habitat and as a result we lost the wolf in Britain and large parts of mainland Europe. Discussions about the reintroduction of predator species and ecological re-balancing would take us too far off track, but there is a bitter irony in the fact that the dog played such a dominant role in the extermination of his ancestor.

In his novel *War and Peace* (1869), Leo Tolstoy gives an expansive account of a wolf hunt which, depending on the edition one is reading, runs for an entire eighteen pages. The Russian wolfhound is the Borzoi and there is no doubt that the working strains are impressively powerful dogs. However, no dog is as strong nor as adept at combat as the wolf. It is for this reason that wolves were seized by sighthounds rather than by scenthounds or mastiffs. Other dogs would not stand a chance in a straight fight with a wolf but sighthounds had a particular technique that gave them the edge. Scenthounds were used to locate a wolf but it was relays of Borzois that took over for the final chase. Being faster, they could catch a wolf on the run, before it turned to do battle, and seizing it by the neck from behind, hold it at a disadvantage until the huntsman arrived with his knife. Borzois were leashed in couples and then slipped to work co-operatively in the chase. In Tolstoy's account the scenting pack numbered fifty-four hounds and the initial number of Borzois setting out was seventy-six. These were then supplemented by an unspecified number of Borzois as more riders joined the hunt as it got under way. This was hunting on a very grand scale.

Whippets and Lurchers

In the popular imagination, Whippets and Lurchers are the dogs of the gypsy, the vagabond and the working man of the industrial north; poachers all, they needed dogs that would put food on the table. Culturally, Whippets are perceived to be as Northern as cloth caps and clogs. The Industrial Revolution peaked in the latter part of the nineteenth and early part of the twentieth centuries. In England it burgeoned most in the Northern towns. Endless rows of small, overcrowded terraced houses provided confined living quarters to the millions of workers who flocked to the smoke-blacked cities for employment. Wastelands adjacent to the factories were poor scrub but they harboured rabbits and these were a very welcome addition to a meagre diet. The Whippet was a small dog, requiring little upkeep and little space but it was a devilishly good rabbit hunter.

Although there is a superficial similarity in appearance, there is a significant difference between a Whippet and a miniature Greyhound, something that can be a source of confusion on today's show benches. Toy breeds of Greyhound can be seen commonly in medieval art, where they appear as ladies' companion dogs. They are their own distinct type and the Whippet is really a different beast. A good rabbiting Whippet needs to have some terrier blood. One might even describe a Whippet as a coursing terrier. Similarly, some terriers, such as the Manchester Terrier, which is the old Black-and-Tan Terrier (now extinct) with an infusion of Whippet blood, might be described equally well as either Whippet or terrier. When it comes to the dogs of the working-man, bred purely for function, with no rules to adhere to, rigid definitions are not appropriate.

In his *Illustrated Natural History* (1862) Reverend J.G. Wood opined: 'the skulking nocturnal poacher is aided in his midnight thefts by the silent and crafty lurcher'.

A pair of Whippets. Note the broad collars, which are necessary to prevent their narrow heads from slipping through. (I-Stock images: Liliya Kulianionak)

Entirely untroubled by breed standards and Kennel Club rules, the Lurcher remains the exclusive province of the countryman. He too is bred for function, not superficial form. Lurchers are the traditional accomplices of men who carry billy-clubs and wear large coats, stitched on the inside with secret pockets for nets and snares, rabbits and hares. However, in Tudor and early Stuart England, there was a notable exception to this stereotype. From the end of the medieval era, around 1500, up until the English Civil Wars was a period in which poaching thrived, not only as a means of vital sustenance for the poor man but also as a risky 'sport' for wealthier citizens. Roger Manning (*Hunters and Poachers*, Clarendon Press, 1993) estimates from local records that fifteen per cent of poachers in Sussex between 1500 and 1640 were from the gentry, noting that 'those from the landed and propertied classes – peers, gentlemen, merchants and yeomanry – organized themselves into poaching fraternities'.

This was a time when vast privately owned estates covered the majority of the country and when private landowners protected these resources aggressively. In places, criminal organization was on a commercial scale in order to supply the markets in the growing cities. Venison, taken by Lurchers, was a prime target. A poaching gang in the New Forest numbered some fifty men in 1620 and in Yorkshire in 1640 a gang of forty poachers was recorded as having killed more than seventy deer in Wortley Park. In 1619 a notorious band of poachers, the Russell Gang, were accused of poaching

John Wilkins with his Lurcher. Wilkins was a gamekeeper who wrote *The Autobiography of an English Gamekeeper* (1892). Although Lurchers are associated commonly with poachers, they were also valued by countrymen of all stamps. (Colin Waters / Alamy stock photo)

327 deer (red and fallow), 1,000 hares, 1,400 rabbits, 5,000 pheasants and 1,000 partridges. In order to harvest such prodigious numbers, the poacher's essential tools were nets and long-dogs.

'Long-dogs' and 'look-dogs' are regional synonyms but the word Lurcher, allied as it is to the word lurk, embodies the essential furtive qualities required of these dogs. They must be able to operate at some distance from their master, be stealthy and sharp-witted and as much on the lookout for the gamekeeper and his night-dog (usually an aggressive mastiff) as for pot-filling quarry. A Lurcher is always a crossbreed; most usually between a sighthound and a shepherding dog such as a Collie to give it that intelligent, independent working spirit. When larger sighthounds, such as the Scottish Deerhound, are recruited into the mix, then the Lurcher is equally capable of putting venison on the table as it is of filling the poacher's pockets with rabbits. Other hybrids include crossing with terrier lines, particularly the Bedlington Terrier. Lurchers are predominantly sighthounds, who hunt by coursing their quarry but they also have good noses and can track and find where the game is lying. Lurchers are truly wonderful dogs and valued by many law-abiding countrymen as well as by more stereotypically miscreant masters. Bred entirely according to function they are more likely to be the sort of long-dog that a medieval huntsman would recognize, compared to the filtered strains that have prevailed since the inception of pedigree breeds in the nineteenth century.

Chapter 9

Scenthounds

'Pour down, like a flood from the hills, brave boys. On the wings of the wind the merry Beagles fly'

—William Somerville (1675–1742)

The author with the New Forest Hounds (Photograph by Ian Potts)

In 1599, Queen Elizabeth I's erstwhile favourite, Robert Devereux, 2nd Earl of Essex, led an army into Ireland with the intent of stamping out a Catholic rebellion against English Protestant rule. His expedition force numbered 16,000 troops. He also took 800 bloodhounds to track and root out rebels in hiding. Essex made poor military decisions and the campaign was a failure. The extent to which this mighty legion of scenthounds were able to do their work is unrecorded but it was common for bloodhounds to be recruited for hunting human quarry in a military context. Robert the Bruce, King of Scotland (r. 1306-1329) was hunted by a 'sleuthhound' – the name for a Bloodhound, in medieval Scotland – whilst waging a guerrilla war in Galloway. He waded downstream to break the scent trail and then crossed to the other bank to escape. Sleuthhounds also tracked that other hero of Scottish independence, William Wallace. The hounds located Wallace and his followers in a small wood. An English detachment of 600 men, under Sir Gerald Heron, surrounded the wood and proceeded to flush them out. The ensuing Battle of Elcho Park (1297) saw Wallace's band greatly outnumbered but he somehow managed to slip the net and escape. Bloodhounds had much greater success when they captured the Duke of Monmouth after the Battle of Sedgemoor in 1689.

A Bloodhound tracking on the leash. This breed has a scent-tracking ability that is many times greater than any other. With his head supported by an immensely powerful neck, the Bloodhound's nose hovers at an optimal height above the ground. In this position he is receiving clues from both air scent and ground scent. (NSC Photography / Shutterstock.com)

Dr Caius, writing in 1576, used the word Bloodhound (rendering it into Latin as *sanguinarius* to give it scientific authority) in his groundbreaking taxonomy of sixteenth-century working dogs, *Of English Dogs*. The name has stuck, though the Scottish 'sleuthhound' is in my view a much better descriptor. It may be that he had in mind that this was the purest form – true blood – of hounds. Even the modern Bloodhound seems little changed in appearance from its lugubrious antecedents depicted in medieval art.

Scenting Ability

A Bloodhound's nose is considered to have 1,000 times greater capacity to distinguish scent than does that of a human. He is capable of detecting and following scent that is almost two weeks old, an ability that results from specialized anatomy. He has approximately 230,000,000 olfactory cells; 40 times more than a human. When an object is sniffed, chemical vapours linger in the mucus of the dog's nose where the olfactory cells detect them. These scent receptors then send a chemical signal to a part of the dog's brain called the olfactory bulb. Here an 'odour image' is created and remembered. For a Bloodhound an odour image carries more detail than does a photograph for the human eye. Not only does the Bloodhound have a greater area of smell receptors in its nose, it also has a greater capacity to receive and interpret those smells in the brain, with around forty times more brain cells connected to scent detection than in a human. When tracking human scent, whether fugitive or missing person, the dog can distinguish between one human and another, provided it has been give an identifying odour image. Any object touched by a person will receive traces of their scent identity and as they move about the world they leave a perfumed trail. This consists of a cocktail of breath, sweat vapour and skin rafts. Skin rafts are microscopic skin cells that carry distinguishing bacteria, sweat, enzymes, hormones and other clues. All humans shed around 40,000 rafts of skin per minute! Some rafts are so light that they are carried in the air, while others, heavier, drop to the ground. Either way they leave a trail – a trail that a Bloodhound sticks to 'doggedly'. Factors that affect scent include weather, wind direction, temperature, humidity, the type of vegetation and the lay of the land. Bloodhounds have a very high tracking drive and have been known to follow a trail for well over 100 miles. However faint the scent, they will filter out any distracting aromas and stay steadfastly on the trail of the target scent. Other types of hound can easily be led astray by recent trails that seem more enticing but a Bloodhound will stick to the trail it was tasked with at the outset.

In addition to its extraordinary nose, far more sensitive than that of any other breed, a Bloodhound's scent detection is helped by its pendulous ears. When hunting with its nose down, these brush close to the ground and waft aromas into the nasal catchment area. Sadly, modern breeders often develop the ears to be too long, a mocking caricature of the true type. Heavy jowls and abundant drool assist in trapping scent particles around the face, though the excessive wrinkle of many present day bloodhounds is yet another aspect of their morphology that has been grossly and unnecessarily exaggerated by show breeders. A Bloodhound needs to be able to carry its large, heavy head near the ground for the duration of a long hunt and consequently possesses a long and muscular neck.

Bloodhounds in the Medieval Hunt

During the Middle Ages, scenthounds almost identical to the modern Bloodhound were used at the beginning of a high-status deer hunt. They were called 'lymers' and the man who worked them was called either a 'lymner' or 'lymerer' ('lyam' is the medieval word for leash). Lymers were worked on-leash to establish the whereabouts of the desired quarry before the subsequent pursuit with the main pack of hounds. Edward, Second Duke of York, in his *The Master of Game* (1406) recommended that the huntsman make his own leashes, spun from horsehair, saying that they last longer than those made from hemp or wool. Images in art show these to be substantial cords, around 1 inch thick, and 10 feet in length. The lymerer keeps around 3 feet coiled over his forearm, so that he has sufficient play to let out line in response to a forward burst of scenting enthusiasm.

For knights and nobility, the hunt was a highly regulated, high-status event and the most prestigious of all hunts was to use hounds to pursue the hart – that is a red deer stag that is more than six years old. When hunting the hart, the hunters would gather in the forest at daybreak and have a formal breakfast. Chairs and tables, bedecked with fine table linens and laid with fine platters and goblets, were

A 'lymerer' from *Le Livre de la Chasse*. In the medieval hunt, the lymerer worked with a bloodhound-type dog on a leash. His mission was to locate the quarry for hunting, before handing over the task of the chase to the pack hounds. (Art Collection 3 / Alamy Stock Photo)

set out for the nobles, and lower ranking hunt servants feasted, picnic style, upon cloths spread on the ground. During this convivial repast the 'harbourer' presented the master of the hunt with a selection of deer droppings, known as 'fumes' or 'fewmets', having first marked the locations in the forest where he found them. The droppings would then be broken apart, examined and sniffed with great *savoir-faire*. According to the smell and consistency of the dung, those that knew could tell the age and sex of the animal, how recently he had passed that way and how strong or weak he was. They selected the biggest, strongest animal to hunt. Any stag less than six years old with ten tines to his antlers was considered a 'rascal' or a 'folly' and not worthy of 'noble' hunting. It was then the task of the lymer (leash-hound) to locate the chosen beast. The harbourer would show the lymerer where the fewmet was found; the hart's last known location. From there, based solely on the odour evidence of the fewmet, the hunt would begin. Lymers were kept on the leash at all times. Their job was to find the quarry not to chase it. A Bloodhound's sense of smell is so great that it can not only follow a cold trail but it can also pick out the scent of a particular deer to the exclusion of all the thousands of other scents on the forest floor. Once it was clear that the lymer had found a hot trail, the rest of the hunt would be summoned by horn; the lymer's work was done.

Of the many medieval dogs for which we still have names but no longer the dogs themselves, the Talbot seems the most likely candidate to have done the work of the lymer. Talbots appear in medieval art a great deal, not least of all because they are a dog that features widely in medieval heraldry. Depictions of them are unmistakably Bloodhound-like. Tradition (though often an unreliable witness) has it that Talbots were a strain of the French St Hubert Hound (also very Bloodhound-like) and brought to England by William the Conqueror in the eleventh century. A seventh-century abbot of St Hubert's monastery, where the breed originated, was called Taillebois and it may be that 'Taillebois' hounds' became known, over time, as 'Talbots'. Pure white was the favoured colour but Talbots also occurred with liver, tan, black–and–tan and even spotted coats. As late as 1615, Gervaise Markham wrote that the 'bigger and heavier Talbot dogs, whatever colour they have, are the best tracking dogs'.

However 'Bloodhound' had already become the more usual term by the time Dr Caius was writing in 1576. Countering a perception that Bloodhounds were overly slow, Caius considered that they applied 'agility and nimbleness, without tediousness' to their pursuit. Certainly there is enormous energy and enthusiasm when a Bloodhound is on a trail but tracking does not necessitate the same turn of speed required for hounds hunting a deer or a fox by pursuit. Nevertheless, Bloodhounds can be, and are, hunted off-leash, even as a pack by mounted followers. In recent decades, pack Bloodhounds have been used for the sport of 'hunting the clean boot' in which they pursue a human runner – a relative dawdler compared to a stag in full flight. However Bloodhounds, and their forbears the Talbot, were leash hounds. Tracking on a leash gave greater control and thoroughness to the process and enabled the human partner to remain more securely in contact with the hunt. It is a mode of canine sleuthing that continues to be used today in hunts for fugitives or in search–and–rescue situations.

Whilst conceding that there is nothing unduly plodding about a good Bloodhound, it is also true to say that there is far greater drive, speed and stamina among packs of staghound/foxhound types who offer a more thrilling, adrenaline-fuelled, dash across countryside in hot pursuit. For this reason, the medieval hunt used entirely different dogs for different stages of the hunt. Establishing the whereabouts of the chosen quarry was just the first stage.

A Complex Ritual

At its core the male hunting party was rooted in prehistory; a tight-knit brotherhood of men who work in strategic co-operation with each other, face danger together and come home with a triumphant kill. This was no less true for the medieval European nobility, despite the fact that many noblewomen also greatly enjoyed the thrill of the chase. It was the men, however, who performed the various designated roles in a formal courtly hunt. In many ways hunting prepared the nobility for war, their principal occupation. A medieval hunt was complex and it reinforced the interdependent hierarchies that are so necessary in battle. Everyone had his particular job to perform. If he failed in that, he let the rest of the team down. Hunting was training for war. It had danger, high adrenaline activity with the camaraderie of others, it conditioned essential muscles to long hours of hard riding and ultimately it was about killing living creatures – blood-letting, and everyday exposure to such things was considered to prepare a man for the rigour and the gore of battle. The bonds forged with such shared endeavours are the bonds that make a man risk his life for his friends on the battlefield. The hunting party and the war party shared the same social dynamic. During the Middle Ages, the two activities were further linked by the coded calls of the hunting horn.

Hunting Horns

The plaintiff wail of hunting horns is an integral part of the soundscape of hunting culture. This also includes the cries of the hounds; the snorting breaths of galloped horses; the creak and jingle of harness on restless steeds; the huntsman's shouts and the rolling thunder of a hundred horses flat out over hard ground on a frosty morning. In manuscript images of the medieval hunt, everyone involved with the hunt, from mounted nobles to hunt servants handling hounds on the ground, has a horn suspended over his shoulder. Most often, several people are represented as blowing their horns

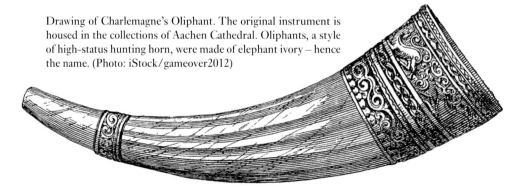

Drawing of Charlemagne's Oliphant. The original instrument is housed in the collections of Aachen Cathedral. Oliphants, a style of high-status hunting horn, were made of elephant ivory – hence the name. (Photo: iStock/gameover2012)

woutter et les fiotter et apsier de
tiestout quant quil pourra luy
z so wrlet ce est de boue litieu.

faut son deuoir.

Cy de aps deuise comet le bo wme doit chasser z prendre le cerf a force.

In this image the huntsmen carry standard medieval hunting horns, fashioned from ox-horn. They follow a pack of both smooth- and rough-coated scenthounds ('brachets'), supported by a sighthound from one of the relays. The hunt servants carry a stick known as an 'estortpoire'. No huntsmen are portrayed carrying whips at this early period. An estortpoire served as an extension to the arm, allowing the huntsman to tap a hound dithering on the wrong scent. It served to exaggerate gestures and to slap against one's boot to make a din of chivvying urgency. After the quarry had been butchered in the field, it was used to spike large cuts of meat, which were then carried home over the shoulder. Mounted hunters are also shown frequently carrying these sticks. Held in front of the face, it was invaluable for warding off the spindlier varieties of low-hanging branches as one galloped through the trees; heavy boughs required more careful avoidance! The deer hunt from a fifteenth-century illustrated version of *Le Livre de la Chasse* by Gaston Phoebus. Bibliotheque Nationale, Paris (World History Archive / Alamy Stock Photo)

French hunting horns. The characteristically extravagant curls of the French hunting horn didn't appear until around 1650, when their raucous rasping refrain first accompanied the hunts of the Sun King's court. It was a stirring sound that continues to echo in the French hunting field. The addition of stops to the 'French horn' has been a more recent addition, solely for the orchestral instrument. (Photo: iStock / carolecastelli)

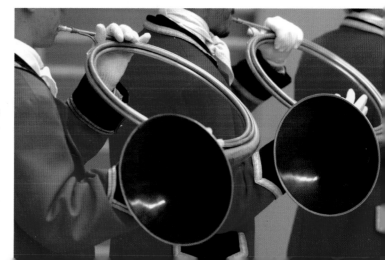

The huntsman of the Duke of Buccleuch Hunt gathers up his hounds by calling them in with his horn. By the eighteenth century, small, straight copper horns like this had become standard for huntsmen in Britain. (Photo: iStock / Chris Strickland)

simultaneously. It was a great hullabaloo and a constant, chattering communication. The types of horn we see in the work of Gaston Phoebus are large ox-horns. Horns of different sizes blew in different keys and this was one way you could distinguish between the horn signals of the lymerer and those of the master. Each stage of the hunt had specific musical signatures, so that everyone would know what was going on, whether they could see the pack or not. Whilst hunting a stag in vast expanses of a French forest offered limited visibility, every stage of the hunt's progress could be followed from these musical cues. At the Battle of Agincourt (1415), the commander of the English archers, Sir Thomas Erpingham, was said to call 'nestroque' as a signal for his men to shoot. It is probable that the word is a contraction of the phrase 'menée strike' and thus was an order to the trumpets to sound the 'menée'. The menée was a call to signal that the hounds were in full flight, in pursuit of their quarry. It doubtless sent a chilling message to the enemy as well as a clear order to the archers.

By the sixteenth century, modest coils of brass tubing allowed for a length of horn that would otherwise be unmanageable on horseback. However, towards the end of the seventeenth century a simpler, short, straight horn of copper or brass was introduced in England and this is the style that remains in use. Whilst the prime function of the horn is to communicate to the field of human followers, some calls were intended for the hounds. Horn blasts are classified as either 'signal' calls or as 'disappointed' calls. For instance two longish single notes, blown in quick succession is the signal for the hunt to set off. It is a rousing sound for both hounds and riders alike. In contrast, a long undulating wail on the horn, its mournful song repeated several times, is a 'disappointed' call to tell the hounds that the quarry, be it fox or deer, is not in a particular covert and that the hounds need to stop scenting it and return to the huntsman. This call is known as 'blowing out'. There seems an easy connection to the modern term 'blown it'. An altogether more exhilarating sound is the 'blowing away' call – a rapid series of pulsating double notes – denoting that a fox has been flushed from covert and is running in the open. This means that the chase is on and everyone is pell-mell in pursuit. So the next time you feel 'blown away' by something, you may appreciate a connection between your ecstatic delight and hounds in full cry. Among other signals and commands, perhaps the most important is a long and even note, which is repeated until there is the required response. It is the signal for the hounds to stop, whether they are chasing a scent they shouldn't, Foxhounds that have got on the trail of a deer, for instance, or, these days, if they are approaching a highway. It is invariably accompanied by loud cracks of the whip, both from the huntsman and his whippers-in, and by stern admonishments. The latter is known as 'rating' the hounds. Back in the days of Gaston Phoebus, when a lymerer blew his horn, it would have received answer and the forest would have echoed with resounding blasts. A military operation ensued. Lymerers were the scouts but there were many others, with different types of dog, who now had to play their part.

Running Hounds and Brachets

Once the hart had been located, relays of fast 'running hounds' were deployed to surround that area of forest. These 'running hounds' were sighthounds – Greyhound/Lurcher types – whose chase response is only triggered if they catch sight of the prey. They were only let slip if the hart passed within their direct field of view. Relays were a safety net to ensure that, if the hart evaded the main pack and was about to escape the area, the hunt could maintain contact. Whenever possible the relays were used to turn the hart back towards the main hunt. A hart is very fast and also has immense stamina. Running hounds (sighthounds) were also fast but of limited stamina. For this reason they were stationed in relays, staggered within the area, so that one could take over from the other. Each relay consisted of two running hounds, called a couple. They were coupled together with a single slip-leash that passed through a ring on the collar of each dog. A loop secured one end of the leash to the handler's forearm and the other end was held in his hand. By letting go, both hounds were instantly slipped and they worked together as a team to course the quarry. Several dozen relay couples might be placed in a 5-mile radius from where the quarry had been located and it could take several hours for all the relays to be in position. Once they were on station the horns cued the main hunting party that it was time to leave their breakfast and mount up.

It was now the turn of the main pack – twenty, thirty, forty hounds who would both track and give chase. Medieval texts refer to them as 'brachets' (sometimes: 'raches') and they are broadly equivalent to today's Foxhounds. They were scenthounds! Brachets hunted off-leash and in a pack, so that they could both spread out, scouring every feature of the land for a scent clue, and so that, collectively, they could hold a large animal at bay at the end of the chase. Fielding a pack with significant numbers offered no advantage in the chase but rather in the ability to fan out and hunt for scent – the greater the number of hounds, the wider net they could cast. These were the hounds the hunters followed on horseback; these were the hounds that delivered the intoxicating thrill of the chase. Their scenting abilities were good, though not as good as those of the lymer – any trail over an hour old was a challenge. Brachets were predominantly scenthounds but they would also pursue by sight if they caught a glimpse of the quarry. They could be quite fast but not as fast as the relays. However they had stamina and a powerful hunting instinct.

Like foxhounds, brachets were spectacular to watch spilling over hedge and ditch, running in full cry over undulating pastureland or running like a river through the obstacle course of an oak forest. A pack is like a single organism, one animal, albeit every single hound has its own distinctive personality and attributes. Like magnetic filings, the pack can divide and disconnect to negotiate the terrain or hunt for scent but it can just as quickly coalesce into a single, tightly packed, entity. Men, and women, rode for the excitement of the chase, for the galloping, the cries and the horns but they mostly rode to get a good view of the hounds at work. Medieval society had a deep appreciation for all the nuances of hound work. Those who followed a particular pack would know the names of individual hounds and observe the progress of their favourite with the ardour of a sport's fan. Depending on the weather – wet, dry, cold, warm, windy or still – the scent will be either strong or weak, lie on the ground or hang in the air. That affected whether the hounds could go fast or whether it was a slow scent to follow. Individual hounds showed greater initiative in different conditions.

English Foxhounds demonstrate athleticism, drive and vigour as they pour over an obstacle. Hounds like this are as close as we have to the medieval brachet. (Mick Atkins / Shutterstock.com)

A core characteristic of brachets and their descendant foxhounds, staghounds, harriers etcetera is that although they are supreme athletes, they are always slower in a straight dash than their intended quarry. Stamina was key and success was eventually achieved by exhausting the hunted animal. In this way the chase was prolonged for the benefit of those following on horseback. It was a fine balance between having hounds that were too slow and would lose contact and using sighthounds that could course and seize the prey in a matter of moments. The relays were there to turn a hind back to the chase, not as an efficiency in catching him. There were many other ways to take wild game; both trapping and shooting with a bow were common options during the Middle Ages. Pursuit with hounds was orchestrated and carefully gauged to create drama and excitement; the hounds were bred accordingly.

In a medieval hunt, once the brachets had run their quarry down, the mastiffs were sent for. These 'catch-and-hold' specialists held large and dangerous game until the huntsman could despatch it with his knife. They are the subjects of a separate chapter. However it was the brachets, highly affectionate dogs, which were ever the huntsman's favourites, and the brachets who were compensated first for their exertions. Gaston Phoebus advocated that at the end of the hunt, the hart should be butchered in the field and that the brachets should be rewarded immediately with bread and scraps dipped in its blood. He argued that associating these morsels with a successful hunt would encourage hounds to stick to a long chase and not give up to make their way back to the kennels in the hope of finding food. The act of dissecting the carcass was called the 'unmaking' and the reward given to the hounds was known, in French, as the *curée*, from which we derive the word 'quarry'. Occasionally the intestines might be fed to the hounds but, more often, they were given to the poorer folk who had assisted with the hunt. A deer's intestines were known as the 'umbles' and a favourite peasant dish was to eat umble pie. The lymer was rewarded separately. Mixing bread with the feed was a common practice and Phoebus even recommended feeding bread alone at the kennels, with the hounds only receiving meat as part of the curée.

Chases, Parks and Forests

Both Greek and Roman aristocrats liked nothing more than to spur their horses to follow packs of hounds in pursuit of game. Throughout the Middle Ages the European nobility shared this passion, almost to the point of obsession. Deer were considered the most prized quarry; be they red, fallow or roe. Hunting by pursuit for such a far-ranging, fleet-footed prey required vast tracts of suitable habitat and by the early medieval period this necessitated the establishment of hunting areas by law. As growing populations began to encroach on the wilderness, these protected hunting lands took various forms. A 'chase' (French '*chasser*' = 'to hunt') was a tract of land, recognized as the hunting domain of a particular person, such as the lord of the manor. Only he, or those operating at his invitation, could hunt deer in the chase. Poaching violations were prosecuted under common law. People were permitted to travel and go about their business in the chase, which might include some villages in its purlieu. Chases, which could cover a substantial area, were also managed to be conducive to a thriving deer population. Although their boundaries were well defined by place names, there were no physical barriers. By distinction a 'park' had enclosed boundaries; in places these were tall hedgerows, in others a wooden paling and, by the Tudor period high brick walls. Majestically antlered red deer still roam, rut and roar in the vast expanse of London's Richmond Park, first established during the reign of Elizabeth I. A few miles south, adjacent to Hampton Court Palace, is Bushy Park, created by her father Henry VIII. Grazing and browsing here are not only herds of indigenous red deer but also fallow deer, the type with the palmate antlers, whose summer coat is characteristically dappled with white spots. Fallow deer were first brought to Britain by the Romans.

Royal Forests, however, were by far the most significant and ubiquitous of these hunting reserves. By the twelfth century, nearly a third of England was designated as Royal Forest. Forests were unfenced but clearly defined areas, with hunting rights strictly protected for the king and for those nobles to whom he extended invitation. Medieval forests were not, as in the modern sense of the word, entirely wooded areas. Forests might contain large open areas of heathland and pastureland, as well as densely wooded zones. Villages and small towns were sometimes within the boundaries of the forest. Forests nevertheless also included extensive woodland; oaks, elms, birches and beeches, were the ideal habitat for deer. One of the most expansive medieval hunting grounds to survive in Britain is the New Forest in Hampshire. Since William the Conqueror first established it as a royal hunting preserve in 1079, there is no longer anything 'new' about it. Boasting many oaks of approximately 800 years in age and some yew trees calculated to be over 1,000 years old, it is a venerable and ancient landscape. Even when the Norman kings first ran their hounds through its dells and clearings, it was mantled with mature trees. The New Forest wasn't a new planting; it was simply new zoning. Forests were governed by Forest Law. In addition to restrictions on the taking of game, there were laws about what weapons could be carried (no sharp arrowheads for instance), the taking of timber and specific laws about dogs (See page 247). A force of Foresters, Agisters and Verderers patrolled the forest; they managed it and prosecuted its laws. Even today there is a Verderers' Court in the New Forest, which has the same legal status as a Magistrates' Court. For a fee, local inhabitants were allowed to bring their cattle, sheep, pigs and horses onto forest land for grazing. Agisters were responsible for administering these rights. To this day assorted farm animals forage, unconfined, in the New Forest. The area also teems with deer and other wildlife. Moreover New Forest Ponies, a semi-wild British native breed, continue to range freely. The grazing and browsing patterns of so many large herbivores have shaped the topography of the forest. Characterized by its pathways and broad clearings, it is a largely medieval landscape.

Although parks covered relatively small areas, chases and forests might cover vast tracts of land and 'the meet', where everyone assembled to begin the hunt, could

Free-roaming horses in the New Forest today. (Photograph by Ian Potts)

be many miles from the kennels. Although a medieval huntsman might ride with his hounds to a meet, there were limits; tired hounds are not an asset for a long chase. For more distant journeys, hounds were carried in horse-litters. Litters were basketwork containers with long wooden poles projecting fore and aft on each side. These poles were suspended by harness straps between two horses; one in front, one behind. Monarchs and high-status nobles were accustomed to take their own packs of hounds with them when hunting in other parts of the realm. For instance, a late thirteenth-century account shows that Thomas de Condovere and Robert le Sanser, royal huntsmen, were paid to transport sixty-six hounds and five lymers in a horse-litter.

Today, hounds are usually driven to the meet in a lorry. In the United Kingdom, hunting wild mammals with packs of hounds has been illegal since 2004. All packs either trail hunt or drag hunt. In a drag hunt, a scent is dragged behind a horse that sets off ahead of the field. In trail hunting, a trail, usually fox urine, is laid by relays of runners just a couple of hours ahead of the hunt. There is no longer a generation of hounds that has been exercised lawfully on live quarry. Despite this, following the hunt is arguably more popular now than ever. In part this may be because many more people find it acceptable to hunt without blood at the end of the chase and partly owing to an increasing affluence amongst a broader spectrum of society, who perhaps did not have the means to hunt in previous eras. Whatever the reason it has thus far been good news for the hounds. With so many paying enthusiasts, the packs are flourishing and these magnificent animals are, as yet, being preserved. Whatever your views about hunting, there can be no doubt that dogs like this will be lost to us entirely, if there were ever to be a ban on trail and drag hunting. It would be the equivalent of condemning a species

Classic English hunting scene from 1910. *Meet of the Quorn Hounds*, painted by Heywood Hard (The Picture Art Collection / Alamy Stock Photo)

to extinction. The type of hound most in use today is the English Foxhound. He is a descendant of the medieval brachet.

Foxhunting

Gaston Phoebus and other medieval authors discuss the hunting of foxes with hounds. They acknowledge that, for them, hunting this clever animal offered both a considerable challenge and enjoyable pastime. Foxes are inedible, however, which seems to be part of a reasoning that did not consider foxhunting on a par with the 'noble' hunt for the hart or hare, or with the pursuit of dangerous game like the wild boar. For medieval man, foxhunting was more of a secondary recreation. Nevertheless it coexisted with the more formalized hunting culture, increasing very gradually in popularity over time. The single greatest catalyst that propelled it to the cultural phenomenon that it became during the eighteenth and nineteenth centuries was sheep. Wool and its associated textile industries were the foundation of England's economic prosperity. From as early as the Tudor period enclosures began to pockmark the land. These were fenced and hedged fields that created restricted, and therefore easily manageable, grazing for sheep. It was more efficient than trying to round up one's sheep over vast commons areas. The trend for enclosures continued, reaching a peak in the eighteenth century. Bit by bit, England was parceled up into tidy fields; a cause of much civil unrest. However, the landowning classes won the day and the effect on foxhunting was two-fold. Firstly there was the perception that foxes presented a significant risk to flocks, especially young lambs. Present day surveys suggest there is only a marginal threat but to an eighteenth century squire, the fox was a predator that needed to be controlled. Secondly, and most significantly, the countryside became criss-crossed with hedges, fences and ditches, creating good galloping pastureland in between. Foxhunting now became synonymous with jumping and new styles of riding,

Foxhounds out with the Holderness Hunt in East Yorkshire. (Mick Atkins / Shutterstock.com)

George Washington riding to hounds. Washington led the life of an English country squire and was an ardent foxhunter. Foxhunting was adopted in America following the English style, though also with French influence. Note the huntsman with the French horn. Colour halftone of a John Dunsmore painting. (North Wind Picture Archives / Alamy Stock Photo)

such as the 'forward seat' developed to negotiate the changing landscape. Foxes have a reputation for cunning for good reason and foxhunts could last a very long time, to the satisfaction of those following on their foaming steeds. In 1739 the Charlton Hunt, one of the earliest foxhunting packs, hunted for ten hours, covering 57 miles.

Hunting Jargon and Hunting Folk

Many traditional activities are garnished with peculiar expressions. Hunting is no exception. In part this reinforces a sort of grammatical tribalism, like Cockney rhyming slang, where only those in the 'know' understand what is being talked about and outsiders are easily identified by linguistic slips. At worst it leads to a silly form of snobbery but at its best it is a treasure trove of poetry, evoking the special rank that hounds hold in the hearts of hunting men. For a start they are called 'hounds', never 'dogs' (other than to specify gender, as in 'dog-hound'). They 'wave their sterns' rather than wag their tails and they 'speak' or 'cry' rather than bark or howl. The metric for counting hounds is the 'couple'. So to say that a pack of 'ten and a half couple' was out that day, would be to indicate a pack of twenty-one hounds. Aitches are dropped, a pronunciation quirk that dates to the accent affectation of the day amongst eighteenth century rural squires. The 'master' is in overall charge and responsible for organizing everything, including the funding of the entire operation. Many modern hunts have joint masters who share this burden. One source of revenue is to have a crowd of people follow on horseback and spectate the hunt. They are called 'the field' and each pays a fee, known as a cap, for the privilege. The 'field-master' controls the field of followers and keeps them back, so as not to distract or endanger the hounds; not all those who ride to hounds are good riders and a hound is easily injured! Hunt staff, under full- or part-time employ of the hunt, include the 'huntsman' and the 'kennelman'. It is the huntsman who is in charge of the pack; indeed he is 'of the pack' – he is its leader. The huntsman is with the pack everyday, whether hunting or on hound exercise. Most hunts, depending on the size of their overall pack, hunt twice a week, each time with a different half of the pack. The entire pack goes on hound exercise on all other days. On a trail hunt, the scent is usually laid over a distance of 25 miles. Every time they lose the scent (and for running hounds the trail goes cold quite quickly, within the hour) the pack has to cast around to re-establish the line. Consequently hounds run between 40 and 50 miles in order to follow a 25-mile trail. In the days of hunting live quarry it could be an even longer outing. To be able to do that once a week requires a substantial level of fitness. Pack hounds are athletes and need regular dietary and exercise regimens.

   A professional kennelman assists the master, with particular responsibilities for feeding the hounds and cleaning the kennels. Both huntsman and kennelman know each hound by name and can also hear subtle differences in the way it uses its voice. The kennelman is also likely to act as a 'whipper-in'. Two whippers-in are a minimum requirement, in addition to the huntsman, to manage a lively pack out in the field. In the United Kingdom's House of Commons, and several other legislatures, the offices of Chief Whip, Deputy Whip and Assistant Whip are appointments made by both governing and opposition political parties. It is a term derived from the hunt. When a vote is 'whipped', a decision made by party leadership, their job is to corral their party members to vote according to party policy. On a hunt the whippers-in are sent ahead, on point, to be a safeguard against hounds going astray. On a trail hunt, for instance, if they see a fox or other animal ahead of the hounds, they will know to ride in, crack their whips and stop the hounds from following its scent. Similarly they are crucial today, to prevent hounds from running into traffic or from trespassing onto land they are not permitted on. Such preventative measures can only be achieved by the whippers-in being ahead of the pack. Whippers-in are also responsible for reuniting a pack that becomes split up. If they get it right, the whippers-in are not seen during a hunt. The shouts of the huntsman or his whippers-in are referred to as 'cheers' and several of these begin with the command 'ware'. It is a contraction of 'beware' and is an injunction to leave or watch out for. ' Ware wire' signals to riders that there is a wire fence they may not see; 'ware cur dogs' tells the pack not to be distracted by the sight or sound of domestic dogs, and 'ware haunch' commands them to come away from a trail of venison.

The Golden Thread

Whether a pack consists of ten, twenty or more couples of hounds, it has the potential to run riot and create havoc in the blink of an eye. In hunting, the word 'riot' is used to refer to a pack that has been distracted from the scent of the intended quarry and, of its own accord, has started to chase another animal; for instance if foxhounds suddenly pick up the scent of a stag and start chasing it. Havoc, incidentally, is of archaic military origin and, during the Middle Ages, it was a call to let an army loose to wreak indiscriminate destruction in enemy territory. An unruly mob of hounds can certainly do the same if passing through a farmer's land or property and, in this modern age, there is great danger to an out-of-control pack should it attempt to cross a road. There are no leashes on a pack of hounds, the hunting drive is very strong and the collective will of the pack even stronger. Control rests solely in the commanding presence of the huntsman, in his relationship to the pack and with three tools of communication: his voice, his horn and the crack of his whip. The extent to which an excited and excitable pack can be checked by a skilled huntsman and his assistant whippers-in is remarkable. Huntsmen refer to the connection they have with their pack as the invisible 'Golden Thread'.

Just Walking the Dog – An Adventure with fifty-six Hounds

Much as I love to ride, and galloping over the English countryside is always a thrill, I didn't feel that 'following' a hunt on horseback would give me much insight into the hounds themselves. I wanted to experience the 'Golden Thread'. With this in mind I contacted the New Forest Hounds and asked if I could accompany them on hound exercise. To my delight they said 'yes'. This would mean that I could spend a maximum amount of time in contact with the hounds and ask questions without disrupting others on a hunting day. My good friend and photographer Ian Potts and

The author takes fifty-six hounds for a walk in the New Forest. (Photograph by Ian Potts)

I checked in at the kennels of the New Forest Hounds late in the afternoon to make plans for the following day. We were greeted by Alan Brown (Joint Master), Michael Woodhouse (Huntsman) and Kieran Hawkes (Kennelman). I had met them all before seven years earlier, when I had filmed with the pack for a television documentary that included images of medieval hunting. It was very good to see them again, true countrymen with immense knowledge, quiet ways and a passion for their hounds.

Whilst the horn is an essential tool of communication on a hunt day, it is not required during hound exercise. Consequently there was no need to give me a crash course in its arcane skills, which was a relief all round. However I did spend some time under Kieran's watchful eye, learning to crack a hunting whip. Since at least the seventeenth century, whips took the place of the long wooden sticks (estortpoires) carried by medieval huntsmen. I should emphasize that a hunting whip is used mostly to open hunt gates. These have a latch system that can be readily lifted by a person on horseback, using the L-shaped hook, usually made from antler, at the base of a hunting whip. Whips can be an extension of the arm for gesturing. Just waving the stock, with the thong furled, is often enough to attract attention. Alternatively the whip can be flicked in vicinity of a hound, even, on rare occasions, to lightly touch but never to strike. That is not what hunting whips are for. Even loosely trailing the whip can help keep hounds from getting under horse's feet where they may get hurt. Cracking the whip is for serious moments, when the pack's attention is required urgently, such as to stop them running onto a busy road. A well-cracked whip is as loud as a gunshot and commands instant attention. Getting a good snap requires not trying too hard. One raises the whip to vertical above the head, no further, not behind. Then with a constant, fluid motion, one brings it down, turning the wrist to the side. So long as the stock is pointing directly away, the thong travels on that line away from the person. Kieran was a patient tutor and I had some success.

We then went to see the pups. There were six, ten weeks old and kept in a separate kennel. They swamped me with affection. Beagles and Basset Hounds make good pets. Bloodhounds, if you can stand the slobber, can also be housedogs. However, for some reason, Foxhounds do not take to domesticity. Not only are they seemingly impossible to house-train but also they just don't settle in a household. The exception to this generalized rule is when they are very young. After ten weeks, individuals are farmed out to 'puppy walkers', who keep them until they are around nine months old, when they are returned to the pack. How anyone could bear to give one back is beyond me but I have to confess to bias. Foxhound types are my favourite dogs; if they made happy pets (which the adult hounds do not), I would have one in a heartbeat. I'd already said hello to the main pack through the railings of their run but before we left, I had to enter the compound and greet them properly. Every hound has distinctly different markings and the hunt staff knows the name of each individual. Not only are they able to identify by sight but they can also tell them apart from the sound of the hound's voice. Hounds from the same litter, irrespective of gender, all have names beginning with same letter and there are usually five to six siblings in a litter; General, Gunpowder, Guinness, Gandolph, Gordon and Gadfly for instance. I wasn't able to

Ten-week-old Foxhound pups. They are about to be given to 'puppy walkers', who will look after them at home until, at around nine months, they are reintroduced to the pack. Adult Foxhounds do not settle in domestic households and unlike some other scenthounds, such as Bassets, Beagles and Bloodhounds, they do not make good pets. (Photograph by Ian Potts)

learn the name of over sixty hounds in a matter of moments but I learned a few and was astonished how quickly they would look up and then come to me when summoned. The pack is divided into two adjacent kennels, bitches and dogs, which have large outside compounds and I spent some time introducing myself to both packs.

The principal breeding line still traces back to Mr Gilbert's Hounds, a foxhound pack that was established in the New Forest in 1781. There have, nevertheless, been frequent outcrosses with hounds from other packs to ensure a healthy pack and militate against inbreeding. Today's New Forest Hounds have a mix of smooth- and wire-coated hounds, owing to an outcross with a wire-coated Welsh foxhound in the 1960s. Performance, not conforming looks is the criterion. Fortunately vintage hunting packs throughout Europe have been immune from the breeding regulation of kennel clubs and breed societies. By adhering to their own breeding traditions, they have succeeded in breeding hounds of great vitality and functionality. Although many of these packs, especially in France, date back to the Middle Ages with unbroken continuity, the dogs themselves look very different to the dogs in medieval art that are performing the

The author meets the dog-hound pack in the run of their kennel, whilst a row of curious females looks on from the adjacent compound. There is a connecting door between the two packs. (Photograph by Ian Potts)

same function. It is yet another reminder that the dogs we have today are not the same as they once were and that the dogs of yesteryear have, in many cases, disappeared altogether. Even so an outing with this handsome pack of hounds was as close as I was ever going to get to an encounter with medieval brachets.

The following morning, Ian and I arrived at the kennels early; all was quiet. In fact it was eerily quiet. I had expected an excited din from the hounds but even our human chatter did not provoke a single interested bark. Hounds milled around silently. Breakfast was long since over; the pack consumes an entire horse per day. These are not killed specifically for the hounds but are old or injured horses that have had to be put down for humane reasons or, tragically in the New Forest, from road accidents with the wild native ponies. This one meal of the day, before exercise, is their only feed, aside from biscuits. Hounds are creatures of habit and a huntsman has no requirement for a timepiece. At 6.45 am, without any human signal, the hounds began their cries. First one, then a couple more, some tentative rejoinders and within seconds a symphonic ululation of howling hounds built to a crescendo as the entire pack enlisted in the chorus. It was their signal for us humans to hurry about our business. It was time for their daily walk! First an adjoining gate between the dog pack and the bitch pack was opened. The New Forest Hounds hunt as a mixed pack. Much excitement ensued as the two packs fused into one. A few hounds were kept back – bitches on heat and a few older hounds, who now only exercised once or twice a week. In all I was to take charge of twenty-eight couple – that is fifty-six individual hounds!

We were at the beginning of the season and for the first three weeks the juveniles learn the ropes by being attached to a senior. Hounds are not taken hunting until they are between eighteen months and two-years-old. For the first season they are taken on morning exercise only. The couples used today consist of broad leather collars attached to each other by a short metal chain. It was easy enough to fasten the collar onto the older hound but, whilst holding on to that one and trying to grab the wriggling fidget of an excited teenager, buckling on the second collar was more of a challenge. Clamping a hound between one's knees helped but it was difficult to remain steady on one's feet. The entire kennel compound was in commotion, as eager hounds scrambled over each other, some pushing through the swarm like eddying tides that threatened to take my legs away. I was swimming in a sea of hounds. Of course Michael and Kieran had the measure of it all and together we managed to weather the hound-storm and get the appropriate pairs coupled. Then the gate was opened and the choppy sea turned into a torrent as the dam broke and a seemingly endless stream of hounds surged into the open. Michael and Kieran were on point to steer them but this was a daily routine and they knew where they were going. First they cascaded through the yard and crowded eagerly by a gate that led to a small field. I opened it and, once through, they dashed around emptying themselves, to be ready for their exertions.

From the field we emerged into the enchantment of the woodland forest. The New Forest is an exceptionally attractive and timelessly tranquil place. A yellow early-morning sun shot shards of dappled light through the oaks. A half dozen New Forest

For the first few weeks of the season, young hounds going out with the pack for the first time are coupled to an old-timer. The older dog shows them the ropes and prevents them from running off into danger. The author negotiates an ebullient scrum of hounds, as he attempts to get a pair coupled. To the centre-right of the image are two hounds that have already been coupled. (Photograph by Ian Potts)

A river of hounds flowing from the kennel with infectious enthusiasm. (Photograph by Ian Potts)

ponies grazed in a clearing to our right. They were only very slightly perturbed by the scurry and hurry of fifty-six hounds, who had now spread out in all directions in search of a scent that might lead to a chase. The ponies trotted off into the shadows. To see so many hounds, busying about their work is a sight and a feeling I will never forget. That it was taking place in such ancient and Arcadian beauty was a prize beyond my dreams. At first Michael took the lead and I walked a little behind him, observing keenly his every action. In order to keep the pack calm, there was minimum chatter and voice commands. There are no horns on exercise. The quieter the handling can be then the more swiftly responsive the pack can be when needed. On exercise, the whippers-in either follow and make sure no hounds wander off at the back, or get up in front to be on point if there is a major road ahead. We had the problem that as soon as my photographer friend, Ian, went on ahead in order to position himself for a shot, the hounds wanted to give chase and follow him, so Kieran went up with him to send them back. We walked through woodland and pasture and then, to my very great surprise, Michael offered me the chance to take charge of the pack. He and Kieran fell way back, almost out of sight and, suddenly I was in front with fifty-six rambunctious hounds under my command. A lot could have gone wrong.

I thought of a passage in T.H. White's 1938 novel *The Sword in the Stone* – a fictional account of the legendary King Arthur's childhood, in which Wart, the future King Arthur, spends much of his time with the dog boy and the hounds in the kennel. In describing the dog boy's manner with the hounds White wrote: 'He talked to them, not in baby-talk like a maiden lady, but correctly in their own growls and barks'. I tried to emulate that. In the absence of knowing every individual's name, my only commands were a gruff 'hold–up', 'wait' and 'get back'. These joined with various growls, 'Oi!' and a sort of 'tssssst' noise that I make with my horse, when working him at liberty. All seemed to work well enough. Just occasionally I gave a gentle flick with the whip ahead of some boisterous rogues wanting to overtake on the outside. It was an exhilarating and fulfilling experience. Although outwardly calm I was on extreme high alert and every sense was sharp and present. It was the first week of November and, though late that year, autumn was in full swing. Above me was a picturesque canopy of gold, brown, green and yellow and beneath my feet a soft carpet of freshly fallen leaves in the same hues. I drank it all in but was not distracted by it; my entire focus was on the hounds. In addition to making our way along woodland paths, we also walked through large fields of open pasture. Here we let the hounds run around, practicing their scouting and scenting. A pocketful of biscuits was a great boon. I could call to the hounds, throw a single biscuit in the air to land in the long grass, and watch them seek it out. Surprisingly they did not have the snarling jealousy that one might expect. It was all good–natured play and many biscuits were thrown.

On the way back, when taking the hounds down a narrow hedge–lined lane, which the hounds crammed from bank to bank, we were confronted with a motor vehicle that needed to get by. Michael stepped to the front and bellowed a sharp 'get over!' With a prompt obedience that would be the envy of many a dog-walker having a single canine in their charge, the entire pack immediately strung out on the narrow strip of verge, allowing the car to pass. Thereafter I led them back into woodland via a clearing, where an old farm building stood. To the far side of the little ramshackle barn was another herd of wild ponies. Once again the hounds took no interest in them and the ponies were unfussed as I led the pack on a circumnavigation of the building. From this spot of glinting sunlight, diffused by the evaporating morning dew and by the light-pierced golden leaves of a majestic beech tree, I piloted the pack though a darker patch of forest. It was densely overgrown with the light barely peeping through. This was the home strait leading to the field behind the kennels.

Calling in the hounds and gathering them for a moment's pause in a clearing. New Forest ponies graze obliviously in the background, behind the trees. (Photograph by Ian Potts)

The hounds were released from my command and had one last pottering about as they headed for the farm gate.

Once back at the kennels, the entire pack was corralled in the run to the dog-hound kennel. They had lost none of their infectious excitement and all mixed together,

Promoted briefly to pack-leader, the author attempts to hold the hounds in check. Whilst distracted by those seeking to get ahead on his left, renegades seize their opportunity to his right. However they only managed to sneak a few paces before a brusque verbal remonstrance had them returning to file. (Photograph by Ian Potts)

Hounds running freely in a field. While the independently minded were content to explore and play, those with a nose for biscuits sought out the author's pockets. (Photograph by Ian Potts)

barging and trampling over each other without offence. There may have been some nascent courtships developing but I couldn't tell. It just seemed like a very genial and sociable pack. We uncoupled the students from their masters. While the hounds were hobnobbing, Kieran hosed and swept the run to the female quarters. All change and the entire pack were sent through the partition gate to associate on the female side, while the male barracks were cleaned. Once that was done, Kieran again opened the gate between the two runs and called 'dog 'ounds!' repeatedly. Without any human contact, the males separated from the females and passed obediently through the partition gate into their bachelor compound. A few Casanovas were more reluctant than others to leave the ladies but Kieran just looked at them and growled 'dog 'ounds' very determinedly and the offenders slunk reluctantly to his bidding. The Golden Thread pulls two ways. I now felt part of the pack. This was now 'my pack' – my tribe. I felt it not as ownership but rather in the sense of belonging. I recalled another passage in *The Sword in The Stone*, where White describes how the dog boy would sleep in the kennel with the pack. He went on to quote the Greek historian Arrian regarding the care of hounds, stating that it was:

> Best of all if they can sleep with a person because it makes them more human and because they rejoice in the company of human beings: also if they have had a restless night or been internally upset, you will know it and not use them to hunt next day.

The kennel bed, where all the hounds huddle together to sleep. The author was swamped when he paid a visit. Well sheltered and raised from the floor, out of the way of draughts, the bed is plumped with fresh straw bedding each day. (Photograph by Ian Potts)

I feared that an overnight stay would have been too eccentric a request. However I did get into each of the kennels. It had been a dream since I first read T.H. White at the age of ten. Each kennel comprised a large, stone-built shelter with plenty of room for a human to stand upright and walk around in. To protect the hounds from drafts, there was a raised bed, also from stone, elevated around 3-feet from the ground. It measured around 12 feet long by 5 feet wide. I jumped up and sat in the far corner. Instantly I was covered in a snug doggie duvet, to the extent that I disappeared from view. What welcoming fellows these were. I subsequently received the same reception in the female quarters. What a day! It was not yet 10 o'clock in the morning but it was time to go. We bade each other 'Good Night'. When parting after being with the hounds, it is the custom in hunting circles to say goodnight whatever time of day it is. After all, when one's time with the hounds is over, what else of any significance could a day hold?

Beagles, Bassets, Harriers and Otterhounds

Foxhounds are only one of several breeds of scenthound and even these vary in form from pack to pack. All scenthounds derive ultimately from a distant Bloodhound-type ancestor. Over time different forms have been bred according to the speed and size of the intended quarry and the terrain over which they hunt it. Staghounds and Buckhounds, a distinction of little difference, are no more than slightly taller versions of the average Foxhound. Otterhounds, on the other hand, have an unmistakably different appearance. They were bred to work muddy banks and streams and they were capable of detecting an otter's scent floating downstream on the surface of the water as well as on land. As one might expect, they have thick, oily wire coats to deal with water and mud and they have webbed feet. Otterhounds are predominantly a cross between foxhounds and coarse-coated water spaniels. There is also much of the French Griffon about them though their doleful eyes hint strongly at their bloodhound heritage; an essential lineage for such refined noses. During the Middle Ages it was not only those who owned rivers in which trout and salmon flourished who considered the otter a predator in need of control, it was also those who kept fishponds. Freshwater fish were a central part of the medieval diet and fishponds, or 'stews' as they were known, were stocked to the gunwales with fish, ready for consumption. Stews existed in monastery and manor house grounds alike and an otter raid could cause considerable depletion. There are records of King John (r. 1199-1215) hunting otter and his grandson Edward I (r. 1272-1307) appointed the aptly named John le Oterhunte as huntsman of the royal pack. Queen Elizabeth I (r. 1558-1603) was appointed the first female Master of the Royal Otterhound Pack, though her role may have been purely titular.

Otter hunting was banned in the United Kingdom in 1978 because otters had become unduly scarce, owing to the effects of pesticides running off into the river systems. Prior to the official ban most Otterhound packs had switched voluntarily to a different quarry – the mink. This invasive, non-native species of riparian mammal

An Otterhound scenting over water. (Tierfotoagentur / Alamy Stock Photo)

from North America was flourishing in significant numbers at the time. By making the change, it was economically feasible to maintain Otterhound packs. However, mink hunting with dogs was made illegal by the 2004 ban. The effect on the Otterhound has been catastrophic and the Kennel Club records them as a 'vulnerable native breed'. At the present time there is only one pack of true Otterhounds in Britain. It is in Wales and financed by an individual, who has no need to rely on hunt subscriptions. Only a very few are kept as individual pets. Estimates account for around six hundred Otterhounds as a total world population. Most of these are in North America, where they are used to hunt coypu.

Harriers were bred for hunting hares. It may seem counter-intuitive but, although the hare is the fastest of Britain's quarry species, it required slower-paced methodical hunters to track it. Three styles of hound were bred specifically for hare hunting – the Harrier, the Beagle and the Basset Hound. Obviously all have a nose for hare. Harriers differ only slightly from Foxhounds in that they are marginally shorter. Traditionally they are followed either on horseback or on foot. Although slower than Foxhounds, Harriers are pretty brisk and, for the packs followed on foot, it requires the vigour of a good cross-country runner to keep up with them (hence numerous running clubs are called 'harriers' and we have the colloquialism to go 'haring after something').

A fine example of correctly proportioned working Basset Hounds, with Norman Matthews, Master of the Woolaston Bassets. These are healthy, fit and agile hounds, quite different to so many that have been bred for the show bench and for an ill-informed public wanting a caricature. (Photograph by Mark Marsden)

Less strenuously athletic, though requiring great stamina, were the slower foot-packs of hare hounds – the Beagles and the Basset Hounds.

Basset Hounds are, or at least were, miniaturized Bloodhound types. I say 'were' because the tendency to breed for over-exaggerated features to please the cosmetic fancies of the pet owner (longer backs, shorter legs, sadder eyes, droopier ears, wrinkled skin and crooked legs with splayed-out feet) has distorted the breed considerably. Technically speaking, it is not a quality in a working breed that it may inadvertently step on its own ears whilst about its business! Amongst hound fanciers, the prefix 'basset' simply denotes that a strain of dogs has been selectively bred to be a more compact version of the parent breed. Only custom prevents us from referring to Whippets as 'Basset Greyhounds' and Pomeranians as 'Basset Chows'. The English Basset Hound is, to all intents and purposes, the Basset Bloodhound. There are several other varieties in France, such as the Basset Artesien-Normand, the Basset Bleu de Gascogne, the Basset Fauve de Bretagne and The Basset Griffon Vendeen. Mechanically, a basset's shorter legs places its nose closer to the ground and slows its pace, advantages both for the serious business of sleuthing the labyrinthine scent trails of the hare and allowing huntsmen on foot to stay with the pack. Properly conformed working Bassets, as distinct from many of the more deformed show types,

Compare this pair of Basset Hounds to the working specimens in the previous photograph. These are by no means the worst examples but their ears are overly long and their torso almost scrapes the ground. They have been bred for comical looks not to be the vigorous hounds they ought to be. (Trybex/Shutterstock.com)

The Reverend Philip Honeywood and his Beagles. Considered at the time to be the most perfect pack in England, these Beagles were sold to the Prince Consort. Standing around 14 inches tall, they were famously fast. Aquatint by B.J. Harris after Harry Hall (1814-1882). (Image courtesy of Reindeer Antiques, London)

can nonetheless be relatively zippy when in pursuit. Such spry energy amongst the working packs has only been made possible by frequent outcrosses, to other hounds such as harriers. The hallmark of the Bassets' hunting style is that they are methodical and painstaking, gleaning clues from both air scent and ground scent. This sleuthing excellence makes them especially suitable for hunting hare, a creature that doubles and re-doubles its tracks. Since the 2004 hunting with dogs ban, sufficiently intriguing trails have to be laid to keep them stimulated.

Standing somewhere in between the Harrier and Basset Hound is the Beagle, a word deriving from the Gaelic '*beg*' meaning small. This beautifully proportioned hound is a bantamized version of the Foxhound, with an especially expressive and slightly rounded face. The Reverend W.B. Daniel (*Rural Sports*, 1801) writes of them:

> Of this diminutive and lavish kind the late Colonel Hardy had once a Cry, consisting of ten or eleven couple, which were always carried to and from the field in a large pair of panniers, slung across a horse; small as they were they would keep a hare at all her shifts to escape them.

Beagles have an irrepressible enthusiasm and a deep well of stamina. They hunt equally well over plough or downland pasture. However, when there are crops or the grass is tall, these pint-pot powerhouses can disappear from view. Like the Basset Hound, the

Beagles are hunted on foot. These lively hounds seem to be enjoying themselves immensely. (Paul Wishart / Shutterstock.com)

Beagle has a white tip to its stern (tail) and, like the Basset, it carries it vertically, waving above the vegetation to the followers behind. In selecting for size, a compromise has to be made between hounds that can travel adequately well over the local terrain and not having hounds that are so fast that foot-followers cannot keep up. So the Beagles for hedge-and-ditch grass country will be smaller than those demanded by a stone-wall and heather topography. Although bred for the purpose of hunting in packs Beagles and, to a slightly lesser extent, Basset Hounds make excellent and affectionate solitary pets. By contrast, Foxhounds can rarely be domesticated successfully. Several types of American scenthound, on the other hand, are more usually lone operators.

Ain't Nothin' But a Hound Dog

In North America foxhunting, very much on the English model, remains popular, especially on the East Coast. George Washington imported hounds from both England and France. However, in addition to foxes, America also has an entirely different range

Sparky, a Black Mouth Cur. This type of scenthound, from the United States, worked traditionally as a treeing hound. In this instance, Sparky, from a rescue shelter, lived with the author and his wife as a gentle companion. (Photograph by the author)

of large fauna to that of Europe. Unique American scenthound types were developed to hunt some of these other species. They are known as 'treeing-hounds'. A treeing-hound, often working solo, finds, tracks and chases its quarry until it takes to a tree for refuge. Treeing-hounds then stand on their hind legs, with their front paws on the tree and give cry. Steadfast in this position, snapping and snarling, they hold the animal at bay until the huntsman can arrive to shoot it. Some treeing-hounds are more specialist than others. There are several that quest almost exclusively for raccoons, such as the Black-and-Tan Coonhound, the Bluetick Coonhound, the Redtick Coonhound, the Redbone Coonhound and the Treeing Walker Coonhound. Treeing-hounds predominate in the South, in areas such as Louisiana, where the influence of French hounds in their ancestry is evident.

The exotically named Catahoula Leopard Dog is also a treeing hound and one with some versatility. It hunts raccoon, black bear, bobcat, cougar, squirrel, and any other tree-minded game. Leopards are not on the list; the reference in its name is to its distinctively spotted markings. Dangerous game is a feature of the North American hunting scene and obviously going after bears and cougars required a dog with significant muscle and grit, as well as scenting ability. Mastiff blood was introduced into some hound strains to establish these qualities. A good example of a hound with some mastiff blood is the Black Mouth Cur. This was a treeing hound that could intimidate the larger more aggressive species including bear, though it was also a general herding and farm dog, popular in the Southern States. We owned one; his name was Sparky. My wife had rescued him from the pound as a puppy, with no idea what breed he was. He grew into a very big dog! However, despite his heritage as a fearless hunter, he was the gentlest, sweetest and most devoted dog you could imagine. For us he was a much-loved housedog, for my Labrador Crockett he was a best friend, and for everyone he met Sparky appeared elegant, majestic and noble. Black Mouth Curs, for all their muscular virility, are known to be very sensitive and Sparky was no exception. He required gentleness, not brusque commands, and in return he repaid it with profoundly faithful affection. We miss him a great deal.

Chapter 10

Mastiffs

That island of England breeds very valiant creatures; their mastiffs are of unmatchable courage.

— Shakespeare: *Henry V*, Act III, Scene 7

The author with two fistfuls of English Mastiffs. (Photograph by Ben Mole)

Holding Mastiffs

Mastiffs and alaunts served the same basic function. They were hunting dogs, of considerable strength and brawn, used to seize large and dangerous game, such as aurochs, bison, bears and boars, lions, leopards and stags, to hang onto it and to bring it down, holding it until the huntsman could arrive to kill it. They can be referred to generically as 'catch-and-hold dogs'; also as, 'catch dogs', 'capture dogs', 'holding dogs', 'seizing dogs', 'pinning dogs' or 'grip dogs'. Their specialities include power and pugnacity, an exceptionally strong bite, reckless courage and unrelenting tenacity. The distinctions between mastiffs and alaunts can blur, as both language and dog morphologies have evolved over the centuries. In general alaunts, often categorized separately as 'running mastiffs', tend to be a little bit lighter, a lot faster and have a longer muzzle. 'Holding mastiffs', on the other hand, are generally bigger, slower and have a distinctively broad mouth. A broad mouth enables a greater spread to the bite, which can assist in prolonged holding. This is augmented by a slightly upturned nose and jaw, which enables the dog to breathe whilst continuing to hold. It is a cruel irony that this functional aspect of the type's anatomy has been turned against it in caricature breeding, smashing the face and creating undershot jaws, so that some animals today can barely breath in any circumstances. Mastiffs have always been brachycephalic dogs, in the sense that they have a shorter, wider muzzle and slightly rounder head. It defines them. However, historical types did not have the appallingly overemphasized flat faces that have so disabled some mastiff breeds for the past century or so. These have been a subsequent imposition by humankind.

Holding mastiffs couldn't keep up with the faster scenthounds (the brachets) at the head of the chase but once the main pack of hounds had its dangerous quarry at bay, be it stag, boar or bear, then they could hold it there for a few minutes until the mastiffs could be brought up. Once slipped from their leashes, these were the attack dogs that leapt fearlessly into the fray, heedless of antlers, tusks, teeth, or claws, to subdue and pin down

The Perro de Presa Canario. This formidable mastiff has been reconstructed in recent decades; however, it is strikingly similar to medieval and Renaissance types. (Photo:iStock. Credit Eponaleah)

the hapless quarry until the huntsmen arrived to dispatch it with his hunting sword, known variously as a 'hanger' or a 'cutto'. Being first in the fray meant that mastiffs were highly vulnerable to being wounded by dangerous quarry and there were a considerable number of casualties. Among the laws of the Welsh King Hywel Dda (r. 942 -948) is one concerning the statutory value of needles. It differentiated between the needles of the queen's serving women and of physicians and 'the needle of the chief huntsman for sewing the torn dogs'. These all had a legal value of 4 pence, considerably more than the 1 pence allotted to the needle of 'any other skillful woman'. The forestry laws of King Cnut (r. 1018-35) required all mastiffs (and Greyhounds) belonging to anyone other than the King or his nobles, to be checked by the tax collector. The requirement was for the dog to be 'lawed' – made lawful. This entailed the middle toe of the front feet to be amputated, so that the dogs could not run fast enough to catch the King's deer.

Bandogs

Dr Caius offered us a comprehensive, albeit somewhat unflattering, description of mastiffs in the Elizabethan era.

> This kinde of Dogge called a mastyve or Bandogge is vaste, huge, stubborne, ougly, and eager, of hevy and burthenous body, and therefore but of little swiftness, terrible, and frightful to beholde.
>
> *(Of English Dogs, 1576)*

The etymology of the word 'mastiff' is uncertain, though it is generally thought to indicate a dog of mixed breeding, whilst conforming to a certain stocky, broad-mouthed type. In medieval literature the alternative nomenclature of 'bandogge' was in far greater common use. A 'ban(d)-dog' is one secured by a band or leash. Although affectionate to their masters, these were deliberately bred as aggressive dogs and they needed to be restrained in the hunting field, lest they attack the scenting hounds or the Greyhounds. Mastiffs were only unleashed when brought up to face down their quarry.

Seizing large and dangerous game was only one of several employments for broad-mouthed dogs. They were equally adept at apprehending human marauders. Bandogges, chained in their master's yard, were prized as watch-dogs. Caius acclaims their role as guardians, not only of 'farmer's houses, but also merchaunts maisons, wherein great wealth, riches, substaince and costly stuffe is reposed'.

The necessity, in earlier ages, for fierce dogs to undertake home protection duty or to accompany travellers, cannot be underestimated. Albertus Magnus (c.1193-1280), the Bishop of Cologne whose prolific writings included a zoological survey, *On Animals*, described the training of a guard dog. He wrote that it 'should be encouraged to attack a man covered in advance with thick hide, which the dog cannot tear. The man should fall and let the dog bite him'.

A signature feature of broad-mouthed dogs is that their jaws close with the sustained pressure of a vice. It is a bite that grips and holds, rather than one intended to tear the victim apart; be that a felon or the hunter's quarry. Whilst the bite of an adult wolf has the capacity to reach 1200 psi and is significantly more powerful than any dog, the broad-mouthed breeds generally have a stronger bite than those with longer muzzles. The bite of a German Shepherd Dog is around 238 psi, whereas a Rottweiler can manage around 328 psi. Topping the scale is the Boerboel, a broad-mouthed homestead guardian from South Africa. These puissant dogs can grip at 800psi! The bite of a strong male human is a trifling 120psi.

Dr Caius lists sundry other occupations suited to the mastiff, together with their appropriate colloquial names. There is 'The Messenger' who,

> At his master's voice and commandment, he carrieth letters from place to place, wrapped up cunningly in his leather collar, fastened thereto, or sowed close therein.

He goes on to explain that the mastiff's suitability for this mission is not only that he would be good in a scrap if set upon but that he is also smart enough, and quick

This Cane Corso, brings vividly to life the words of the eighteenth-century poet John Gay:

A Mastiff pass'd inflam'd with ire
His eyeballs shot indignant fire (*Fables*, 1727)
(Photo:iStock. Credit Linas Toleikis)

enough, to make a run for it if the odds were against him. Mastiffs, by virtue of their strength, were also used for drudgery. Caius records that the 'greater and the weightier sort' were used to draw water from wells by turning a wheel. As we have seen in the chapter on draught dogs, mastiff types were the most common between the shafts of a cart. Dr Caius informs us further that the mastiff was sometimes known as 'the butcher's dog', a role assumed most famously by the Rottweiler (a broad-mouthed mastiff) which I also touched upon in the draught dogs chapter. Some mastiffs, the good doctor goes on to tell us, were called 'tyncker's curres' because they accompanied tinkers (itinerant tradesmen, who repaired pots, pans and other metal household effects). The dogs wore large panniers in which they carried all the tinker's tools and materials. In addition to functioning as beasts of burden, these mastiffs were also personal guard dogs. Travelling alone, often in remote areas, with their goods and their takings, tinkers were vulnerable to thieves. Caius observed that these dogs 'love their masters liberally. And hate strangers despightfully'.

In later centuries such dogs became known as 'night dogs' and were the companions of gamekeepers as they patrolled their isolated country beats after dark, on the lookout for poachers. Not only would the night dog be expected to seize and hold a potentially violent and armed marauder but it might also be required to first tackle the poacher's dog. It was a fine balance for breeders to produce dogs for this work that had the necessary assertiveness and determination, ferocity even, without the dogs having an unpredictable temperament and unmanageable aggression that could not be controlled by their master. Night dogs had a deservedly fearsome reputation. The English Bull Mastiff, a brawny and bellicose behemoth, was bred especially to be a gamekeeper's night dog. In his book *Dog Breaking* (1909), General Hutchinson concluded that a fierce looking night dog,

> was the terror of all the idle boys in the neighbourhood. Every lad felt assured that, if once 'Growler' were put upon his footsteps, to a certainty he would be overtaken, knocked down and detained until the arrival of the keeper.

The Bull-Biters
Gripping and pinning dogs were also recruited for the abhorrent business of bull-baiting, as well as for managing bulls around both farm and market, and for the equally repellent activity of bear-baiting. Deriving from Ancient Rome's obscene animal spectacles, bull- and bear-baiting remained widely popular public attractions throughout Europe until the nineteenth century. In Britain, these contests were outlawed by The Cruelty to Animals Act of 1835, although sadly the law was little regarded at first. The last recorded bull-baiting in Britain was in West Derby in 1853. In many instances the event took place in a town square or village green, although a number of cities had elaborate, purpose built bullrings and bear pits, where these cruelties took place. In either circumstance, the bull was tethered to an iron ring that swiveled around a central iron stake. He could move around freely on a long rope but was unable to break free and run amok in the crowd. A number of dogs were set to bite

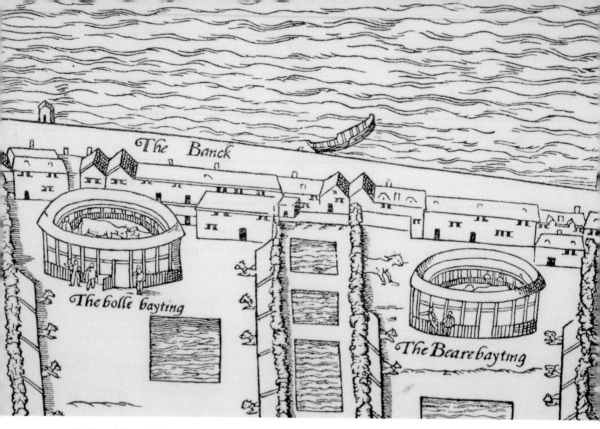

Bull- and bear-baiting arenas shown on a map of London from 1560. They are situated on the South Bank, close to where Shakespeare's Globe Theatre was erected in 1599. The architecture of both theatre and animal circuses appears remarkably similar. These depraved spectacles were a leading form of entertainment at the time. Note the extensive kennels in the surrounding area. (Wikicommons)

and hang onto the enraged bull, while the poor tortured beast did its best to dislodge their powerful jaws and toss its tormentors to the ground or flying through the air. Bulldogs would drop into their shoulders like setters and creep low to the ground as they approached, ever wary of the horns hooking beneath them. The main target was the bull's nose. If a dog could take him by the nose, he was usually able to subdue the poor creature. It seems unimaginable but such degraded spectacles drew large crowds of onlookers. While the struggling bull writhed in fitful agonies, men would place bets on which dog would maintain its hold the longest. Bulls were also abused in this way at the livestock market and in the butcher's yard. There existed an entirely erroneous theory that the meat on a tough old bull would be tenderized by having adrenaline course through its veins.

During the medieval period, the bulldogs used for baiting were broadly similar to the catch dogs used in the hunt. From the late seventeenth century however, to satisfy the 'sporting' demands of the bullring, multiple relays of smaller dogs began to be favoured. This led to the development of types like the English Bulldog. These were a class of holding mastiff, more compact than those used in the hunting field, which offered the public faster and, in their eyes, more thrilling sport with more flying dogs.

After the 1835 ban on bear- and bull-baiting, all the bull types were out of a job and their numbers declined rapidly. Whilst we can rejoice at the redundancy

The bulldog. From Thomas Bewick's *A General History of Quadrupeds*, 1790. This is the typical form of an eighteenth century bulldog, as seen in numerous works of art. Note that he has straight legs, is of athletic build and, although broad-mouthed, his face is not smashed in. Bulldogs can be seen in the background chasing and seizing a runaway bull in the farmyard. (Alamy Stock Images)

of their grisly occupation, what befell the poor Bulldog was that, with function abandoned, he was redesigned for purely cosmetic reasons. People decided his head should become rounder, and larger, a bit more human if you will, together with various alterations to his skeleton. It was gradual, each little tweak making a slight adjustment on the last, so that each generation began to think that a Bulldog's appearance was normal for the breed. This transformation was achieved by crossbreeding with little flat-faced Pugs from China and then piling exaggeration upon exaggeration. People think he looks 'cute' and are able to anthropomorphize his chubby humanesque features, forgetting that this is not how functional bulldogs appeared. Today the English Bulldog has become an absurd caricature of its former self. One only has to compare the images of bulldogs in eighteenth- and nineteenth-century art with modern specimens to see how much his form has been degraded. Bulldogs were broad-mouthed dogs, mastiffs, but never flat-faced dogs. They were of stocky build with straight legs, capable of a predator's springing leap, not rotund dogs on crooked legs and with chests splayed open so wide that the animals cannot walk normally. Nevertheless, despite my concerns for the anatomical problems inflicted on them by humans, I recognize that Bulldogs are the most wonderful and affectionate characters, who make heartwarming companions. I have met several over the years and I understand perfectly how people can become so devoted to them. With just a few old-fashioned specimens left, I daresay it was the loyal and loving nature of their engaging personas, that so energized nineteenth-century breed enthusiasts to set about turning hapless bulldogs into a new breed of companion dog, not understanding the mistakes they were making.

A modern English Bulldog, showing the unnaturally flattened face, undershot jaw, wrinkled skin and excessive bulk that has become fashionable. Compared to many, this dog has relatively moderate problems and might be considered normal until he is compared to the historical type. (Photo:iStock. clauds)

The story of the modern Bulldog is a shameful chapter in canine husbandry and a cautionary tale for the future of all breeds. While it is undoubtedly sickening to contemplate the depraved cruelty of bull-baiting, it is nonetheless important to understand the task for which these types were developed. Bulldogs had to be as quick on the dash as they were tenacious for the hold. They needed to be sturdy and athletic, able to withstand and bounce back from being tossed high in the air by an irate bull. It is right that we no longer use dogs to do this work. However for the breed to be healthy, the design features of its original function cannot be ignored. In morphing the bulldog into a new dog, breeders have taken as their template, not his former functionality, but rather the imaginings of artists, who took licence to exaggerate aspects of his form in order to suggest qualities of tenacity, resilience and fight. A Bulldog was the ever-present companion of John Bull, a fictional character representing a jingoistic English archetype, equivalent to America's Uncle Sam. John Bull was envisaged as a bluff eighteenth-century farmer, fond of ale and roast beef, a no-nonsense, anti-intellectual patriot. He first became a national symbol of stubborn defiance during the Napoleonic Wars and his Bulldog remained an iconic symbol of 'British pluck' until beyond World War II. Despite this nationalist appropriation, the working bulldog was by no means an exclusively English type. The Dogue de Bordeaux is a fearsome French mastiff of similar build and the Rottweiler is a German broad-mouthed bull breed. There were a number of *'bullenbeisser'* (bull-biter) breeds, now extinct, popular throughout the German-speaking lands. The Boxer was developed in the nineteenth century by

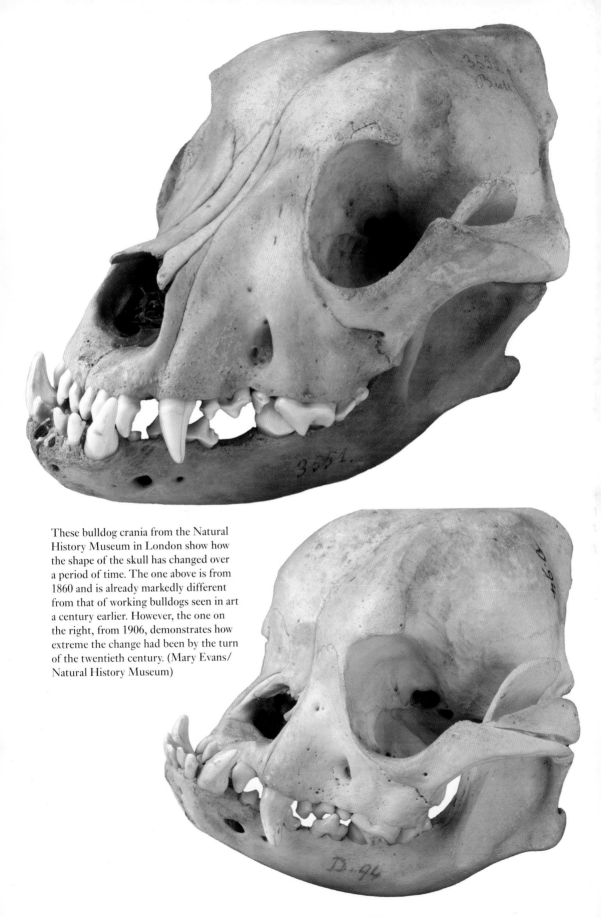

These bulldog crania from the Natural History Museum in London show how the shape of the skull has changed over a period of time. The one above is from 1860 and is already markedly different from that of working bulldogs seen in art a century earlier. However, the one on the right, from 1906, demonstrates how extreme the change had been by the turn of the twentieth century. (Mary Evans/Natural History Museum)

A Boxer. Whilst retaining the defining broad mouth characteristic of a mastiff, this Boxer still has some muzzle length. Poor examples of Boxers with overly-squashed faces do exist but, generally, this breed has fared better than others of the type. (Photo:iStock. alberto clemares expósito)

A Boxer. Although compared to historical types the modern Boxer is considerably less aggressive and more slightly built, many examples, such as here, have retained an athletic conformation and powerful musculature. (Photo:iStock. Credit alberto clemares expósito)

mixing several of these old *bullenbeisser* types. Originally Boxers had more substance than today's specimens and a good deal more aggression. They worked as butcher's dogs and were used to control cattle in slaughterhouses. In their homeland, Boxers also became the dog of choice for both police and military service. During World War I they were employed for guarding and patrolling and also acted as messenger dogs. It is generally thought that a Boxer takes longer to train for police duties than does a flock guardian such as a German Shepherd Dog or a Malinois. However, once trained, Boxers do extremely well at this work and their numbers are increasing in *schutzhund* competitions. These are working trials that take place in Germany for the assessment of protection dogs. Seeing a fit Boxer sprint across a field and take a flying leap to bring down a fugitive is a sight to behold and reminds us of what athletes the bull breeds once were. By reputation, most Boxers bred outside Germany have been made too docile to be suitable for this work, but in Germany more assertive working strains still survive.

Alaunts: The Running Mastiffs

A variation on the broad-mouthed holding mastiff was known in the Middle Ages as an 'alaunt'. Today's bold Spanish mastiff, the Alano Espagñol, retains an echo of that name. Alaunts may be distinguished from holding mastiffs, by their longer muzzles and by the fact that they were better runners. A mastiff was unleashed at close quarters to a hunted animal that was being held at bay; whereas an alaunt could pursue over distance. His longer muzzle was better able to snatch quarry on the move than was that of a broad-mouthed dog. Although powerfully muscular, alaunts had a conformation more suited to the chase. This style of hunting by pursuit with heavy dogs was known as hunting 'par force' and it depended on these 'nose-up' running hounds. Alaunts were nonetheless a class of seizing dog, similar to mastiffs, and once they caught a prey animal, they would pull it down and hold it. The name alaunt is thought to derive from the idea that these were a type of dog introduced to Western Europe by the Alans (Alani). This Migration Period people, mighty horse warriors who originated in the East, moved into Southwest France and Spain in the fifth century. Place names such as Alençon and Valencia echo this heritage. During the Middle Ages some authorities made a distinction between alaunts as a general type, which could include watchdogs, and 'alaunts gentle'. In its medieval usage, the word 'gentle' was applied to anything that had associations of good breeding or nobility – hence 'gentleman'. There was nothing 'gentle' in the modern sense about an alaunt. These were vicious dogs; only an alaunt could drive a wild boar from its covert. According to Edward of Norwich in *The Master of Game* (fifteenth century), alaunts will:

> run gladly and bite the horse…run at oxen and sheep and swine and at all other beastes or at men and other hounds. For men have seen Alaunts slay their masters. In all manner of ways Alaunts are treacherous and evil

Despite these seemingly disqualifying traits, alaunts gentle were used extensively in the medieval par force hunt. Quite simply they could manage dangerous game in a way that was beyond the capabilities of either brachets or Greyhounds and at a sustained pace unachievable by a mastiff. Naturally they required strong and expert handling.

Hunting the enormous wild boar that still roamed Europe's forests was their primary function and it required several alaunts to take on a big tusker, an animal that could exceed 200 pounds of squealing rage. In subsequent centuries other breeds were developed in Europe specifically for the boar hunt, although they were all far more biddable and domestically docile than the fearsome alaunts that Edward of Norwich cautioned about. The Great Dane (known in Germany as the Deutsche Dogge = German Mastiff) is close to an example of an alaunt type, which was developed as a big, powerful, athletic hunting dog, intended to tackle wild boar. Although the Great Dane is German rather than Danish, there is a Danish equivalent. Stockier and heavier, a real hunting alaunt type, it is called the Broholmer. These powerful seizing dogs were virtually extinct but enthusiasts are reviving the breed from a small stock that had been preserved at Broholm Castle. Another modern example of an alaunt type is the Rhodesian Ridgeback, which was bred by European settlers in Southern Africa, using a mix of European imports and native dogs. It was native dogs that passed on genes to give this breed its distinctive ridge of spinal hair

The Dog Argentino, developed as a boar-hunting dog in Argentina, is a reasonable approximation of what a medieval alaunt may have looked like. (Photo:iStock. Credit Lunja)

An old-style Great Dane photographed by Thomas Fall in1897. This is another boar hound that is representative of the medieval alaunt type. Although this breed have now been bred to be docile and with exaggerated height, in order to maintain its status as the tallest breed, the power and rippling muscle mass of this nineteenth century specimen is imposing and would impact with quite a punch when launched with intent. The cropped ears were common on mastiffs who had to engage in dangerous combat, as the ears were especially vulnerable in such a situation. (Mary Evans Picture Library/Thomas Fall)

that grows in the opposite direction to the rest if the coat. Ridgebacks have immense stamina for hunting all manner of African game and are large, solid dogs.

The Molosser Fallacy

Mastiffs are not necessarily gigantically massive. They do require a certain amount of bodyweight to perform their function but their greater need is to be supple and athletic. When hanging on to a larger and enraged animal by its teeth, a mastiff would be swung and shaken violently for a considerable length of time; if its spine were not supported by a prodigiously strong and supple musculature it would snap. Great forces would be at play in such an encounter. Moreover a mastiff needed a sprinting dash and a flying leap in order to launch himself at his foe. Mastiffs did not have the running of an alaunt but they had an impressive explosive power at short range. Being sturdy, strong and muscular is an identifying characteristic. However, the trend since the nineteenth century has been to exaggerate the fact that they are larger dogs and turn them into lumbering giants, who couldn't possible do the jobs they were first intended for. As early as 1888, Hugh Dalziel was complaining in his book *British Dogs* that:

> a desire for immense bulk seems to have led exhibitors of mastiffs to obtain this by fleshiness rather than increase of frame. This is done at a loss of symmetry and activity of action.

A century later, in 1989, an English Mastiff called Zorba entered the record books, weighing in at 330 pounds. I doubt his jaws would have been strong enough to hang his vast weight onto anything. It may be shocking and repugnant to think of a mastiff's purpose being for such objectionable activity; however, it is a historical fact. Moreover that function determined his anatomy and by ignoring the balanced requirements of his traditional work (even though we no longer wish to use him in this way) we have done a great disservice to the dog. Now we breed simply for the novelty of size and disregard all the discomforts that may bring.

Several Kennel Clubs place a number of the larger breeds, both mastiffs and flock guardians, under the banner of 'Molosser' dogs, as if this were a genuine zoological entity; it is not. By doing so, they imply falsely that these dogs have a direct lineage to a distinctive landrace of dogs from ancient Molossia that were extolled at the time by a host of Greek and Roman writers. Molossia was an independent kingdom on the Greek peninsula, at its ascendant between the fourth and second centuries BC. Molossians were famed for their large dogs. However Aristotle, a contemporary who knew Molossian dogs first hand, is clear that, although the Molossians also had hunting dogs just like everyone else's, it was their flock guardians that were famously large and ferocious.

> In the Molossian race of dogs, those employed in hunting differ in no respect from other dogs; while those employed in following sheep are larger and more fierce in their attack on wild beasts (*History of Animals*, fourth century BC)

Molosser and mastiff should not be confused. Molossers were not the original mastiffs. Muscular, broad-mouthed hunting dogs (mastiffs) can already be seen in Assyrian art several centuries earlier and in Sumerian art from as early as the second millennium BC. As Aristotle tells us, the Molossians' unique strain of dogs were livestock guardians. Like all livestock guardians, they could also do duty as house-dogs. Virgil, a poet of the first century BC, noted:

> Never with them on guard, need you fear for your stalls
> a midnight thief or onslaught of wolves,
> or Iberian brigands at your back.

Some years ago I was filming in Rome for a television documentary that featured a sequence about the fighting dogs of the Roman army. Little is known about such

Hunting mastiffs from the court of the Assyrian King Ashurbanipal (r. 661–631 BC). Relief carving from the North Palace, Ninevah, now in the British Museum. The dogs are held on leashes and the hunt servants carry nets and stakes for creating an entrapment area into which to drive the game. Ashurbanipal was a devotee of the lion hunt and this may be the intended quarry here. (Photograph by the author)

dogs, though the column of Marcus Aurelius in Rome (erected in AD 180) does tease with what look like attack dogs in the midst of a battle. Certainly fighting dogs have been a feature of a number of militaries and Pliny the Elder (AD 23-79) recorded that the Colophonians kept squadrons of mastiff dogs to use against their enemies. I was taken to meet a pair of Neapolitan Mastiffs that the programme's researcher had been misled into thinking were of the appropriate historical type. These poor wretches were the saddest canine specimens I have ever encountered. Victims of atrocious modern breeding fads, their size had been so excessively over-exaggerated that they were barely able to support their own weight for more than a few strides. The day was warm but nothing out of the ordinary and it proved difficult to keep them on their feet. It was quickly apparent that these were not an approximation of an ancient Roman type, despite the fact that the American Kennel Club still peddles this fantasy on its website. These were not the dogs of the Roman army, nor were they even fit to be regular domestic guard dogs, although some may find their appearance off-putting. An excess of wrinkled skin further afflicted these poor animals. It was necessary to wipe between the pendulous folds at regular intervals to

Neapolitan Mastiffs. These Leviathans had been so overbred for size that they were barely able to move. (Photograph by Ben Mole)

deter skin infections. To a lesser extent, surplus folds of skin are common on several mastiff types. There is a somewhat spurious argument, which suggests that dogs who are bred for aggressive situations, may need some loose skin, so that if they are bitten it does not reach the muscle. What may have started off as a very subtle characteristic has, in this case, been so amplified for human amusement, that it is a welfare problem.

We left the poor Neapolitans behind to flop in the shade and went elsewhere to inspect some English Mastiffs. There is no doubt that they were impressive and, holding them on leashes, I was keenly aware of their intimidating power. Even so they had been bred to such an enormous size, perhaps just for the curiosity of being extra-large, that it was difficult to imagine them being useful as battlefield dogs. Bandogs, guarding a yard on a chain, yes, but it took too much effort to shift their excess bulk for them to have the stamina to keep going throughout a military campaign. I doubt that the historical types carried such bulk.

Battle Mastiffs

From the tomb of Tutankhamun (r.1334 -1325 BC) is a casket that features painted panels of the young Pharaoh in battle on his chariot. He is accompanied by a pack of large hunting dogs, off leash, who fly at his foes. In some instances they have taken the enemy's heads in their jaws. There is no evidence for Tutankhamun ever having fought in a battle, so these images are purely symbolic. Throughout history dogs had various military functions including as messengers, as sleuthhounds to hunt fugitives and as camp guards but there are only occasional glimpses of them being used to attack the enemy directly. As in the case of the Tutankhamun casket, the evidence of art is insufficient on its own, since hunting is a common metaphor for the subjugation of an enemy. The evidence from antiquity still rests behind a veil and requires deeper enquiry than space permits here. From the circumstantial evidence of the column of Marcus Aurelius, the dogs are being held back on leashes with individual handlers. This would make sense to prevent them running around in a disordered, snarling, out-of-control frenzy, where they might be as much danger to friend and foe alike. Training them to attack forward and only slipping them when in direct contact with the enemy would make sense but this is purely speculation.

Some Roman writers, such as Grattius (63 BC – 14 AD), author of *Cynegeticon*, described dogs from Britain in a way that suggested they were broad-mouthed mastiffs. These dogs were much sought and, although Grattius labels them as ugly, he heaps praise on their valour. Even so it is difficult to discern whether their value was in the hunting field or on the campaign trail. By virtue of their courage, strength and ferocity, mastiffs and alaunts would certainly seem to be the most suitable dogs for the battlefield, whether as attack dogs or as personal wardens. Lysimachus (360-281 BC), one of Alexander the Great's Successor generals, who with ruthless ambition became *basileus* (effectively king) of Thrace, Macedon and eventually much of Asia Minor, was killed at the Battle of Corupedium in 281 BC. Although his body was not found for days, it remained recognizable. His faithful dog had stood guard, shielding him from the tearing talons and eviscerating beaks of the vultures. We do not know the type of dog, was it his hunting hound or a mastiff type taken into battle for personal protection? Perhaps it fitted both descriptions? There is a similar tale from the European Middle Ages. Sir Piers Legh of Lyme Hall was wounded at the Battle of Agincourt (1415). His mastiff remained steadfastly guarding his body, which lay undiscovered as night fell. He was not found until the following day. Subsequently he was taken to Paris, where he made a full recovery. In the case of Sir Piers, we know his dog was a mastiff and at his ancestral home the Lyme Hall strain of English Mastiffs were claimed to have an unbroken line from this female right up until 1900. Moving though these stories are, they pose more questions than they answer. What were these dogs doing on the battlefield? Were they running around loose? Did others at the same battle have their dogs with them? Did loose dogs fight each other on the battlefield? Alternatively were they kept back at the camp, possibly chained and guarding their master's tent. Were they then released to find their master's body when he went missing in action? This seems slightly more plausible but even so, imagine dozens of mastiffs roaming a battlefield looking for their masters - what fights would then ensue? How common was it for a warrior to have his own protection dog on the battlefield? Lysimachus and Sir Piers Legh are separated by seventeen centuries. There is much we still don't know.

There are apocryphal accounts perpetuated in a number of online breed histories that in 1518 King Henry VIII presented 400 battle mastiffs, with iron collars, to King Charles V of Spain (r.1516-1556). I have been unable to find any primary source to confirm this. Furthermore it is improbable. The Calendar of State Papers only reveals a rather more modest gift from Henry of 'some' hunting Mastiffs to the Marquis of Mantua in 1526. What is more certain, is that the Spanish made brutal use of large packs of dogs in their conquest of the Caribbean and the Americas (as did the Portuguese in Brazil). Mastiffs and alaunts were unleashed on native populations in barbarous and frenzied attacks, which rank among the worst of the Conquistadors' atrocities. Dogs were set onto civilian populations in villages as a terror tactic and they were also used to hunt out the unarmoured natives as they attempted to resist invasion with ambush. It was an especially dark chapter for both humans and canines.

Armour for Dogs

Whether going into battle or, more usually, hunting deadly game, mastiffs were frequently armoured to afford them some protection. This was despite the dismissive attitude expressed by Edward of Norwich in the fifteenth century. In writing of mastiffs, he declared, '*they are so heavy and ugly that if they be slain by the wild boar it is no great loss*'. Others thought differently and went to considerable lengths to safeguard a daring and loyal mastiff. All-encompassing dog armour, of leather, layered canvas or mail, offered significant protection against the tusks of a wild boar, the teeth of a wolf, the claws of a bear, the horns of wild ox or antlers of a giant stag. Seizers didn't have to be as swift as the hounds that chased down the prey initially; they were only required

These Sussex Bulldogs (a recreated breed) appear similar to hunting mastiffs depicted in medieval art. One wears a spiked collar, which was a standard defence for going up against dangerous game such as boar, bear and wolves. Their stocky frame, powerful neck and muscular body give these dogs the strength to wrestle large quarry to the ground and to hold it. They are broad-mouthed but the face is not so squashed as a modern Bulldog. (Photograph by Adam Schuch-Des Forges)

to make a short-distance flying lunge at an almost-stationary animal, already held at bay. Where greater mobility, or less expense, was desired, broad iron collars or leather collars equipped with spikes furnished protection for the vulnerable throat in the same way that they did for flock-guarding dogs. Elaborate dog armours, fashioned from plates in imitation of knightly forms, did exist. There is one in the Royal Armoury of Madrid and images in art of others. It is improbable that such armours suggest the use of dogs on the battlefield and more likely that they were parade novelties. Mail, textile and leather armour, however, was an essential working tool for those dogs that faced real danger in the hunt.

Our dear old dog Sparky modelling a type of armour commonly worn by alaunts and mastiffs during the Middle Ages for hunting dangerous game. A mail collar and mantle (made by Nick Checksfield) defends the vulnerable throat, neck and chest areas. Mail is an interlocking web of iron rings, each secured with a rivet, which gives good protection against teeth, tusks or horns. The metal component is just the outer layer of a composite construction; mail always works in combination with a thick textile lining that helps to absorb the force of any attack. A significant advantage of mail is that it is flexible and so doesn't impede the dog's running. In order to keep the overall weight down, the body armour is wholly textile. In this case it consists of twenty-four layers of strong linen, gathered together by stitching and studding patterns to create a denser matrix of fibres. It is the same principle as a medieval soldier's gambeson. Textile armours were often worn alone and acted as a reasonable barrier to the worst of claw and gore. (Photograph by Kim Hawkins)

Japanese dog armour, certified to date from the mid- to late-Edo period (c 1750-1850). This armour was not suited to either battle or the hunting field, since the helmet prevents the dog from using its jaws. Moreover protection is absent from the crucial areas of the chest and throat. Such armour can only have been intended for parade and display. (Images courtesy of Trevor Absolon)

Chapter 11

Terriers

Outspeaks the Squire, 'Give room I pray
And hie the terriers in:
The warriors of the fight are they,
And every fight they win'.
—'Ring-Ouzel'

Jack Russell Terrier (Photo: iStock.com / K_Thalhofer)

A popular and widely accepted view is that the word 'terrier' derives from the French '*terre*', meaning earth. Certainly many of these 'earth dogs', as they are also known, go underground in pursuit of their quarry; whether it is rabbits, badgers or foxes. However earth-work is not all they do and there are a number of larger terriers who are not expert tunnelers (though of course all dogs *can* dig!). David Hancock in his excellent book *Sporting Terriers* (2011) suggests that 'terrier' might have derived, not from the French '*terre*' but from the Latin '*terrere*', which means to frighten. Certainly terriers are known for their fierceness. They undoubtedly frighten and 'terrorize' their subterranean victims and their tenacious ferocity knows no bounds when it comes to ridding a grain store or stable of rats. In the home, of course, these 'terrors' soften into very friendly fellows and loyal companions. Having said that, digging is a signature for a majority of the terrier breeds. Their front paws are shovels and they can claw their way through a tunnel with astonishing speed and efficiency.

Earth Dogs

Foxes create underground labyrinths – dens, where they sleep, store food and seek refuge. From a nondescript aperture at ground level, a main passage leads to the nesting quarters. Angled at roughly forty-five degrees, this burrow can reach up to 50 feet in length and 8 feet in depth, though most are less than half this size. Extending from the main passageway are two or three other burrows, which connect to the surface at extremely steep angles. These are the escape hatches, into which a hunted fox can plunge and instantaneously disappear from sight. Prior to a foxhunt, huntsmen block off these bolt-holes in the hope of keeping the fox on the run for the sport of the hounds. However in a landscape honeycombed with multiple dens and plunge-holes, there are usually some that are missed. The primary hunting function of a terrier is to drive a fox from his lair in the event that he 'goes to ground' during a hunt with hounds. Before putting a terrier to earth, the huntsman must first ensure that the other exits are unblocked. In this way the fox can be bolted, that is forced to flee his hole, and the hounds can resume their chase. Since 2004, such practices are no longer legal in the United Kingdom but they are the reason why many terrier breeds were bred the way they were. Terriermen also work to catch foxes independently of hounds, in the name of 'pest control'. In precisely defined circumstances, this activity is still sanctioned by law in the UK. When operating with just a terrier, terriermen stake nets at the escape holes. Once a bolted fox is caught, it can either be killed or transported to another area.

Terriers do not dig fresh tunnels but rather scratch, scrabble and wriggle their way along the pipes that the fox has already excavated. Steadfast courage, determination and a well-regulated circumference are prerequisites for a good earth dog. Mostly a fox is bolted. The worst of situations is when a fox and a terrier come into contact underground; terrible wounds can ensue for both. There are other jeopardies. Over-enthusiastic terriers can get wedged in too tight a tunnel. It is the terrierman's chief responsibility to know exactly where his dog is, to be attuned to its voice and to be able to bend his back to a shovel effectively and urgently, as soon as needed. At all times terriermen carry with them a round-pointed spade and a digging bar, together

The Earth Stopper by J. Clark 1820. Accompanied by his mongrel dogs, the earth stopper cuts a solitary and sinister figure as he makes his rounds under the cloak of darkness. He uses a spade to stop up the foxes' network of escape holes before they return from their nocturnal explorations. The idea is that once a fox is being pursued later that day, he cannot disappear and go to ground. The earth-stopper seldom manages to find all the holes. If a fox finds an open one, that is when they send for a terrier to dig him out. (Smith Archive / Alamy Stock Photo)

with a brush hook to clear away dense undergrowth from the entrance to a pipe. Since the invention of tiny radio transmitters, collars with these attached have become an essential safety precaution for all who engage in this form of hunting. Smaller-chested dogs have the advantage. The less they have to excavate, the less they will tire. A smaller dog can negotiate tight turns more easily and a slightly longer spine has more flexibility when negotiating tight angles, though it is a weakness if it is too long. A fox's tunnel narrows as it descends and when a larger dog has to expand the passage in order to move forward, it accumulates an earth build-up behind. This can lead to 'bottling', whereby the dog can neither go forward nor back. Another consideration is air-flow; if a dog is too portly for the work, it risks suffocation because, acting as a plug, it can limit its own air supply. As many a terrier pet-owner will tell you, some terriers get stuck underground on a regular basis, especially those that dive down rabbit holes. If they can be located, they have to be dug out but if they make it to depth in a large warren, they can seem to disappear. Terriers frequently emerge from underground forays after several hours and they can survive below ground for days, even for a week or more. In the latter case, dehydration and time serve to reduce their body mass by just enough that they can get themselves turned around.

As with any athlete, natural ability is one thing but it has to be honed with constant practice. Earth-dog trials involve man-made underground tunnels that the dogs must negotiate, while scenting a rat. The dog must follow the scent to the quarry and then 'work' the quarry. Depending on the officiating organization, 'working' means barking, scratching, staring, pawing, digging; any active behavior. The quarry is protected at all times by wooden bars across the end of the tunnel. The hunting encounter is controlled, and organizers claim that neither the dog nor the quarry are endangered by the activity. I have not witnessed it and so cannot offer an opinion on the matter.

Terror Dogs

All dogs will go after rats but only a terrier has the specialist skills to catch and dispatch them dependably. Rats operate in the small, dark, confined spaces of farm buildings and storehouses. They jump, they run, they turn, they dart and they disappear. Terriers have agility, drive and lightning reflexes that are more than a match for a rat. Indeed they can be a match for dozens, even hundreds of rats. Once stimulated they have an insatiable prey drive combined with seemingly limitless energy. A ratting terrier is a force to be reckoned with and it can kill its quarry with a single quick and powerful bite. Terriers also kill by shaking their victims violently to break their backs and then tossing them into the air. Although terriers work perfectly well as soloists, they can also co-operate as a pack. Countrymen often unleash several dogs, when seeking to clear a barn of vermin.

A distinction may be drawn between a terrier working to keep down the rodent population on its home turf, in the same way as does a domestic cat, and a terrier being used for the depraved sport of rat-baiting. Rat-baiting reached a peak of popularity in the nineteenth century after the Cruelty to Animals Act of 1835 put a stop to bull- and bear-baiting but left rat-baiting unregulated. By mid-century London alone boasted around seventy rat pits. These tiny amphitheatres were approximately 6 feet in diameter with sheer wooden walls that rose to elbow height. Spectators stood around the pit, which was lit dimly by gaslight and often situated in the back room of a public house; some pits had bleachers rising steeply to the rafters. The smell of beer competed strongly with the gaslight, the musty odours of the unwashed crowd and the piled carcasses of dead rats. A hundred live rats were put into the pit before each terrier was entered. People gambled on how many rats could be killed in a set amount of time. Without any exits or hiding places, the terrified rats leapt and ran in all directions, while the terrier whirled and whipped, jumped and jack-knifed as it seized and shook its hapless victims in a frenzy of killing. Records from these macabre circuses show that it took a terrier an average of between three and five seconds to assassinate one of his foes. In 1849, a Manchester Terrier called Tiny famously killed two hundred rats in an hour at the Blue Anchor Tavern in Bunhill Row, London. Thankfully, by the end of the nineteenth century, rat-baiting had been outlawed in both England and the United States.

In the United States there is a type called simply the Rat Terrier. It has distinctively large prick ears. Keen hearing is a key feature in rat detection, though such prominent

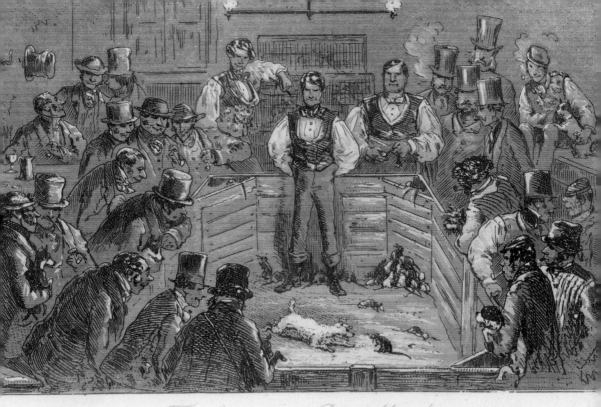

The Great 100 Rat Match.

A nineteenth-century cartoon depicting rat-baiting. Bets were placed on how many rats a single dog could kill within a set amount of time. (Chronicle / Alamy Stock Photo)

A fine pair of Manchester Terriers, bred by Sabra Weeks. During the heyday of rat-baiting contests in the nineteenth-century, Manchesters were considered to be the very best for competition. (Photograph by Brandee Massey)

A pair of Yorkshire Terriers. The pink bows, apparently mandatory on these poor dogs, belie the origins of this breed, which was once employed to wage war on the rat populations of the Industrial North of England. (Eve Photography/Shutterstock.com)

antennae would not suit a dog for earth work. Other ratting virtuosos include the West Highland and Cairn Terriers, the Norwich Terrier and, perhaps surprisingly, the ancestors of the Yorkshire Terrier. No amount of tying ribbons in the hair can disguise the underlying belligerent tendencies of the Yorkie. Yorkshire Terriers exist now only as a 'toy' breed; selective breeding has diminished their size considerably. Although they make extremely affectionate companions, make no mistake; beneath all that frou-frou hair beats the heart of a rodent-slaying warrior. Although the original breed, before it was bantamized, was known for its somewhat long, sleek coat, the excessively exaggerated extra-long coats are relatively recent. Halifax Terriers, sometimes known as Blue-and-Tans, were a Yorkshire breed that appeared in wire-, smooth- and long-haired varieties. It is from the larger, long-haired Halifax Terrier that the present-day Yorkie descends. In the mines and mills of the Industrial Revolution, these silken-haired dervishes, their tasseled jackets swirling, flew at the rats as fiercely as any other type of terrier.

Historical Shadows

There are faint glimpses of terriers in the art of the Ancient World, but they are fleeting apparitions that defy clear identification. Archaeological excavations at Roman sites occasionally reveal canine remains, which are recorded as 'the size of a terrier'. In 2018 such a find was made at Vindolanda on Hadrian's Wall. Unfortunately, size is no indicator of type; terriers and 'toy' companion dogs fit snugly into the same basket.

What is almost certain though is that the Romans, and other earlier civilizations, whilst not using terriers as the enablers for fox-hunting with hounds, did require them for controlling vermin and also, quite probably, as companions.

In the prologue to *The Master of Game* (fifteenth century), Edward of Norwich teases at the end of a list of dog types that he will also tell us of 'small curs that come to be terriers and their nature'. Disappointingly, he does not deliver on this promise. It may be that the terriers of his day were little mongrel terror dogs but not yet specialized as earth dogs. The evidence is unclear and either way, humble terriers were not yet considered fit study for aristocratic hunters. Terriers (spelled 'teroures') are nonetheless mentioned in a list of dog types featured in the fifteenth-century *Boke of St. Albans*. Here we have recognition of the type by name but no account of its duties. Occasionally images in late-medieval art hint at a dog of terrier sort, though invariably of a longer-legged variety. Whether these dogs went to ground is conjectural. However, we can be sure that terriers were used as earth dogs by at least the sixteenth century. Dr Caius (1576) described how they

> creep into the grounde, and by that meanes make afrayde, nyppe and byte the Foxe and the Badger in such sort, that either they teare them in pieces with theyr teeth being in the bosome of the earth, or else hayle and pull them perforce out of their lurking, darke dongeons, and close caves.

Caius' description paints the terrier as an agent of pest control, rather than as an essential accomplice to the hunt with hounds. Wherever there were meadows and ponds nurturing farmed chickens, geese and ducks, wherever gamebirds were plentiful on heath and moor, there was a perceived need to control the population of their chief predator – the fox. He was inedible and, although occasionally hunted by a pack of hounds, not yet the prestige quarry he was to become. Culling foxes with terriers and nets was the everyday work of the yeoman classes. Accordingly, terriers did not merit more than passing mention in the hunting literature of the medieval nobility.

A change in attitude towards foxhunting in Britain occurred following the rapid increase in land enclosures that began in the seventeenth and peaked in the eighteenth century. As a consequence of these alterations to the British topography, it became necessary for horses to jump obstacles in order to travel cross-country. The thrill of fast riding, combined with frequent jumping, made foxhunting all the rage amongst the landed classes. Hitherto, terriers had been merely useful as the exterminators of vermin but now they became an integral part of an elite pastime. It is from this period that we start to see passion applied to the breeding of the 'perfect' terrier; dogs suited not only for their intended quarry but also for the terrain in which they were to be hunted. Finally terriers had status, elevated to the ranks of the other hunting dogs of the aristocracy. Terriers began to be written about and with that came all manner of pronouncements as to which line was superior and what breeds of outcross should be sought to infuse certain qualities. The terrier had arrived as a specialist, even though he had probably always been there as a general factotum to the lower ranks of society.

A Very British Breed?

It is sometimes claimed that terriers are a uniquely British style of dog but that isn't entirely true. In 1575 the Elizabethan courtier, poet, soldier and scholar George Gascoigne translated a work on hunting (*La Venerie*) by the French author Jacques du Fouilloux. His translation appeared bound with another work (*The Book of Falconrie*) by George Turbeville. As a result, Gascoigne's work has often been misattributed to Turbeville. Be that as it may, in Gascoigne's translation of the Frenchman's work, we read:

> There are two sorts of Terriers…one sort came out of Flanders or the Low Countries, as Artoyes or thereabouts and they have crooked legges and are short heared…Another sort there is which are shagged and straight legged.

Gascoigne/Fouilloux doesn't tell us where the shaggy, straight-legged type originates from, though by implication they are native French dogs, since that is the perspective Fouilloux was writing from. This description of the two types is repeated, almost verbatim, by Nicholas Cox in *The Gentleman's Recreation* (1674). However, he omits the assertion that the shorthaired, crooked-legged variety originated in Flanders; perhaps some nationalism was already creeping into the story. The accuracy by early writers on such matters is not dependable but it is notable that Gascoigne acknowledged the existence of some form of terrier type on the Continent. Closely related to terriers are the German Pinschers. These too were bred predominantly to keep down rat populations on farms. Their name probably derives from the French '*pincer*' meaning to pinch or nip. When he appears as a wire-haired variety, the Pinscher is called a Schnauzer. He received this title, which means 'snouter', in recognition of his exuberant moustaches. The German Teckel/Dachshund can also be classed as terriers. There are some false trails, however. The Czech Cesky Terrier was not developed until 1948, using bloodlines from the Sealyham and Scottish Terriers; and the German Jagdterrier, developed in the 1920s, was a cross between the English Fox Terrier and the English Black-and-Tan (now the Welsh Terrier). These are Continental dogs but made with British breeds. An especially wide range of terrier breeds developed in Britain owing to the national obsession for foxhunting and we may say that although terrier-style dogs were not unique to Britain, British strains were nevertheless highly sought after.

Victorian art gives us occasional glimpses of a long since extinct variety of terrier, the English White Terrier. Although no longer with us it was the foundation stock for many varieties we have today. An interesting insight into how dog varieties are made comes from the writings of Darley Matheson. In his book *Terriers* (1922), he bemoaned the loss of the English White and argued that it could be reconstructed by crossing a Bull Terrier female with a Whippet dog and then outcrossing the progeny to a Manchester Terrier. Such gene-pool jiggery-pokery serves to remind us how fragile the concept of a 'breed' can be. Standing up to 18 inches at the withers, the English White was too tall to be a useful earth dog but was considered an excellent ratter and rabbit dog. Judging by Matheson's reverse engineering, it may have had Whippet in its original mix, giving it the turn of speed required for coursing rabbits. Certainly it was an elegant dog.

A Standard German Pinscher, called Tuli. This beautiful medium-sized dog is a classic German terrier type, which was used traditionally to control vermin in farmyards. (Image by Bob and Pam Langrish, KA9 Photo)

W.E. Mason in *Dogs of All Nations* (1915) opines of the English White that 'this terrier should resemble the Manchester Terrier in every respect excepting in regard to colour, which should be pure white'. Though they are less stocky than they once were, Manchester Terriers are representative of an old type of English rat terrier. They have short-haired, black-and-tan coats. References to 'black-and-tan terriers' crop up frequently in nineteenth-century canine literature, implying this was a distinct breed – sometimes called the Old English Black and Tan – but the evidence is hazy. These were working men's dogs, not bred with pedigree credentials in mind. Manchester Terriers, with their sleek coats, may have been a cross between smooth-coated Black-and-Tan dogs and Whippets. There was also a broken-haired Black-and-Tan Terrier, which must surely have been a close ancestor of today's Welsh Terrier. Another aspect of coat colour that we see in terriers today is the presence of hound markings – white with black and tan splotches. This may be the result of black-and-tan terriers mating with white terriers or, more probably, there has been some hound infusion in those strains. Some early literature on the subject conflates the words 'beagle' and 'terrier' ('beagle' derives from the Gaelic '*beg*' meaning small). It is one thing breeding for size but quite another to develop temperament and skillset. As well as being able to scent and track and sight and course, a terrier required a strong bite and bottomless courage. That is where bulldog and mastiff genes were required. The terrier stock of the British Isles has been assembled from a motley genetic cocktail.

A photograph dated to 1890 of the now extinct English White Terrier. These smooth-coated white dogs were a significant foundation strain for many British terriers. (The History Collection / Alamy Stock Photo)

Welsh Terrier. These rough-coated black-and-tan dogs are closely related to the now-extinct Old English Black-and-Tan Terrier, which was the foundation stock for several other terrier breeds. (Photo: iStock.com / CaptureLight)

Terrier-type dogs were once bred with no thought of conforming to a standard. They were the working man's mutt; good for taking rabbits for the pot or keeping down foxes in sheep country. Working ability and companionability was all that counted. Every small district had its own distinct type, breeding from the local gene pool of proven workers. There were once so many varieties that it seemed as if every village had its own. Even during the past century several new 'breeds' have been established. For instance: the Plummer, the Dekker, and Lucas Terriers. In truth these dogs (all named after their personal Doctor Frankenstein) manifest with only minor modifications to existing breeds. Like the Parson Jack Russell, they are differently sized varieties of the Fox Terrier. Once the cocktail mixing has achieved the desired result and if, a few generations later, a Plummer female mated with a Plummer sire produces Plummer pups, then the strain is said to breed true; hey presto, it is a new breed. Overall, however, there have been more losses than gains. Moreover, a number of terrier breeds exist in name only and are no longer representative of a working type. In many cases they have been miniaturized beyond their original compact stature and now function purely as companions – a valuable job that they do extremely well. There is not space to examine every named terrier but what follows is a selection of the more capable working strains that remain.

The Borderers

Separating England and Scotland lies a rugged no-man's-land, the Borders. It was formerly a buffer zone between these two, frequently hostile, nations. The accession of James VI of Scotland to the English throne as James I in 1603 resulted in the Union of the Crowns and, eventually, the Act of Union in 1707. Border folk have a characteristic toughness, resilience and a strong sense of independence, wrought of centuries of living in an area enmeshed in conflict and with an often bad-tempered climate. Their dogs are no different to the people. Among the surviving 'fell terrier' types are Border Terriers, Lakeland Terriers and Patterdale Terriers. The latter are really just Border Terriers with a skinhead buzz cut and an attitude to match. There is a terrier spirit – it is courageous, resolute, defiant, gutsy and loyal. In my opinion, no other terrier embodies these qualities in greater measure than does the Border Terrier. Fierce of face and brave of heart, these perennially unkempt tangles of wiry hair are as tough as they come. Impervious to the driving rains and the blustery winds of the harsh border country between England and Scotland, they are equally at home squeezing between crags to get to the entrance of a foxhole as they are ratting in a barn or giving chase to rabbits in a thicket. A Border Terrier will pile-drive into a rabbit hole with no thought to a reasonable exit strategy. They have enough leg to bound effortlessly over heather and will splash through tracts of swampy bog all day without complaint. Biting cold and diamond-sparkling, frost-clad pastures do not elicit so much as a shiver. All that excites them is prey drive, together with a deep affection for their owners. I have known many Border Terriers that have belonged to friends. When curled on one's lap being scratched, they are gently peaceful and affectionate. Yet one can sense them on constant alert, never knowing when they will spring into action at the slightest sound from a possible foe outside.

A small pack of Border Terriers crossing a burn with fierce determination. (Photo: iStock.com /shellhawker)

A Border Terrier – always on the alert. (Photo: iStock.com /shellhawker)

Fox Terrier

Compared to other varieties of earth terrier, the Fox Terrier is longer-legged. It is commonly suggested that this is so that they can keep up with a mounted hunt. Nobody would dispute the determination of a terrier to do this; terriers have zip, zest and can-do in abundance. However their stride just doesn't have the reach to maintain pace with galloping horses or with much larger foxhounds over distance. Even if it were possible for a short distance, an exhausted dog would be extremely vulnerable if it were put to ground after a chase. For mounted hunts, terriers were carried on horseback in a satchel, whatever the breed. Today, they are more likely to hitch a ride in a Land Rover or on a quad-bike. Of course any terrier can keep up with pedestrian huntsmen.

Both wire- and smooth-haired types exist and it is axiomatic that a sure way to produce a tough, wiry, weather-resistant coat is to cross a rough with a smooth. Despite this, Kennel Clubs class them as two distinct breeds, thus narrowing the gene pool for each. As a consequence the wire-haired variety have developed a number of over-exaggerated features, while it is more common to find a viable working type among the smooth-haired variety. Fox Terriers tend to have square features and have been known popularly as 'bricks with the four corners knocked off'. In nineteenth-century paintings of the breed, this rectilinear tendency is subtly apparent but nowhere near as extreme as the rigid box-like creations of today. Together with unnecessary, and

A smooth-coated Fox Terrier (Photo: iStock.com /LexussK)

A wire–coated Fox Terrier (Photo: iStock.com /DevidDO)

A Scottish Terrier, popularly known as a 'Scottie'. The old working varieties, whilst undoubtedly hirsute, had far shorter overcoats than that being worn by this show ring type. Such profusion of hair on both body and face disguises the regular terrier shape beneath, though it gives good protection against the weather and for running through wet heather. (Pukhov K / Shutterstock.com)

absurdly long, brick-like faces that are almost entirely without stop (the naturally indented angle between the muzzle and the forehead), today's specimens have ramrod-straight front legs. Moreover there was a muscularity to earlier types that is absent from the modern show dogs. With terriers, there is always a fine balance regarding chest size, known as the 'span' of a dog. If the ribs are too broad, then a dog can be too easily wedged in a burrow; if too narrow then the dog may lack essential lung power. In common with a number of other terrier breeds (the Kerry Blue, the Sealyham, the Lakeland, the Welsh and the Scottie), Wire Fox Terriers have extravagant beards that obscure and alter the natural profile of their faces. Such hirsute augmentation can be reasoned as part camouflage and part armour. When it came to a fight in a tunnel, then a bite to the face would, as likely as not, be rewarded with a mouthful of hair. Although one can see potential functional merit in these hairy adjuncts, it should be noted that they are absent from images of the breed in its nineteenth-century heyday. A nineteenth-century Fox Terrier looked like a larger version of a Jack Russell Terrier.

The Milkman's Dog – The Jack Russell

The Reverend John 'Jack' Russell (1795-1883), known also as Parson Russell, was an eccentric and colourful foxhunting man who lived on Exmoor in Devon. I have ridden with friends on Exmoor many times. With its vast expanses of unfenced moorland, it is to my mind the perfect terrain for bold and thrilling gallops. Being a sporting parson (he was vicar of Swimbridge and rector of Black Torrington) at the height of foxhunting's popularity, and in an area of such natural beauty, incubated a passionate enthusiasm that bordered on obsession. In that place, at that time, hunting was central to the community. Reverend Russell was also a breeder of dogs, especially Fox Terriers. Despite his considerable gambling excesses, his marriage to a wealthy heiress allowed him to continue his sporting life unencumbered. In 1819, according to legend, he was very taken with a small terrier type owned by the local milkman and bought it from him. The dog, a female named Trump, was a diminutive of the standard Fox Terrier sort; a mostly white dog with dark tan spots over her eyes, ears and at the tip of her tail. He bred from her carefully, seeking to retain the type, and within a few generations the 'Jack Russell Terrier' was an established and recognizable variety. Although the foxhunting reverend was a founding member of The Kennel Club, and an author of the breed standard for Smooth-haired Fox Terriers, he did not show his Jack Russell strain, nor endorse others doing so. Despite the utility displayed by these little dogs, Russell claimed that the distinction between them and standard Fox Terriers was 'the difference between wild and cultivated flowers'. Such narrow snobberies were endemic to the thinking of the time.

The first breed standard created for the Jack Russell was by the Devon and Somerset Badger Club 1894. It favoured these tenacious little dogs for badger-digging, rather than foxhunting. This was an appallingly vicious activity in which both dog and badger were almost invariably hurt. Badgers are immensely powerful with a strong bite and a swipe from one of their puissant digging claws could rip a dog open. To breed greater fighting spirit into the strain, the Jack Russell line was infused with

A smooth-coated Parson Jack Russell Terrier. (OlesyaNickolaeva / Shutterstock.com)

Bull Terrier blood, resulting in dogs with shorter legs. Over time there was further crossbreeding, including with Chihuahuas. In addition to their value as working terriers, Jack Russells – dogs of exceptional intelligence and engaging character – became popular as family companion dogs. It wasn't until 1990 in the UK and 1997 in the USA that the respective kennel clubs recognized Parson Jack Russell Terriers. As I write it is 200 years since the milkman's dog was first noticed for his admirable qualities. Since then there has been two centuries' worth of constant outcross breeding, creating a variety with great vigour. Like the Fox Terrier parent strain, there are both rough- and smooth-coated varieties of Jack Russell and there is a pleasing variation in size, markings and conformation between the many dogs that come under the Russell umbrella. Jack Russells are renowned as first-rate ratters and are much loved both as working dogs and as pets. They are the universally ubiquitous terrier of our times.

Not Terriers

When developing breeds that require grit and ferocity, traits that are innate to the terrier character, then terriers have been top of the list for the breeding admixture. Paying homage to the importance of their influence, the word 'Terrier' (or the German equivalent: 'Pinscher') has been retained in the name of the new breed. However, whether or not the resulting dog should be classed correctly as a terrier is open to question. Wilfred Holmes developed the Airedale Terrier in 1853. He crossed local terriers with Otterhounds to produce a larger, stronger type to hunt otters in the nearby Aire, Colne and Calder rivers. Common sense suggests that these dogs are really too large for this taxonomy. The Airedale has proved itself to be an admirable all-round working dog, far beyond a terrier's normal duties. During the First World War, Airdales served as sentry dogs and messengers, earning great distinction for their capability and bravery. At a time when the British public was hostile to all things German, it was the Airedale, not the German Shepherd, that acted as the arrest dog for the civil police. Airedales were also used on the farm to herd and guard and as the farmer's shooting companion, where they proved themselves to be competent retrievers. As hunting dogs, Airedales achieved star status in the United States. In 1925 Airedales were the most popular dogs in America. American hunters used them as treeing dogs for raccoon, retrievers for ducks, and tracking dogs for a range of dangerous game such as bear and bobcat. Airedales are versatile dogs but can hardly be classed as terriers, despite the fact that there is terrier blood in their origins.

In the 1880s, a German tax collector (or rent collector – the story varies), Karl Doberman, bred a larger, stronger pinscher dog for personal protection – the Doberman Pinscher. The standard German Pinscher was the basis for the breed and by far the most influential and common of the outcrosses was the Manchester Terrier from England. However, other non-terrier, and much-larger, breeds were also enlisted to develop an imposing and intimidating dog. These may have included German Shepherd Dogs and Rottweilers among others. Herr Doberman's dogs have earned a fearsome reputation as protection dogs. However despite the word 'Pinscher' in

An Airedale Terrier. Bred for otter-hunting in the North of England, these versatile dogs have been used for a variety of tasks from sentry dogs to shooting companions. (Photo: iStock.com / Farinosa)

A Doberman Pinscher. The influence of the Manchester Terrier in the development of Herr Doberman's breed is evident. Although pinschers, like some terriers, were bred originally as ratting dogs, this larger version was created as a protection dog, intended to seize humans rather than rats. (DragoNika/Shutterstock.com)

the name, they can no longer be considered a true pinscher/terrier type. Similarly the Black Russian Terrier was 'invented' in the 1930s by the Soviet army, combining numerous European breeds including the Airedale Terrier, from which it took the type name. Black Russians are large dogs (standing around 30 inches), which are used for border patrol and as prison guards. They are not terriers in any meaningful sense of the word, nor do they perform terrier work.

Otter Terriers

Digging out foxes and killing rats were the signature roles of the terrier but they were also employed in otter-hunting in the days when it was legal. Otters live in a holt in the riverbank, which like the den of a fox has several tunnels and entrances. Terriers were just as necessary to flush an otter from its holt, as they were to bolt a fox from its den. Captain John Edwardes (1808-91) lived at Sealyham House, a well-appointed mansion near the banks of the River Sealy in Wales. He had a pack of Otterhounds and he bred a particular strain of terrier – the Sealyham Terrier – to assist him with his otter hunts. Sealyhams are a rare sight these days, though I remember them being popular when I was a child. My kindergarten teacher had one and I remember it being only slightly less scary than she was. W.E. Mason in his *Dogs of All Nations* (1915) describes the Sealyham as having a 'punishing jaw', with the implication that such a thing was a

A Sealyham Terrier. These fierce little dogs were bred to hunt otters in Wales. (Photo: iStock.com / CaptureLight)

virtue. It was a more muscular age. The breed is now in considerable decline, a mere ornament of the show ring with exaggerated whiskers. Other waterproof breeds such as the Border Terrier, who looks like an improbable cross between an otter and an Otterhound, were also strong on otter as was the Scottish Terrier. However in the nineteenth century, a Scottie's coat was not the floor-length clown's cape it dons today but rather a serviceable, rugged overcoat with longish hair. Otters are captivatingly enchanting animals and it is difficult to understand the extent to which they were hunted and trapped because of their depredations on fish stocks. However they were; it is part of social history and certainly part of canine history.

Feisty Fellows

In North America, there is a strain of dogs known as 'feists'. Their ancestry is connected directly to British terriers. Used predominantly for hunting squirrels, feists track silently and then, upon sighting their quarry, give energetic chase until they put one of these arboreal acrobats up a tree. Only then do they bark, calling the hunter to come and shoot it. Squirrel-hunting was, and remains, a widely-practised field sport in America. At a time when the development of terriers was all the rage in eighteenth-century Britain, these versatile and tenacious dogs also became increasingly popular with the hunting fraternity in the New World. Imported terriers were outcrossed with other breeds, creating a distinct range of North American types. Feists today manifest in around twenty different varieties. Mountain Feists, popular in the Appalachian and Ozark Mountains, are notably similar in appearance to a Jack Russell Terrier. Feists occur in a variety of colours and coats. Galla Creek Feists are sometimes pure white and images of them are strikingly similar to those of the now extinct English White Terrier.

In early references the spelling of 'feist' varies. Writing in the 1930s, the American novelist and chronicler of Southern life William Faulkner used both 'fice' and fyce' in relation to these dogs. George Washington's diary of 1770 refers to 'a small foist-looking yellow cur'. There is also mention of these 'feisty' canines in Abraham Lincoln's poem *The Bear Hunt* (1846):

> The tall fleet cur, with deep-mouthed voice,
> Now speeds him, as the wind;
> While half-grown pup, and short-legged *fice,*
> Are yelping far behind.

Completing this feist-fancying presidential trinity, Teddy Roosevelt often hunted with a feist named Skip, although the dog actually belonged to his son Archie. The 'feist' is a very American dog, though in all but name it is a terrier.

A Treeing Feist. This North American branch of the terrier family is used for squirrel hunting. He is wearing a locator collar because these dogs work far ahead of their handlers in dense woodland. (Photograph courtesy of Gala Creek Feist)

The Bull-and-Terrier

There is nothing new about designer dogs. Labradoodles and Cockapoos are in a long line of arranged matchmaking intended to engineer an ideal dog for the requirements of the day. In the early nineteenth century a demand arose for a 'gentleman's companion' dog. Those owning country property wanted a multi-purpose dog that would control the rats in the stables, be a loyal house dog and be a deterrent to burglars or poachers; young bucks about town wanted a dog that would be a convenient size to keep in their rooms, accentuate their swagger and protect them from ruffians. The answer was a cross between the bulldog and the terrier. At first these were know as 'bull-and-terrier' dogs. Eventually this became contracted to the more familiar 'bull terrier'

Brave, staunch and frightening to strangers, bull-and-terrier dogs became equally in demand by thugs and villains. Bill Sikes, bully and burglar in Charles Dickens' novel *Oliver Twist* (1839), famously owned a dog called Bull's-eye, which has invariably been portrayed in subsequent dramatized versions by an English Bull Terrier (notwithstanding that all Dickens tells us is that he was a white, shaggy dog). Bull's-eye was a literary device, 'having faults of temper in common with his owner' and the reputation of these dogs as intemperate and aggressive has suffered, in part, as a result of this association in popular culture. They have also suffered from a bizarre change in morphology that occurred during the first decades of the twentieth century. Images of bull-and-terrier dogs from the nineteenth century show animals with perfectly

A modern English Bull Terrier showing the rugger-ball shaped head developed in recent years (Photo: iStock.com/iko636)

normal canine heads – some with more of a terrier head; others having a wider early bulldog head. However, in 1914, the Kennel Club breed standard stated that a Bull Terrier's head should appear 'oval, almost egg shaped'. It was nothing more than a cosmetic design fancy from which developed a dog with a head that now resembles that of a Cheviot sheep. Such an absurdity of ovine/canine fusion only serves to make the breed appear alien and unnatural. Pinprick eyes that leave no scope for expression compound this impression. The reason for such shielded eyes was that these dogs soon became the favoured contenders for public dogfights. These despicable events, in which people gambled on the outcome, had been popular for centuries. However there was a combination of athleticism, tenacity and scrapping ability that made bull-and-terrier types especially entertaining for the depraved spectators.

A Staffordshire Bull Terrier. This regional variety of bull terrier is a broad-mouthed dog that has still retained a healthy amount of stop. This head-shape is more similar to the original bull-and-terrier types than is that of the modern oval-headed specimens. 'Staffies' are the progenitors of Pit Bull Terriers in America. Contrary to popular prejudice, they are extremely affectionate. (Photo iStock.com : redstallion)

An offshoot variety became known as the Staffordshire Bull Terrier. It can be said that 'Staffies' are more similar in form to the original bull-and-terrier types than are those with sheep's heads. Bull-and-terrier types brought by migrants to the United States in the nineteenth century led to the development of an American version: the Pit Bull Terrier. These plucky dogs found fame in the dogfighting pits of the New World. Perhaps counter-intuitively, all these dogs, so often mistrusted by an uninformed public as 'dangerous dogs', show gentle affection and loyalty to their owners. At the time, aggression to other dogs was bred in to those intended for the wretched life of the dog pits but even these were required to be non-aggressive to humans. An owner had to be able to step into the pit and separate two fighting dogs without fear of being bitten. They also lived as family dogs in what were often cramped quarters. Aggression wasn't an acceptable option for a dog in a household of numerous children. From time to time there are tragic cases, where these dogs attack people. Abuse and neglect will make any dog dangerous; it is not an inherent fault in the breed.

Teckels and Dachshunds
The Dachshund and his alter-ego the Teckel are a distinctive terrier type that flourished in German lands. '*Hund*' is German for 'dog'; the word does not mean 'hound' (a dog that tracks or chases its prey), though it does not preclude some hound ancestry. '*Dachs*' is German for badger. Dachshunds were used extensively to

An example of a robust, well-built Long-haired Dachshund. The body is long but not overlong and the dog appears to be fit and athletic. (Petra Wegner / Alamy Stock Photo)

A fine Smooth-haired Dachshund specimen with a noble head. The hound ancestry is apparent. (Photo: iStock.com / Gorlov)

dig poor brock out of his sett. An alternative name for them was once '*dachskrieger*', which means 'badger-warrior'. Miniature '*wiener*' dogs, so popular as companion pets, are a dwarf variety of the standard working Dachshund and would stand little chance against a badger. However, Standard Dachshunds weigh around 25 pounds and so constitute a substantial slab of fighting muscle, despite their short legs. When not bred with over-exaggeration, the longer back can be powerful and flexible, offering exceptional agility underground. Although a dog the size of a Standard Dachshund is necessary for hunting larger game, the miniature varieties have been used to hunt rabbits. Sadly, too many Dachshunds are caricatures of the original working type, having absurdly long backs together with crooked legs that are too short and unable to reach forward sufficiently to support the spine in motion. The result is an animal destined for a lifetime of unnecessary discomfort. However, working strains of sensibly proportioned dogs do exist and they are superb dogs.

Dachshunds (badger dogs) may have developed from a type known as the *Dachsbracke* (badger hound). The German word for hound, '*Bracke*', has clear associations with the medieval word for a pack scenthound – 'brachet'. These *Dachsbrackes* were similar in size to an English Basset Hound, though they sported the rich red, black and tan jackets of the Bloodhound. A quick glance at a Dachshund reveals that there is a great deal of hound about them. They occur in three coat variations – smooth-, long- and wire-haired. The wire-haired variety were not created until 1925, when

Leutnant Klaus Graf Hahn introduced crosses with British Dandie Dinmont Terriers. The latter, also known for a longer body, owe their fanciful name to a character in a Sir Walter Scott novel; today they owe their over-exaggerated fanciful shape (including a silly top-knot that didn't exist in the historical type) to the excesses of the show ring. Despite the detrimental impact that show breeding has had on the production of healthy Dachshunds, strains of working, hunting dogs have been preserved. Today these are most often the wire-haired variety.

The word '*Dackel*', an obvious contraction of '*Dachshund*', is used colloquially for all Dachshund types in Germany and a slight variation of that, '*Teckel*', usually

A working pack of Teckels run by Des Landes de Saint Martin hunt in France. The pack has been selectively bred to produce hounds with strong bite, scenting ability and obedience. They track and hunt both foxes and wild boar. (Photograph by Stephan Levoye)

This is Jimi Hendrix von der Rauhhaarmeute, a classic example of a strong and athletic, working, wire-haired Teckel (Photograph courtesy of Peter Dolecek)

denotes working specimens. As well as badger, they hunt fox and rabbit in their earth-dog role. However they are also excellent tracking dogs and are used in the forests of Europe to track both stags and wild boar. In many areas, Dachshunds are still used in large packs to hunt for wild boar, their low-slung, torpedo bodies being ideal for getting underneath the brambles and tangles of a dense forest floor. They have excellent noses for finding their quarry, which they then surround and hold at bay until the hunters arrive. It is said that if the boar charges them they will lay on their backs playing dead and that if he rushes over them, they leap up and bite his testicles. Whether or not this is entirely true, I have a deeply ingrained instinct to never step over a Dachshund!

Turnspit Dogs

In Charles Darwin's *The Variation of Animals & Plants Under Domestication* (Volume 1), published in 1868, he refers to the 'turnspit-like German badger hound'.

A turnspit dog in its wheel on the wall from Henry Wigstead's *Remarks on a Tour to North and South Wales in the year 1797* (Wikimedia Commons)

The author with Whiskey, a taxidermed turnspit dog in the Abergavenny Museum (Photograph by Ian Potts)

The turnspit dog, now extinct, was so similar in appearance to the Dachshund that it must have shared a good deal of common lineage. Sadly, however, while one was out in the forest having a fine time procuring game for its master, the other was in the kitchen turning the spit for its mistress. Turnspit dogs ran in little wheels, like hamster wheels, that, via a series of chains and cogs, turned the spits for roasting meat over great open fires. In the Abergavenny Museum is a taxidermic specimen of a turnspit dog – a little chap by the name of Whiskey. He is the only surviving example of his kind. When I visited the museum to see him in person, I found the stuffed and posed cadaver extraordinarily lifelike. There was inevitable sadness in thinking of the hard life he and his kind must have endured but there was also a deep soulfulness in his face that moved me. His connection to the wider terrier family was obvious and I could picture him down a rabbit hole just as easily as in the kitchen with rabbit pie.

Tobias Smollett in his novel *Peregrine Pickle* (published 1751) has his eponymous hero, a foppish, scatter-brained prankster, play a trick on the residents of Bath. On a visit to the city Mr Pickle stole all the turnspit dogs and locked them up. He had observed that in that part of the country the turnspits were accustomed to making their own way to the kitchens in time for preparation of the evening meal. When it was time for the cooks to put in their skewers, they were alarmed by the absence of the turnspit dogs and whistled for them in vain. The whole town was in uproar and they had to resort to turning the spits by hand. Once the meats were cooked young Pickle released the dogs. A contemporary French commentator on the novel, Madame Fréron, remarked:

> the turnspit dogs of England must be better trained than ours; for in France these animals are careful to hide when they sense that the hour of work is at hand.

When not required for kitchen duty, turnspit dogs might be taken to church to act as foot-warmers for the kitchen servants. One anecdotal story has it that at Bath Abbey, when the bishop was sermonizing about Ezekiel's vision of a wheel, he said the word 'wheel' rather forcefully. All the turnspits in the congregation heard it as the familiar command to jump to their duties and ran out of the church.

There are horrific accounts of sadistic cooks putting hot coals in the wheel to make weary dogs run faster, literally dancing on hot coals, but there is also reason to believe that in kinder households the dogs would go to their labours, if not willingly, then at least compliantly. According to Rev J. G. Wood in *The Illustrated Natural History (Mammalia)* (1853):

> As the labour would be too great for a single Dog, it was usual to keep at least two animals for the purpose, and to make them relieve each other at regular intervals. The dogs were quite able to appreciate the lapse of time, and, if not relieved from their toils at the proper hour, would leap out of the wheel without orders, and force their companions to take their place, and complete their portion of the daily toil.

In addition to this system of alternating labour, larger houses, with multiple turnspit dogs, might have a rotation system that allowed each dog to have at least one day off on a regular basis. The saying 'every dog has his day' derives from this idea. In Shakespeare's *The Comedy of Errors* (Act III, Scene ii), Dromio of Syracuse remarks: 'She had transform'd me into a curtal dog and made me turn i' the wheel'. 'Curtal' or curtailed refers to a short or docked tail (French 'court' = short). Whiskey's little fly-whisk is neither short nor docked but we may imagine that docked tails would have been common for turnspit dogs. Certainly Shakespeare's reference establishes that turnspit dogs were already in use by the sixteenth century, a fact confirmed by their passing mention by Dr Caius (1576):

> a certain dogge in kythchen service excellent. For where any meat is to bee roasted they go into a wheele, which they turning rounde about with the weight of their bodies

To what extent all turnspits looked like Whiskey is hard to know. Whiskey certainly seems to have the long body consistent with Darwin's comparison of the turnspit to the Dachshund. Terrier types in general obviously fitted the size requirement

An original turnspit's wheel in the Abergavenny Museum. (Photograph by Ian Potts)

and had the energetic vim for such labour. However, it is possible that this was a very distinct type that has now been lost to the world. The turnspit dog was made redundant by technology – the smoke-jack used convection heat from the chimney to turn the wheels, the weight-jack relied on a descending weight and complex gears and the steam-jack, patented in 1792, speaks for itself.

Treadwheels operated by dogs were also in use in America as late as the nineteenth century. They were used as the engines for domestic fruit presses, butter churns and water pumps, and in many cases were rather larger than a little turnspit could spin. In 1874 Henry Bergh, the founder of the American Society for the Prevention of Cruelty to Animals, saw a dog from his New York window operating a cider press with one of these wheels. He was horrified by the wretched state the animal was in and had the owner prosecuted. Burgh was known to storm into saloons using dogwheel-driven presses and demand that the dogs be relieved of their duties, invoking animal cruelty laws that he had been instrumental in securing. In many cases, wheel-dogs were replaced by child labour! The cruelties of hot coals and excessive hours, of poor rations and lack of care are unacceptable horrors for any dog. However, maybe, just maybe, in households that fed them well and treated them kindly, a rare few of these little turnspits sprang to their work with an eagerness we find hard to imagine. After all they were bred for it and it is hinted at in the contemporary accounts. I am also quite sure that many a kitchen maid took pity on her little co-worker, fed him tidbits from the pantry and snuck him into her chamber at night.

Chapter 12

Companion Dogs

Animals are such agreeable friends. They ask no questions, they pass no criticisms.
—George Elliot

Wolf-dog pups are fearless, curious and affectionate. (Photograph by Kim Hawkins)

Dancing with Wolves

The bond between human and dog begins with the contract between human and wolf – or at least human and proto-dog (see Introduction). There is something about the wolf that speaks to our souls. In search of greater insight into that primordial connection, I visited Coleen and Jeffrey Burnham-Gladstone at Singing Moon Wolfdogs. They live in the beautiful mountain country of Shasta County, California, just outside the hamlet of French Gulch. Established by French prospectors in 1849, this was once one of California's major gold-producing areas. It is a picturesque place that still oozes with history and character. Coleen and Jeffrey live on Lost Bridge Road. Fortunately, by the time we arrived, the bridge had been found and we drove over it and onto their charming property.

A wolf-dog is a domestic dog, usually a Malamute or Husky or German Shepherd, crossed with a wolf. Wolf-dogs can also be bred with each other. They are classed as low-, mid- and high-content, according to the percentage of wolf they contain. The wolf-dogs that I met were ultra-high-content, between 95 per cent and 98 per cent pure wolf, which is as close as genetic testing can determine. Nevertheless, that 2-5 per cent of genetic difference is crucially important and enough to account for a tendency towards greater docility, provided that the animals receive the appropriate nurture. There are controversies about wolf-dog ownership. Indisputably the higher-content specimens do require expert knowledge, care and the right facilities. These include

With her head held low and her tail between her legs, Maeve, an adult wolf-dog, approached the stranger in a manner that appeared threatening but was in fact no more than wary caution. (Photograph by Cyrena Rose)

adequately large, secure pens and access to open countryside, where they can be taken for a walk of several hours, on a long leash, each day. They will neither suit an urban apartment nor an inexperienced owner. However in the right hands they are perfectly safe and that was certainly the case here. It is also a question of degree and the lower the wolf content, the greater the docility. When I stopped for a break on the way back from French Gulch, there was a low-content wolf-dog (part Malamute) tied down and sitting in the bed of a truck in the car park. He was magnificent, large and very wolf-like. As the owner returned I asked about the dog. 'Oh you can pet him if you like', he said. Now most domestic dogs, however docile they may be around strangers in general, will erupt aggressively if you approach them whilst guarding their owner's vehicle. However this 'demi-wolf' (as Shakespeare called them – MacBeth, Act III, Sc.1) just wagged and wiggled, enjoying every smidgeon of attention on offer. This was a pet dog, a companion dog and certainly no big bad wolf. Having said that, his owner told me that he would never let him off leash. Wolf-dogs do not have recall, certainly not if faced with temptation like a deer getting up in the woods. They have a very high prey drive. So that they can roam, scent and explore naturally, wolf-dogs are usually exercised on 30 ft long leashes. They adapt from an early age to be able to step over the line and disentangle themselves without fuss or interruption to their activities. In the hands of responsible owners, who have both the time and the facilities to give these dogs the attention they require, a wolf-dog can become a profoundly meaningful companion.

Wolf-dogs, in essence tame wolves, go to the very heart of humankind's social connection with the species. I wanted to meet a creature as close as possible to the original 'man's best friend' and that quest is what took me to French Gulch. For these ultra-high-content types, the pups are taken at just six days old, bottle-fed and reared by loving humans. Although they do not take instructions, such as 'sit', 'stay', 'fetch' and 'come', as do domestic dogs, they do learn strict regimens of social behaviour. First and foremost of these, because of the enhanced power of a wolf's bite, is 'no mouth'. High-content wolf-dogs are more tamed than trained but constant daily interaction with humans ensures that these 95+ per cent genetic wolves turn out well-socialized and affectionate. Nevertheless, before visiting I did take the precaution of tallying all my appendages and extremities, so that I could account for them when I left.

The prime adult grey wolf-dog was called Maeve. Wolf-dogs, like wolves, come into season just once a year and when I telephoned Coleen, Maeve was showing signs. She would be on heat the following week. That and an impending snowstorm in the mountains required a quick decision and two days later I was there. Coleen had warned me that it was unlikely we would get Maeve's co-operation. Although normally sociable she was now moody, highly strung and decidedly anti-social. In fact the day before she had given Coleen an irritable nip, nothing serious but a reminder that her disposition was currently unpredictable. Coleen has other wolf-dogs but they were not grey wolf types. I was determined to meet a grey wolf-dog, as the closest ancestor to our domestic breeds. So we decided to see how Maeve would react to me. After a cursory inspection of the spacious and well-appointed enclosures, I made my way down to the dry creek bed, where hardy adventurers once panned for gold. I wanted Maeve to meet me on neutral ground rather than in her compound, so I sat on a driftwood log and waited. Jeffrey brought her down and we left it to Maeve to make the first moves.

For the first several years of her life Maeve's sole companion had been Coleen. As a consequence she was much more wary around males. She stalked, she slinked and she prowled around me, with her tail tucked, her back arched and her long, stilt-like legs striding with the sultry stealth of a tango-dancer. Haltingly, she edged ever closer. First a paw struck out across my knee; it was a fleeting slap and she was gone. She was testing me. I remained static, murmuring singsong words of gentle encouragement. Again and again she returned, scratching my foot with her paw, or flicking an arm with her nose or, eventually, stealing a quick lick on my face. I am used to moving slowly when around young and skittish horses but Maeve's reactivity to movement, or even thoughts of movement, was so much more sensitive. Wolves in the wild are hyper-vigilant. Even for a predator, there is always danger. In her first approaches, not only did she drop between her shoulders, whilst fixing me with her wolfish eye – it was an eerie feeling to be on the receiving end of such predator behaviour – but, as she drew closer, she serpentined her spine in such a way that she appeared to be simultaneously advancing and retreating. I didn't perceive this as nervousness, more as a highly-tuned and responsive reflex system, ready to spring in any direction at the first flicker of movement. One's natural instinct when meeting a dog is to put out one's hand in an offer to pet. This does not work with a high-content wolf-dog. They make the choices;

Maeve prowled and circled as she edged ever closer. I had to sit stock still for fear of startling her. Although I knew she was well-socialized, the skulking menace of her body-language was a little intimidating. (Photograph by Kim Hawkins)

they come to you. Once full connection is made, there can be stroking, scratching and even belly rubs if the wolf-dog trusts you enough to submit to that extent. However such intimacies are not on immediate offer.

Time and again, even when she had stretched her neck in to give my face a tentative lick, I thought I could slowly reach my hand to touch her, only to be rewarded with an instant darting recoil. Then the whole process of prowling and stalking would begin again. Treat inducements, in the form of diced hot dogs, were on offer from my pocket but her lightning in-and-out forays to steal these from my outstretched palm were less rewarding than if I stayed perfectly still. When sheer curiosity was her dominant motivator, and as she gradually became more confident around me, she lingered in close proximity, sometimes inches from my face, staring at me with her hypnotic eyes. It was mystic, mysterious and, for me, also profoundly spiritual. I have always been drawn to wolves. Those eyes, that distinctive mask and the long narrow muzzle emanating from a broad forehead were a powerful sight to confront at such proximity – this was iconic wolf. All my cultural conditioning suggested this should be a moment of danger and yet I could see the innate sociability, the would-be friend behind the predator's gaze. It was like meeting the first dog. We decided to trust each other.

She would remain in physical contact for only a few seconds at a time but after a while she let me reciprocate her face-licking, nosing and pawing by giving her scruff

'Are you looking at me?' After nearly an hour, Maeve made the choice to come into my space and stay there for protracted moments. The slightest move and she would run away but if I held steady, she remained, growing more and more confident in my presence. (Photograph by Kim Hawkins)

a good scratch. I never tried to restrain her though. It was always her choice to stay or go. Despite repeated injunctions of 'no mouth' from her owners, she at various moments took my hand into her mouth and, at one stage, my nose. This is what we see them do with each other when at play. They explore their world and communicate a great deal with their mouths – their feet ever ready for escape. I knew it could go wrong if I moved suddenly and startled her but I felt entirely safe; she was a sweet and gentle lady and I felt privileged to receive her attention.

I was curious to see what she would do if I lay on my back. She approached the feet first and gave my left foot a hefty swipe, jumping back as she did so. Emboldened by my lack of response, she took my foot in her mouth. I was wearing hiking boots, which wolf-dogs are notoriously fond of eating. The 'no mouth' refrain sounded again. Next she shoved her nose up my trouser leg, using it to lift my leg up and down with some vigour. Then, after a few slightly concerning moments while she investigated my groin, she moved onto my stomach. She jabbed her nose into my guts with considerable force; it was almost like receiving a strong punch. When wolves devour a carcass, they start with the viscera. She was just testing to see if I was dead or alive. I don't think she really had plans to dine on me but the instinct to scrutinize my prone body was strong. After all you don't want to bite into something that may then sit up suddenly and attack you back. We spent over an hour together before it was time to give her a break.

Finally, after a great deal of prowling and darting in and out, Maeve tolerated staying close to me and allowed me, very slowly, to raise a hand to stroke her muzzle It was a moment of trust for both of us. (Photograph by Cyrena Rose)

Next I was introduced to two seven-month-old pups, Druid and Claddagh. The young of a wolf, like those of a dog, are known as pups. It is bears that have cubs; Baden-Powell got it wrong. It was tremendous fun to have a romp with the pups but also informative. Coleen's wolf-dog pups already had their prick ears and were quite a size but their soft fluffy, downy coats and their exuberant playfulness marked them as juveniles. They had no suspicions or inhibitions and just piled on me. It was challenging for the photographers, my wife Kim and local photographer Cyrena Rose, because I was buried beneath an intense wolf-dog scrimmage for extended periods of time. This was puppy-love on steroids. When I was kneeling, they enjoyed using their bodyweight against the head, in an effort to wrestle me fully to the ground; an endeavour in which they succeeded frequently. I also presented them the novelty of a bald head, which they licked with an enthusiasm that they might otherwise bring to a discarded dinner plate. In between mauling me, they played with each other, using exactly the same play stratagems, dominated by facial contact. They pawed and pressed and licked and nibbled with such joyful relish that one might have thought they were just over-sized Labradors. However, these were high-content wolf-dogs. This was it; this was that timeless connection and at the heart of it was playfulness and fun.

'They call it puppy love.' Although of adult size, Druid and Claddagh are in fact only 7-month-old pups. Without fear they piled in instantly to jump all over me. There can be little doubt that the earliest physical contact between man and wolf/proto-dog must have happened first with pups. The contrast between Maeve's tentative hyper-vigilance and the confident high spirits of these affable pups couldn't have been more marked (photograph by Kim Hawkins)

When they needed a rest, they were happy to flop by my side or nearby, just like any domestic dog on the hearth rug. Just being there is really the essence of all companionship.

While we were clowning around down in the creek, a lyrical chorus struck up, initiated from the pens above us. Maeve and her partner Nashoba, a magnificent black–phase timber wolf, began howling. The humans joined in (very convincingly), as did the pups. It was a social call, everyone just saying 'we're here'. It was a wonderful sound and I was struck by its similarity to whale song. It was a blithe moment that reinforced the sense that I was among wolves in a wilderness landscape. After playing with the pups, I visited Maeve in her pen. As well as shaded areas, it has two very large water troughs. Wolves, and wolf-dogs, love water, not least because it is a useful cooling system after exertion. After her earlier outing with me Maeve had plunged into her trough to cool down. Personally I am rather fond of the smell of wet dog but that is probably because it has associations with invigorating outdoor days in the company of a water-loving canine, rather than any innate aromatic pleasantness. However the coat of a wolf, or wolf-dog, does not give off any odour whatsoever, not even when wet. It was just one more remarkable thing about these extraordinary animals. Another point of note is that wolf-dogs live far longer than domestic canines. As a general rule of thumb for dogs, the larger the breed, the shorter the lifespan. Gauged by size, one might not expect a wolf-dog to live more than seven or eight years and yet they consistently live healthy lives to well over twenty years. There are those that claim that an occasional judicious and dilute infusion of wolf-dog blood into some of the more over-bred specimens of domestic dog might right some of the genetic defects that are starting to occur and produce healthier dogs with greater genetic integrity. I have no expertise to comment on the validity of the case but it seems an interesting and logical proposition.

Mankind has ever had a conflicted view of the wolf. He has been demonized and feared, the big bad wolf of nursery rhymes, and yet there is a parallel story, exemplified by Romulus, the legendary founder of Rome. As infants, he and his twin brother Remus were cast adrift in a basket on the River Tiber. Their mother, a Vestal Virgin, had been imprisoned for breaking her vow of chastity. Legend has it that the basket got caught in some reeds and that a she-wolf rescued them and then suckled them for days, until they were found by humans, who took them in and raised them. It is a story that resonates with the idea that dogs, originally wolves, have a unique connection to human beings. My time with the wolf-dogs certainly reinforced that perception.

Chamber Dogs

All types of dog can, and do, make the most wonderful companions. The shepherd in his bothy or the hunter in his hide has no other company, save his dog. Consequently many working dogs also have a bonding streak of amity bred into them alongside their signature skills. Some pet dogs are chosen purely for their looks. Voguish trends create a market demand for breeders. In a letter to a society friend in 1897, Florence Amherst lauded her beloved Salukis commending them as ideal 'drawing-room dogs'. The elegance of an exotic sighthound laying majestically by the hearth, bestowed qualities of refinement and pedigree upon the owner. The idea of the dog as fashion accessory is not new. It has led to many of the excesses of over-exaggerated features that manifest in far too many breeds today. However, dogs bred solely as household companions – 'chamber dogs' - have been a feature of human society throughout recorded history. Books advising which breed to choose exceed the breeds available. There is little I can add to that lexicon but from a social history perspective the story of these little companions is every bit as rich as it is for the working breeds.

In 1855, the city of Paris levied a tax on dogs. It was a response to an expanding 'pet dog' population, which the authorities considered competed with human inhabitants for food resources. Taxes were applied on a sliding scale with one franc for certain working dogs at the lower end and a top rate of ten francs for hunting dogs and pleasure dogs (*chiens d'agrément*). Citizens accounted for the number and type of dogs under their care on their tax return and tax assessors arbitrated on the charges to be made. Entries such as 'Inexact declaration with regard to the function of dogs' indicated that there was a great deal of obfuscation about when a dog was a working dog. Even the tiniest of parlour pooches can be considered a guard dog if it barks at strangers. Following the harsh puritanism of the Revolution, this was an age of a rising bourgeoisie, who took to the new status-enhancing fad of pet ownership with enthusiasm. Dog taxation was seen as moral interference by municipal authorities who disapproved of the notion of 'luxury' dogs. Despite the tax, dog ownership expanded exponentially. Because of the tax, which in time spread to the rest of France, we have a reasonably accurate census of the dog population at the time. By 1896 there were over 3,000,000 dogs in France. Alfred Barbou (1846-1907), author of *Le chien; son histoire, ses exploits, ses aventures*, wrote:

> We now turn to the role the dog plays in the home. Good to all those who approach him, always ready to defend the weak, and the children, friend of the house and recognizing only friends of the house, he plays a large part in family life. Often he proves himself not only a supporter, but a consoler. More than any human being, the dog is able to give his master, after the most dreadful misfortune, brief moments of joy.

His words still resonate.

Little Dogs and Lapdogs

Although today we refer to our canine companions as pet dogs, medieval texts reference 'little dogs' and 'lap dogs' as the generic types. In an inventory of goods belonging to Charles V of France (r.1364-80) are a 'collar of silver with bells for a little dog' and 'a very small dog collar of blue cloth, with a gold fleur de lys and three gold bells, with a gold buckle'. I am not sure how widespread or long-lived was the trend for bedecking little dogs with bells but, rather than bringing joy, I would find their constant jangling an annoyance. Charles, however, was presumably anxious to know the whereabouts of his little dogs and was cheered when hearing them approach.

Portrait of a Man with a Dog by the Venetian artist Giovani Cariani (c. 1520) now in The National Gallery of Art, Washington DC. The dog is of an old-fashioned Maltese type before they were crossed with long silken-haired dogs of the East to produce today's specimen with its exaggerated coiffures. Maltese types like this were among the most common companion dogs from the Roman period to the Renaissance. Here we see a male, sword-bearing nobleman, confidently masculine, and yet clearly fond of his little chamber dog. Contrary to the misogynistic nonsense which pervaded the writing of the age, it is evident that male courtiers were equally attached to their companion dogs as were the 'daintie dames'. (Artokoloro Quint Lox Limited / Alamy Stock Photo)

In a list of extant dog types, which includes Greyhounds, mastiff, spaniels and terriers, *The Boke of St Albans* (1486) included 'small ladies popis that beere away the flees'. It is clear from art and literature that, even in an age in which hunting dogs were given exalted status, little dogs were immensely popular with the courtly classes. Then, as now, their mistresses pampered them to excess. John Bromyard, a fourteenth-century Dominican Friar, considered such spoiled creatures a useless and immoral indulgence, on a par with actors and prostitutes! He chided further:

> The wealthy provide for their dogs more readily than for the poor, more abundantly and more delicately too; so that, whereas the poor are so famished that they would greedily devour bran-bread, dogs turn up their noses at the sight of wafer bread, … They must be offered the daintiest flesh, the first and choicest portion of every dish.

Neither were these denunciations the sole province of the church. Dr Caius (1576), in discussing the Maltese dog, which had become popular in England, delivered a somewhat mixed message when he wrote of them:

> These dogs are little, pretty, proper and fyne, and sought for to satisfyie the delicatenesse of daintie dames, and wanton womens wills, instruments of folly for them to play and dally withal. To trifle away the treasure of time, to withdraw their minds from more commendable exercises

He continues in this vein but such diatribes had no effect. The fondness for little dogs as companions for wealthy patrons was undiminished.

Many of these were dwarfed or 'basseted' varieties of a familiar hunting type. Miniature white greyhounds, for instance, appear often in medieval and Renaissance paintings. Today's Italian Greyhound (a toy breed) is probably a descendant of these dogs. Today we have a large coterie of 'toy' breeds that are miniature versions of standard dogs and which do lapdog service; Toy Poodles for instance. Terriers, by dint of their profession, are equally small but not always as suitable for the more genteel parlour. However there is a wide variety of dogs that have been developed purely to function as lapdogs or 'chamber companions' as Dr Caius termed them.

Comforter Spaniels

An especially popular candidate for basseting was the spaniel. The Romans had small spaniels as pets and 'little spaniels' became firmly established as a distinct type of companion dog in their own right. The heyday of these small spaniels was during the Tudor and Elizabethan periods. In 1526, Henry VIII issued an ordnance for his palace at Eltham that gave a special dispensation for ladies to bring their little dogs into court:

> No person whatsoever he be, presume to keep any grey-hounds, mastives, houndes or other dogges, in the court other then som few small spaniels for ladyes or others.

One of the ladies at Henry VIII's court, Catherine Brandon, had a pet spaniel, which she named Gardiner. Bishop Stephen Gardiner was a prominent Catholic who opposed Henry's ideas on the Reformation. Consequently when Lady Brandon called for her little spaniel - 'Heel Gardiner!' – it amused the other courtiers immensely. During the sixteenth century these basset spaniels were known either as 'Comforter Spaniels' or 'Spaniels Gentle' and it was not unusual for one of these little fellows to spend much of his day tucked up beneath a lady's skirts, where it did her the added service of keeping her legs warm. Comforter Spaniels were commonly nick-named 'feet warmers'. Notwithstanding his prejudices against the Maltese dog, Dr Caius was keen to point out a singular benefit of small dogs, with regard to Comforter Spaniels. He conceded that they were,

> good to assuage the sickness of the stomach, being oftentimes thereunto applied as a plaster preservative, or borne in the bosom of the diseased and weak person, which effect is performed by their moderate heat.

Mary Queen of Scots (1542-82) had a particular affinity with Comforter Spaniels and other little dogs. At five years old Mary was packed off to France, where she grew up in the French court, betrothed to the Dauphin, the future Francis II of France, a year her junior. She and Francis were permitted to play together but she spoke no French. Her companions, her confidantes and her comforters were a pack of twenty-two lapdogs

A descendant of the Comforter Spaniel – a modern Cavalier King Charles Spaniel. The flat face and exaggerated ears are much later modifications to the type. Images in Renaissance art show Comforter Spaniels with heads that are proportioned in the same way as a standard spaniel. (iStock/ Bigandt_ Photography)

that included Maltese, Pugs and Comforter Spaniels. In later years Mary was known to be especially fond of a little black and white spaniel. It may be assumed that the affection was reciprocated since, according to legend, this wee dog was discovered, hiding in her skirts, after she was beheaded!

Mary's grandson, Charles I, had a Comforter Spaniel as a child and passed on his fondness for them to his son. When Charles II came to the English throne, following the restoration of the monarchy in 1660, his court bustled with scores of scampering spaniels. As a consequence Cavalier King Charles Spaniels, as they became known, enjoyed a boost in public popularity. Their descendants remain a primary choice of companion breed. Queen Victoria's (1819-1901) Comforter Spaniel, Dash, sat next to her on the throne and was immortalized in many a royal portrait. By that time, however, a dramatic change in the appearance of these dogs had occurred. During the latter part of the nineteenth century, Cavalier King Charles Spaniels were crossed with Pugs from China, resulting in the flatter face and upturned nose that is so characteristic of the breed today. In subsequent manipulations, their ears have been bred ever longer. They are nevertheless happy companions, who like nothing more than to nestle close to their master or mistress.

The Influence of the East

While Europe's diminutive dogs were essentially compact versions of well-known hunting types, in China and Tibet the emphasis was on creating entirely unique looking dogs. Here they developed animals that displayed eye-catching, ornamental

A Chinese Crested Dog. Once known as the Chinese Ship Dog. On board it served double duty as companion and ratter. Its hairlessness was considered a boon because it did not harbour fleas. Chinese traders took Cresteds all over the world and their similarity to the Mexican Xoloitzcuintli is obvious. There is, at present, no known pre-Columbian link between China and Mexico and it is entirely possible that the breeds are unrelated. However it would be strange if there were no connection whatsoever. (iStock/zuzule)

flourish. Perhaps the most bizarre was the Chinese Crested Dog but there were other, better-known ornamental varieties that all had one thing in common – a squashed face. Chinese and Tibetan breeders were the masters of miniaturization and signature breeds such as the Lhasa Apso, Shih Tzu, Pekingese and Pug came to have a strong influence in changing the morphology of companion dogs in the West.

Bred by Tibetan monks as monastery dogs, the long silken coat of the Lhasa Apso had some function in protecting these small dogs from a harsh mountain climate, although it has been much exaggerated in recent decades. It is likely that they also bred the similar but slightly shorter-haired Shi Tzu, meaning 'lion dog', as a variant. These Shih Tzu dogs were given as gifts to Chinese royalty, where they became known as the 'Chrysanthemum-faced Dog'. Shih Tzu dogs appear in art from at least as early as the Tang Dynasty (618-907). They were among the favourites of the Empress Dowager T'zu-Hsi (popularly known in the West as Cixi) who ruled China from 1861 to 1908. She presided over a court culture that held chamber dogs in the highest esteem. Ownership of certain breeds – Shih Tzu, Pekingese and Pug – was limited to the nobility and theft was punishable by death. Built between 1406 and 1420, the imperial palace complex, known as the Forbidden City, contained nearly a thousand buildings. Among these were richly-decorated, marble-floored pavilions, where the palace dogs lived. These cossetted canines slept on plump, silk cushions and were looked after day and night by eunuchs who worked for the Dog Raising Office. It is said that the

The Shih Tzu, also known as the Chrysanthemum-faced Dog, because its flattened face, with hair radiating in all directions, bore a resemblance to the flower. Chrysanthemum flowers enjoyed a prominent status in Chinese culture and were considered one of the 'four gentlemen' or 'noble ones' of Chinese art. The others were the bamboo, the plum blossom and the orchid. Chrysanthemums are a symbol of nobility and longevity. (Photo: iStock/ Fran Montes)

dogs were trained to raise a paw, whenever the Empress entered. Ladies of the court amused themselves by walking and playing with these little dogs, although, since the courtly fashion of the day was to have finger-nails in excess of six-inches, one might imagine that their ability to pet the dogs was limited.

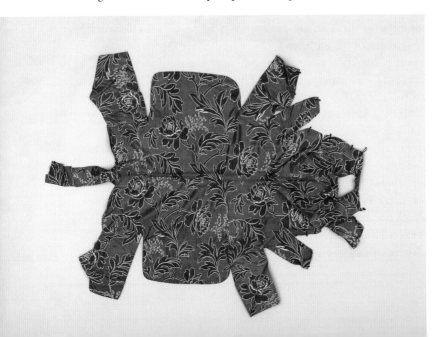

This Chinese silk coat for a dog was made during the reign of the Guangxu Emperor (A.D. 1875-1908). It features a peony pattern and has the name of the dog embroidered on its lining. His name translates as Big Luck. (Image courtesy of The Palace Museum, Beijing)

They also delighted in dressing their dogs. Today we see crass excesses of anthropomorphism as people dress their dogs in the most tasteless and cringe-worthy of costumes, often emulating human attire. It affronts the dignity of these noble creatures. I acknowledge the hypocrisy of my attribution of nobility here but I find it deeply degrading to see a dog dressed as some little person. Whilst dressing our dogs is nothing new, at least the ladies of the Chinese court did so with style. They had hundreds of opulent outfits made for their decorative companions. For the culture of the time, appearance was everything and when that could be combined with symbolism, so much the better.

Pekingese

Although there was a long tradition of short, flat-faced dogs in China, it is impossible to say how early the Pekingese, as we would recognize it, was developed. It seems likely that it was established by cross-breeding long haired Lhasa Apso and Shih Tzu types with perhaps some flatter-faced Pugs and the Maltese dog from Europe. The Maltese was an ancient breed, mentioned in the writings of Aristotle, Martial and Strabo. It was once known as the 'Roman Ladies Dog'. In AD 620, the Byzantine Emperor Heraclius (r. 610–41) sent a gift of two dogs (a male and female) to the Tang Emperor Gaozu (r. 618–26). Their description is similar to that of the 'Melitaei' – the Maltese dogs that were so popular among Roman matrons. It remained a court favourite in Europe throughout the Middle Ages and the Renaissance. Maltese were formerly a general type of small white dog – Bichons are closely related – that had a coat of modest length. However the appearance of the Maltese today, with its preposterously long, silky coat, would be unrecognizable to Mary Queen of Scots, who played with one during her infant exile. It was when the Maltese returned from the East, after centuries of crossbreeding with longer-haired varieties that it appeared in its current form with an over-long coat. Meanwhile, in the East, it passed on some of its excellent companion genes to the Pekingese.

Whenever the Pekingese was first established, the breed was refined and codified under directions from Cixi, in the years before she became the Dowager Empress. She inspected litters personally and with ruthless zeal; pups not to her liking were euthanized. Her ambition was for these little dogs to resemble the lions guarding the gates of the Forbidden City. They were thus imbued with associations of good fortune. Many Pekingese breed histories cite a list of Cixi's guidelines. Its provenance is slightly spurious, with no original Chinese source cited, but nonetheless it probably captures the essence of what was being sought. The following extracts may give insight to her intentions, especially the last item!

> Let the Lion Dog be small… Let its face be black… Let its eyes be large… Let its forelegs be bent; so that it shall not desire to wander far… Let its feet be tufted with plentiful hair that its footfall may be soundless…Let it be dainty in its food so that it shall be known as an Imperial dog by its fastidiousness; sharks fins and curlew livers and the breasts of quails, on these may it be fed… and let it learn to bite the foreign devils instantly.

A Pekinese, coiffed and sheared to maximize its resemblance to a lion. (iStock/Vera Nazemkina)

Pekes had a trilogy of familiar names: Lion Dogs (an appellation they shared with the Shih Tzu), Sun Dogs and Sleeve Dogs. This last because their owners were apt to carry some of these dogs concealed within the ample sleeves of their court robes. Those destined for this mode of transport were miniaturized versions of what was already a small dog. Cixi's purported list also addressed the practice of carrying dogs in the sleeve insofar as it related to a dog's colour. She suggested different coat colours be bred in order to fashion coordinate with whichever robe the canine was to inhabit that day:

> And for its colour, let it be that of the lion – a golden sable, to be carried in the sleeve of a yellow robe; or the colour of a red bear, or a black and white bear, or striped like a dragon, so that there may be dogs appropriate to every costume in the Imperial wardrobe.

In 1860, British troops, commanded by Lord Elgin, stormed and sacked the Summer Palace during the Second Opium War (1856-60). This was a reprisal for the torture and execution of a delegation sent, under a flag of truce, to negotiate with the Regent Prince Li (r.1825-1861). Despite the heinous nature of the provocation, the three days of burning, killing and looting was an act of cultural atrocity on a horrific scale. The Imperial family had fled and only maids and eunuchs were left to guard the exquisite

A classic Pekinese, with a full coat. The shared lineage with the Shih Tsu is clear. Curiously, both dogs are considered to have a genetic signature that is closer to the wolf than other breeds. (Photo: iStock / Gwenvidig)

purlieus of this enchanted place. Many treasures were taken as spoils. The pillage included a number of Pekingese Dogs, taken not only by soldiers but also by a few opportunistic court eunuchs. Shortly afterwards, the first Pekingese was brought to England by Admiral Lord John Hay. He was given the unusual name of Schlorff, which I can only surmise was an onomatopoeic rendering of the sound made when the poor animal, with its squished-in face, attempted to breathe. A number more were imported shortly afterwards as prestigious symbols of Empire, and the breed soon attained a faddish popularity.

Although the Pekingese of the mid-nineteenth century did have a face flatter than nature intended for a dog, images in art show that it was nowhere near as flat as it has now become. There are serious health concerns relating to shorter-muzzled dogs, which need addressing, but where did all these flat faces come from in the first place? Small dogs with compressed faces were coveted as early as the Zhou Dynasty (1050-256 BC). Known as '*haba*' dogs, the Imperial Court demanded them as tribute from the Southern Provinces. These little 'square-mouthed' canines were also described as 'under-the-table dogs' and on hunting excursions, while larger hounds ran beside the chariots, the under-the-table dogs were permitted to ride on board alongside their masters. They were the distant forerunners of the Pug and it is Pug genes that have been the dominant force in compressing the muzzles of so many of our breeds.

Pugs

When the Dutch East India Company began trading in the Far East in the seventeenth century, among the cargoes of exotic spices and fine silks that it brought back to eager European markets was a small, round-headed little dog from China – the Pug. Brachycephalic (round-headed) dogs have a particular appeal as companion dogs because the flatter face with its centred round eyes elicits similar care responses to that of a human baby. Perhaps the most childlike of all dogs is the Pug. In addition to its diminutive size and flat, humanesque face, the Pug has smooth skin, wrinkles, an infant chubbiness and a toddler's waddle. These features combined with the little snorting noises it makes as a result of its truncated nasal passages, reminiscent of a baby's gurgling, endear it to many. At first sight it might appear like a basseted Bulldog but in fact it was Pug genes, introduced into Bulldog bloodlines, which began the flattening of that poor creature's face to such an uncomfortable extent. Early images of Pugs in art show that their face has not always been as flat as they are now.

From the moment the first Pug disembarked in Amsterdam, the breed became popular in Royal circles. Referred to ironically as 'Dutch Mastiffs', Pugs not only

The Painter and his Pug, 1745. Self Portrait by the artist William Hogarth. Hogarth was a celebrated devotee of Pugs. Note that although the dog has a foreshortened muzzle its muzzle is significantly longer than is commonly found today. (The Print Collector – Alamy Stock Photo)

A modern Pug. Compare its wholly compressed face, which results in breathing problems, with that of a typical eighteenth-century Pug painted meticulously by the artist Hogarth. (Photo: iStock/ Anna Cinaroglu)

found favour at the Dutch court (the court of the House of Orange, destined for export to Britain by the end of the century) but also across the North Sea in Britain at the (for the time-being) presiding Stuart court. Pugs reached their peak of fashionability during the eighteenth century. This was the age of the Grand Tour, when young, well-to-do English gentlemen travelled Europe by coach in extended cultural forays to see the sights of Ancient Rome and Greece and to imbibe the artistic glories of the Italian Renaissance. Both compact and warming, with a snuggling, sedentary nature, a Pug made an ideal carriage companion. A first-hand observer of this peripatetic traffic, Mrs Piozzi, wrote in her journal, 'The little Pug dog or Dutch Mastiff has quitted London for Padua, I perceive. Every carriage I meet here has a Pug in it.'

She wrote this in 1789, the year in which the French Revolution began its chaotic and tortuous unravelling of all that had gone before. In 1794, during the 'Reign of Terror' Joséphine de Beauharnais, later to become the wife of Napoleon Bonaparte, was incarcerated in the Carmes Prison in Paris. It followed the guillotining of her first husband, Alexandre de Beauharnais. Bringing her comfort through this ordeal was her Pug, Fortune. In fact Fortune brought her more than comfort, he brought and delivered messages to and from her children, Eugene and Hortense. The clandestine epistles were concealed in his collar. It was common for prisoners to be allowed their dogs but it seems that Fortune had unusual privilege by being granted visiting rights to come and go as he pleased. Happily, both for Fortune and Madame Josephine, their ordeal didn't last long. Robespierre was assassinated five days later, the Reign of Terror was over and Josephine released.

It is a curious contradiction of revolutionary principles that so many aristocrats were permitted canine company during their time in gaol. The dogs of the aristocracy generally suffered at the hands of revolutionary fervour quite as much as their masters. Le Comte de Buffon's *Histoire Naturelle*, published in 1788, advanced the theory that dogs had learned to be 'civilized' through living with humans. It followed, he argued, that the high-bred dogs who lived as the favoured companions of the nobility were therefore 'more civilized' than the mutts who toiled for the lower classes. A tragic consequence of this idea during the Revolution was the persecution of dogs owned by the aristocracy. This often necessitated packs of noble hounds being kept in hiding, though how they kept them quiet is a mystery. There was a brutal mass murder of dogs in Paris. The Place des Grèves, a traditional venue for executions, saw hundreds of aristocratic lapdogs burned there on a great bonfire in 1790. Their aristocratic owners, who had fled without them at the first sign of trouble, had already abandoned the poor animals.

Royal patronage of the Pug, and consequent public popularity, was re-invigorated during Queen Victoria's reign. She kept packs of Pugs. It was during Victoria's reign, in the 1860s, that a fresh wave of imports from China introduced a shorter-legged and shorter-muzzled variety; a type which was to predominate thereafter. Queen Victoria's love of Pugs was passed down to both her grandson, George V and her great-grandson, Edward VIII. Wallis Simpson, wife to the Duke of Windsor, who had abdicated as Edward VIII in 1936, was well known for her fondness for the breed and during their exile in Paris she doted on a nursery of Pugs.

The Little Dogs from Central America
In 1520, the conquistador Hernan Cortés wrote a letter to Charles V of Spain (r.1516–56) chronicling details of everyday life in the Mexican city of Temixtitlan. He reported: 'There are also sold rabbits, hares, deer, and little dogs, which are raised for eating'.

These 'little dogs' are often thought to have been Chihuahuas, since these are famously Mexico's, and the world's, smallest dog. However it was probably the Xoloitzcuintli that Cortés saw in the market. The Xolo (pronounced 'Cholo'), as it abbreviates, is an entirely hairless dog. From the evidence of primitive art, similar dogs are believed to have existed more than 3,500 years ago. Among the Mayans and the Toltecs, these hairless dogs were sacred animals. They were fed lavish meals of corn cakes and guinea pig stew and slept in their owners' beds. Such cosseting came to an end if their owner died before them, because the poor dogs were then sacrificed to serve as the deceased's guide in the afterlife. Even more tragic was the fate of the Xolo after the Aztec Empire was established in the fourteenth century. Although on the one hand Xolos were revered as the earthly embodiment of Xolotl, the Aztec god of death, and valued for their supposed healing properties, they were at the same time raised for their meat. They were served as a delicacy at banquets and mass sacrifices of these innocent creatures occurred on religious feast days or to appease the gods at times of disaster, such as crop failure.

The Xoloitzcuintli. This entirely hairless breed, once sacred to the Mayans and the Toltecs, as well as being a sacrificial animal to the Aztecs, is today hailed as the national dog of Mexico. (Photo: iStock/ Ирина Мещерякова)

A red-coated Chihuahua with dark markings that resonates with early depictions. It has the ears of a ratter and although these little fellows make ideal chamber dogs, they are also known to be keen rodent hunters (Photo: iStock/Laures)

Ceramic pot in the National Museum of Anthropology, Mexico City depicting a Techichi. Highly valued by the Toltec civilization, this dog is strikingly similar to the Chihuahua and is its probable ancestor. (Photograph by Juan Carlos Fonseca Mata, Wikimedia Commons)

Appearing in both long- and short-haired coats, Chihuahuas are an entirely different strain of dog from the same region. It seems probable that the modern breed descended from a type called the Techichi. Both apple- and deer-headed Techichis/Chihuahuas appear in ceramics from the Toltec period (900-1168) and also as wheeled toys. Like the Xolo, the Pugs of China and the Comforter Spaniels of Europe, Chihuahuas have been appreciated as living hot-water bottles for the infirm. They have also been accredited with healing powers. Many books and online entries suggest that Chihuahuas were sold as meat and in ritual sacrifices but this seems to be a conflation with the history of the Xoloitzcuintli. Perhaps both breeds suffered the same fate but it is more probable that the Xolo was the canine demi-god, experiencing both an exalted status and a cruel fate, while the Chihuahua was a favoured housedog, who also kept the vermin at bay. Chihuahua history becomes more certain around the 1880s, when Mexican traders began selling these tiny dogs to American travellers, who took them home as pets. The novelty of their diminutive size and characterful personalities made them much sought after. Initially they were known in the USA as the Arizona Dog, the Texas Dog or the Mexico Dog before the name Chihuahua took root. Chihuahua was the northernmost border state in Mexico. However the Chihuahua was never unique to that region, but rather distributed throughout Central America.

A trinity of long-haired Chihuahuas, showing variations in size and coat. (Photo: iStock/cynoclub)

Mongrels, Tykes, Mutts and Curs

Crossbred dogs have been given many names. These tend to carry pejorative connotations as if there were innate virtue in pure breeding. Genetically speaking, such unscientific snobbery is a complete fallacy. It ignores the crucial phenomenon of 'hybrid vigour', which results in more resistance to disease, lower incidences of physical and temperamental defects and greater longevity to dogs (or any organism) that draw on a wider gene pool. Consequently purebred/pedigree dogs have a far smaller reservoir of genetic diversity, which is why there is such a health crisis in so many of our modern breeds. The viability of a species depends a great deal on its physical health and functionality. It must surely be obvious that the first responsibility of a breeder is to breed healthy specimens above any considerations of coat colour, the length of the ears or shape of the head. In celebrating the diversity of classic dog types and their partnership with humankind, it has never been my intention to under-value the mongrel. They too can perform tasks. In most parts of the world, shepherds manage to get their flocks to pasture perfectly well, using dogs whose parentage is neither recorded nor certified. Their merit is their ability to do the job. Mongrels can also make the most characterful and nurturing of companions.

Stray dog populations are a significant problem in many areas of the world. I remember visiting Bucharest fifteen years ago and being astonished at the size and number of thuggish feral dog gangs roaming the streets at that time. Dogs breed in prolific number and an urban dog population, feeding on the abundant food debris

Milo is a mongrel adopted by the book's editor at ten weeks old. His mother, a Border Collie, was abandoned while pregnant and Milo was born in an RSPCA centre in Surrey. DNA testing later revealed he has Alaskan Malamute, Akita, White Swiss Shepherd and American Bulldog genes from his father's side! He has grown into an intelligent, playful but gentle family pet with boundless energy.

of over-consumptive societies, can quickly become out of control. Programmes of neutering and spaying are essential. Educating people about the responsibilities of dog ownership is also fundamental to the problem. Meanwhile our shelters are full of mutts and mongrels, as well as abandoned and neglected purebred dogs. Every single one needs a loving and responsible home. Mongrels can be the best of dogs but let us not forget the abandoned 'purebreds'. They too are worthy of love and care; they too have been let down by humans. Too often humans recruit dog types as surrogates for their own tribal identities. Championing the mongrel at the expense of the purebred dog is not the equivalent to standing up for the disadvantaged and downtrodden in human society. The circumstances that bring a dog to a shelter are not the dog's fault. A purebred dog in a shelter is in equal distress and equally deserving of compassion and nurture.

For all their extraordinary abilities and the multitude of ways in which dogs have assisted humankind, there can be no role as important or meaningful as that of companion. In the big cities of the world, many homeless people have a dog. These are people who have been abandoned by their own species but who receive unquestioning love, companionship and comfort from their loyal and non-judgmental canine friends. It is right that there should be concern for the welfare of these dogs (though I acknowledge there are controversies) but I think that most fare reasonably well and their devotion to their humans is plain to see. Their plight tells us much about dogs to their credit and much about humans to our shame.

Epilogue

Breeders are not the enemy. The Kennel Clubs are not the enemy. Bad breeders, puppy mills and nonsensical breed standards are the enemy. There needs to be more outcrossing to promote hybrid vigour and to expand the gene pools. Should that happen then expert breeders, with all their specialist knowledge, passion and dedication, could become the guardians of wonderful strains of healthy dogs. Many already are. Similarly the Kennel Clubs might consider reducing the number of breeds that they recognize, in order to concentrate on some basic types, giving access to a wider gene-pool. They have the potential to become the champions in the quest for a healthier dog population in the future, whilst at the same time conserving all that is best about our primary traditional breeds. There are far too many 'micro-breeds', founded upon the merest splash of a gene pool. So many dogs that the Kennel Clubs recognize as breeds are really just a variety of a primary breed; they do not require their own breed category. There needs to be wider awareness of how recently our dogs have come to look the way they do. It is we humans who have changed them and regulated their appearance. Continuing to breed from shallow gene pools and pandering to ever-changing whims of fashion about how we want these dogs to look is not sustainable and we owe our dogs a better future.

At the time of writing there are laws in Germany, Austria and Switzerland that penalize those whose deliberate breeding choices result in offspring that endure a lifetime of discomfort. In German it is given the name '*qualzucht*', which means 'torture breeding'. It is considered equally as cruel to engineer an animal with anatomical abnormalities, as it would be to harm it directly by human hand. Chief among the culprits are the breeds that have an over-exaggerated flat face, causing chronic breathing difficulties. When this is combined, as is so often the case, with the animal having a heavy coat, then there is the compounded problem of the dog not being able to regulate its temperature in hot weather. Hip problems, over-long spines, kangaroo hocks and bowed legs are all skeletal defects that affect functional capacity and which can also cause chronic pain. Exophthalmos (bulging eyes) is a common problem in small breeds and sight and hearing problems are rampant across many breeds, as are malformed teeth and deformed skulls. Most heinous of all is the situation of certain breeds, which having distorted proportions, are unable to give natural birth. Some breeds can only deliver their young via Caesarean section. Such a state of affairs is shameful.

I believe we have a serious problem concerning the future of our dogs and that, in order to find a path forward, we need to balance what may seem like competing notions. Clearly the pedigree dog institutions have failed some breeds. However that is only part of the story because the system, especially when it comes to working dogs, recognized additionally by their performance in Working Trials, has also produced the most magnificent specimens of health, vitality and type. Too much reactionary pushback against the mistakes of the pedigree system risks destroying that which is good about it. Much as I love mongrels, it would be an unthinkable tragedy to lose our classic breeds altogether. It would be too sad to live in a world entirely without Labradors, Spaniels or Beagles. The mantra of 'all shelter mutts good; all bred dogs bad' serves neither man nor dog. I believe that the system needs adjusting, not breaking. Yes, do take in a rescue dog if you can – our dog Sparky was a rescue and brought us immeasurable joy. No, do not buy from a puppy mill – they in-breed and overproduce to excess. Yes, do buy from reputable breeders – wise breeding choices, especially when backed by proven performance in Working Trials, still produce dogs that are not only healthy but that also have reasonably predictable character traits. You owe it to the dog to choose one that will fit well with your lifestyle and family situation. Knowing what sort of dogs a particular breeder produces can aid that selection.

My criticisms of distorted forms and some current breed standards should not be taken to imply that these dogs are any less loveable. I have met many dogs that would fall into the category of 'poorly bred'. All have had wonderful and endearing personalities and have been wholly deserving of the love that they receive. However we must ask ourselves if we think it right to deliberately perpetuate the breeding mistakes of the past, when we know that we have a choice to favour breed standards that put the animals' health and comfort first. Whilst urging greater emphasis on welfare in the regulation of breed standards, I intend no disrespect to those humans, whose compassionate hearts are drawn to the misfits that are the innocent offspring of poor breeding decisions or accidents. Such people give essential love to sentient creatures that need and deserve it. There is a paradox in 'the curse of cute'. It seems to me to be a boon that some people favour dogs that waddle and snuffle and look a little bit funny. Those motivated by such empathy may be the best of us. By the same token, we must also be mindful of *qualzucht* and in future avoid deliberately breeding dogs whose form has been distorted in order to exploit the market for 'cute'. There is a middle path: cherish the dogs that exist but broaden awareness, so as not to repeat mistakes. The little toy breeds and other companions bring so much joy and meaning into people's lives and their occupation is as vital as any other. All that is required is that we breed them prioritizing health over looks. I wouldn't be at all averse to having a cheerful little Pug around the house, provided that it could breathe properly and run around, and that it looked like the longer-muzzled Pugs so doted on by Mr Hogarth in the eighteenth century.

Our requirements for function have changed; the role of dogs in our society has changed. There are still plenty of dogs working in traditional roles such as herding but for every Collie with a flock of sheep there must be several hundred more dogs with a nursery of humans. The principal function of dogs in today's society is to be pets. Accordingly we are breeding more and more dogs created specifically for that purpose. In recent years we have seen the emergence of so-called designer breeds such as the 'Labradoodle' and the 'Cockerpoo'. All dogs are ultimately 'designer-breeds' and these new hybrids, just like the strains of old, have been bred with a view to a purpose, in this case to be household companions. In some cases they are hypoallergenic (or at least carry that claim), in others they address size, exercise requirements and the needs of the city dweller. Of course, the idea of mixing breeds deliberately is heresy to those who advocate a wholly rigid adherence to written breed standards. Paradoxically such zealots are probably unaware of the tenuous historical lineage that their own preferred breed enjoys. Too often the call of history, under a cloak of tradition, is invoked to resist the tide of change. Surely if history teaches us nothing else, it should teach us about the inevitability and the energy of change. The human story, like the universe we inhabit, is in motion. For me an appreciation of history is about being part of the story, part of the continuum of the human experience and feeling connection to it. That means having knowledge and appreciation of what has gone before; it does not mean lamenting the passing of an imagined golden age. I want to see our classic breeds conserved but that is not the same as being inflexible to any changes in their form. Contrarily I believe that it is some nuanced change that will save them.

Inevitably we will continue to develop new and different types of dogs as our uses for them evolve. I have no quarrel with that. Dogs will change in the future, just as they have changed in the past. However, the addition of new types need not mean that we throw our hands up and let our current breeds disappear entirely. On the one hand our traditional breeds are under threat from too much in-breeding and overly stringent breed standards; on the other hand they are in jeopardy from those who think that all dogs should be allowed to breed without any thought to the qualities of the progeny. Neither camp serves the best interests of dogs. We should be more aware of the fragility of breeds, lest we surrender them too casually. Our traditional breeds will not disappear tomorrow but, unless we rethink our approach to dogs, there will be a steady decline and we will lose them in the end. First to face extinction may be the mastiffs, then possibly the hounds; which next I wonder? Their demise will only be in part owing to occupational redundancy. It will also, in some measure, be because of misshapen mutations. There has already been too much damage and we owe it to our dogs to have a new conversation. That may mean countenancing adjustments to the status quo. In fact, accepting a modicum of change may be precisely the recipe required for the long-term preservation of that which is most excellent about our breeds. The experiment of freezing the gene pools is relatively recent. I would suggest that we need to become more tolerant of out-crossing and more mindful of breeding according to original purpose, whether or not the dogs are used in this way. They were developed to be the way they are for a function. It is once we start to ignore this that the problems set in. It is also to be hoped that, by promoting wider understanding of the issues, the public demand for cosmetic exaggeration can be moderated and that the worst of *qualzucht* can be eliminated.

The beauty of classic dogs is sublime, forged from generations of careful breeding. They are a treasure of incalculable value. I derive tremendous pleasure, not only from the dogs that have been in my care, but also from seeing supremely beautiful dogs, owned by others, as they go about their business in the world. Such sightings are as magical to me as seeing other species in the wild. In addition to possessing stunning good looks, purebred dogs also have widely differing characters, temperaments and abilities according to type. These attributes enhance our unique and sacred inter-species relationship in so many different ways. I hope that, whilst we will come to accept some gently modifying changes – changes that widen the gene pool and improve the fettle of our dogs – we will also hang on to as many of our classic breeds as possible in a form that is both recognizable and sustainable. Classic dog breeds are a living heritage. I believe that it is a heritage worth conserving just as much as the priceless legacy of animals in the wild.

(Photograph by Kim Hawkins)

Bibliography

Aristotle, trans. Richard Cresswell, *History of Animals* (Elibron Classics series, reprinted 2005).

Bise, Gabriel (after Gaston Phoebus), trans. J. Peter Tallon, *The Hunting Book (Livre de la Chasse)*. (Geneva: Miller Graphics, 1978).

Brewer, Douglas, Terence Clark and Adrian Phillips, *Dogs in Antiquity* (Oxford: Oxbow Books, 2001).

Caius, Johannes, *Of Englishe Dogges* (1576; reprinted Alcester: Vintage Dog Books, 2005).

Coppinger, Raymond and Lorna, *Dogs – A New Understanding of Canine Origin, Behaviour and Evolution* (Chicago: The University of Chicago Press, 2001).

Corin, Stanley, *The Pawprints of History* (New York: Free Press, 2003).

Cummins, John. *Medieval Hunting* (Edison, New Jersey: Castle Books, 2003).

Edward of Norwich, ed. William A. and F. N. Baillie-Grohman, with a foreword by Theodore Roosevelt, *The Master of Game* (1413; edited 1909 and reprinted Philadelphia: University of Pennsylvania Press, 2005).

Hancock, David, *The Mastiffs* (Ducklington: Cherwynne Dog Features, 2000).

Hancock, David, *The World of the Lurcher* (Wyeky: Quiller Publishing, 2010).

Hancock, David, *Terriers* (Marlborough: The Crowood Press, 2011).

Hancock, David, *Sighthounds* (Marlborough: The Crowood Press, 2012).

Hancock, David, *Gundogs* (Marlborough: The Crowood Press, 2013).

Hancock, David, *Hounds – Hunting by Scent* (Marlborough: The Crowood Press, 2014).

Hancock, David, *Dogs of the Shepherd* (Marlborough: The Crowood Press, 2014)

Hull, D.B., *Hounds and Hunting in Ancient Greece* (Chicago: The University of Chicago Press, 1964)

Huntington, Sidney and Jim Reardon, *Shadows on the Koyukuk* (Alaska: Northwest Books, 1993)

Mason, W. E., *Dogs of All Nations* (1915, reprinted London: Forgotten Books, 2015).

Maxwell, C. Bede, *The Truth About Sporting Dogs* (New York: Howell Book House Inc, 1972).

Secord, William, *A Breed Apart* (Woodbridge: The Antique Collector's Club, 2001)

Thurston, Mary Elizabeth, *The Lost History of the Canine Race* (Kansas City: Andrews and McMeel, 1996)

Xenophon. trans. Dansey, William *The Cynegeticus* (Bibliolife, reprint of 1831 edition).

Index